Advanced Databases

We work with leading authors to develop the
strongest educational materials in computing,
bringing cutting-edge thinking and best
learning practice to a global market.

Under a range of well-known imprints, including
Prentice Hall, we craft high quality print and
electronic publications which help readers to understand
and apply their content, whether studying or at work.

To find out more about the complete range of our
publishing, please visit us on the World Wide Web at:
www.pearsoned.co.uk

ECDL
Advanced Databases

**Judith Cuppage
and
Paul Holden**

Approved
Courseware
Advanced
Syllabus AM 5
Version 1.0

PEARSON

Prentice
Hall

Harlow, England • London • New York • Boston • San Francisco • Toronto • Sydney • Singapore • Hong Kong
Tokyo • Seoul • Taipei • New Delhi • Cape Town • Madrid • Mexico City • Amsterdam • Munich • Paris • Milan

Pearson Education Limited
Edinburgh Gate
Harlow
Essex CM20 2JE
England

and Associated Companies throughout the world

Visit us on the World Wide Web at:
www.pearsoned.co.uk

First published in 2004

ISBN 0-131-20240-5

British Library Cataloguing-in-Publication Data
A catalogue record for this book is available from the British Library

10 9 8 7 6 5 4 3 2 1
08 07 06 05 04

Typeset in 11pt Times New Roman PS by 30.
Printed and bound in Great Britain by Bell & Bain Ltd, Glasgow

The Publishers' policy is to use paper manufactured from sustainable forests.

Contents

Chapter 3: Table design: data types, field sizes, field formats   18

Chapter 4: Table design: advanced field properties   34

Chapter 12: Form design: calculated controls   177

Chapter 13: Form design: subforms   189

Preface

What is ECDL?

ECDL, or the European Computer Driving Licence, is an internationally recognized qualification in information technology skills. It is accepted by businesses internationally as a verification of competence and proficiency in computer skills.

The ECDL syllabus is neither operating system nor application specific.

ECDL Advanced Database module

ECDL Module AM5, Database, Advanced Level, requires you to operate a database application effectively, at more than a basic level of competence, and to be able to realize much of the potential of the application.

It requires you to be able to use the database application to organize, extract, view and report on data using advanced data management skills, and also to create simple macros, and to import, export and link data.

For more information about ECDL, and to see the syllabus for ECDL Module AM5, Database, Advanced Level, visit the official ECDL website at www.ecdl.com.

About this book

This book covers the ECDL Advanced Database syllabus Version 1.0, using Microsoft Access 2000 to complete all the required tasks. It is assumed that you have already completed the database module of ECDL 3 or ECDL 4 using Microsoft Access, or have an equivalent knowledge of the product.

The chapters in this book are intended to be read sequentially. Each chapter assumes that you have read and understood the information in the preceding chapters.

Most chapters contain the following elements:

- **New skills:** This sets out the skills and concepts that you will learn in the chapter.

- **New words:** A list of the key terms introduced and defined in the chapter.

- **Exercise files:** A list of the exercise files that you will work with in the chapter (see 'Exercise files' below).

- **Syllabus reference:** A list of the items from the ECDL Advanced Database syllabus that are covered in the chapter.

- **Exercises:** Practical, step-by-step tasks to build your skills.
- **Chapter summary:** A brief summary of the concepts and skills covered in the chapter.
- **Quick quiz:** A series of multiple-choice questions to test your knowledge of the material contained in the chapter.

Case study

The exercises in this book guide you step-by-step through the tasks you need to be able to perform, using a library database as a case study.

The database in the case study is used by a village library that serves a small but growing local community. Library staff use the database to maintain information about the books available in the library and about loans of books to library members.

At present, all information is maintained manually, using a variety of paper forms, card indexes and ledgers. This system was adequate while the membership and library holdings were small. Now the membership is growing steadily and the library is expanding. It has been decided that a relational database system is necessary.

In the exercises in this book you will design and build the village library database, and the various queries, forms and reports needed to support the library services.

Note that the case study has been designed to illustrate the features necessary to cover the syllabus. It is not intended as a complete functioning database for a real library.

Exercise files

The CD accompanying this book contains a database file for most chapters. In each case, the database file provides the starting point for exercises in the chapter. For example, you work with the following database file when doing the exercises in Chapter 3:

- `Chp3_VillageLibrary_Database`

For some chapters, additional files (such as spreadsheets or text files) are provided for use with the exercises.

Before you begin working through the exercises, you need to copy all of the files from the CD to your computer. To do this, create a working folder anywhere on your computer and name it something like `ECDL_Database_Advanced`. Then copy all files from the CD to that folder.

Text conventions

The following conventions are used in this book:

- **Bold text** is used to denote the names of Access menus and commands, buttons on toolbars, tabs and command buttons in dialog boxes and keyboard keys.

- *Italicized text* is used to denote the names of Access dialog boxes, and lists, options and checkboxes within dialog boxes.

- The | symbol is used to denote a command sequence. For example, choose **Tools | Macro | Run Macro** means choose the **Tools** menu, then the **Macro** option on that menu, and finally the **Run Macro** option on the **Macro** sub-menu.

- Field names are often prefixed by the name of the table to which they belong. For example, Books.ISBN refers to the ISBN field in the Books table.

Hardware and software requirements

Your PC should meet the following specifications:

- Microsoft Access 2000 (including the Northwind sample database) (see next section)

- Microsoft Word 2000

- Microsoft Excel 2000

- 10 MB hard disk space for exercise files

Access 2000 service packs

Your Access 2000 installation must include the following service packs:

- Microsoft Office 2000 Service Release 1a (SR-1a)

- Microsoft Office 2000 Service Pack 3 (SP-3)

A service pack contains a collection of product updates that enhance, extend, and fix known errors in the original product. If you do not install the Microsoft Office 2000 service packs, you may encounter problems when creating and using the sample forms, reports, and macros in this book.

To check your version of Microsoft Access, start the application, and choose **Help | About Microsoft Access**.

- If both service packs have been installed, **SP-3** will appear as part of the version number at the top of the *About Microsoft Access* dialog box, and you do not need to take further action.

- If Service Release 1 or 1a has been installed, but not Service Pack 3, SR-1 will appear as part of the version number at the top of the *About Microsoft Access* dialog box. In this case you need to install Service Pack 3 and possibly Service Release 1a.

- If neither SR-1 nor SP-3 appears as part of the version number, you need to install both service packs.

Note that the installation procedure requires access to your original Office 2000 CD.

Installing the service packs

To update a single, stand-alone computer, you can download both service packs from the following Microsoft website:

```
http://office.microsoft.com/officeupdate/
default.aspx
```

The website provides a utility that scans your computer to detect which Office updates you need. The results list available updates for all your Microsoft products.

- If a Windows Installer update is included in the list, download and install this first, following the instructions on screen.

- If Office 2000 Service Release 1a (SR-1a) is included in the list, download and install it following the instructions on screen. You must download this update separately from other updates.

- If Office 2000 Service Pack 3 is included in the list, download and install it following the instructions on screen.

To update Office 2000 on a network, go to the following website:

```
http://www.microsoft.com/office/ork/2003/
admin/97_2000/default.htm
```

This lists administrative updates for Office 97–2000. The following items provide information on deploying Service Release 1a and Service Pack 3:

- Office 2000 Release 1a Now Available

- Office 2000 Service Pack 3 (SP3)

Access environment defaults

Access's *Options* dialog box presents a wide range of options that enable you to customize your Access working environment. You can, for example, specify the default formatting for datasheets, define the default field type and size for new fields in a table, and change the default behaviour of the **Enter**, **Tab** and **Arrow** keys in forms and datasheets.

The exercises and illustrations in this book assume that all the options have their original default values. To use the same settings, open the *Options* dialog, by choosing **Tools | Options**, and then apply the following settings:

Option	Settings
View tab	
Show in macro design	
Names column	Not selected
Conditions column	Not selected
Double-click open	Selected
General tab	
New database sort order	General
Use four-digit year formatting	
This database	Not selected
All databases	Not selected
Edit/Find tab	
Confirm	
Record changes	Selected
Record deletions	Selected
Action queries	Selected
Keyboard tab	
Move after enter	Next field
Behaviour entering field	Select entire field
Arrow key behaviour	Next field
Forms/Reports tab	
Form template	Normal
Report template	Normal
Always use event procedures	Not selected

Option	Settings
Tables/Queries tab	

Default field sizes
    Text
    Number
	
	50
	Long Integer

Default field type	Text

Query design
    Show table names
    Enable AutoJoin
    Output all fields
	
	Selected
	Selected
	Not selected

Windows Regional Settings

By default, Access displays numbers, currencies, and dates in the format specified in your Windows Regional Settings. The examples used in this book assume that your Regional Settings are set to *English (United Kingdom)*, that the default currency symbol is £, that the default date sequence and display format is dd-mm-yy, and that commas are used as the thousands separator.

It is recommended that you use the Regional Settings listed here. Otherwise, dates and numbers may display differently on your screen than in the examples and illustrations in this book. You can access your Regional Settings from the Windows Control Panel.

Note that, depending on which operating system you are using, the order and names of Regional Settings options may differ slightly from those listed here.

Setting	Value
Regional Settings	
Regional Settings	English (United Kingdom)
Number	
Decimal symbol	.
No. of digits after decimal	2
Digit grouping symbol	,
No. of digits in group	3
Negative sign symbol	–
Negative number format	–1.1
Display leading zeros	0.7
Measurement system	Metric

Currency	
Currency symbol	£
Position of currency symbol	£ 1.1
Negative number format	–£ 1.1
Decimal symbol etc.	Same as for numbers.
Date	
Short date style	dd-MM-yy
Date separator	–
Long date style	dd MMMM yyyy

1

Database development: overview

In this chapter

Creating a relational database requires careful planning and preparation. You need to understand not only how to create the database in Access, but also how to design the database so that you can quickly and easily retrieve any information you want.

This chapter provides an overview of the steps involved in creating a database and explains the benefits of good database design.

New skills

At the end of this chapter you should be able to:

- Explain what a relational database is
- Explain the advantages of good database design
- List the typical steps involved in designing and creating a relational database

New words

In this chapter you will meet the following terms:

- Relational database
- Relationship

What is a relational database?

A relational database consists of a collection of data organized into tables. Tables are linked together by defining relationships between them. These relationships are based on the tables having a common field, and they allow you to bring together data from different tables.

As an example, take the Books and Publishers tables shown below. Each record in the Books table has a related record in the Publishers table that provides details about the book's publisher. The relationship is established by including a PublisherID field in the Books table as well as in the Publishers table.

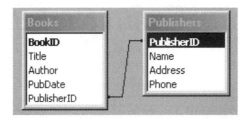

Knowing the PublisherID value for a particular book, Access can find the publisher with that PublisherID and so bring together the records from the two tables. In the example here, Access has retrieved the title and author of a book from the Books table and the name and address of the book's publisher from the Publishers table.

Title	Author	Name	Address
Mansfield Park	Jane Austen	Penguin	London, England

Relational database

A collection of data organized into tables.

Relationship

A connection between two tables that allows them to share data. It is based on the tables having at least one field in common.

Overview of database development

Developing a database involves a design phase and an implementation phase. In the design phase, you decide on the structure of the database. In the implementation phase, you build the database by using a Database Management System (DBMS) such as Microsoft Access.

Design phase

The object of the design phase is to determine a suitable structure for your database by answering the following questions:

- What tables do I need to create?
- What fields do I need to include in each table and what are their data types?
- What is the primary key of each table?
- What are the relationships between the tables?

It is important to spend time on this phase. A poorly designed database makes it difficult for users to retrieve certain information and may return inconsistent and inaccurate results. A well-designed database, on the other hand, provides the following benefits:

- The database will be compact, efficient and easy to modify.

- Data will be consistent, accurate and easy to maintain.

- Users will able to retrieve whatever information they want now and in the future.

Pen and paper or a word processing application are the best tools for roughing out and refining your database design. Only when you are satisfied with your design should you start to create the tables and enter data.

Implementation phase

In the implementation phase you use Access to create the tables you identified in the design phase, and to create the queries, forms and reports that you need to input data and retrieve and present information.

> **Data and information**
>
> *Data is the values that you store in the database. Information is data that you retrieve from the database in some meaningful way.*

Steps for building a database

Here is an overview of the typical steps involved in designing and building a database.

1) **Determine the overall purpose and specific objectives of the database.** Establishing the purpose of your database provides a focus for your design. Establishing the specific tasks you want to accomplish with the database helps you to identify the main subjects of the database and the facts that you need to store about each subject.

   The subjects you identify are all candidates for tables in your database. The facts about a subject are all candidates for fields in that subject's table.

2) **Determine the tables and fields you need.** In this step you establish a preliminary set of tables and fields based on the subjects and facts you identified in step one. You then apply a set of design principles to these tables and fields in order to determine the final set of tables and the primary key for each.

3) **Determine the data type and properties for each field.** A field's data type determines the kind of data that the field will accept. A field's properties control such attributes as field size, default value and display format.

4) **Determine the table relationships.** In this step you determine how one table is related to another and the type of relationship in each case. You may need to add new fields or create new tables at this stage in order to define the relationships correctly.

5) **Implement the database design.** In this step you create the tables and relationships you identified during the design phase.

6) **Enter the database records.** Because it is much easier to change the database design before you have filled the tables with data, it is a good idea to first test the design. You can do this by entering sample data and checking that you can get the results you want. When you are satisfied that the database design suits your requirements, you can begin entering data in the tables.

7) **Create queries, forms and reports.** This final step involves designing and creating the queries, forms and reports you need for inputting data to the database and retrieving information from it.

Chapter 1: summary

A relational database consists of a collection of data organized into tables. You can retrieve a combination of information from different tables by defining relationships between the tables.

There are two main phases in creating a database: design and implementation. In the design phase you decide on the tables, fields and relationships you need. In the implementation phase you create the tables and relationships, and also the queries, forms and reports you need for inputting data and retrieving information.

2

Table design: what tables, what fields?

In this chapter

Designing an appropriate set of tables for your database is an essential first step in building an effective and efficient database.

In this chapter you will learn the principles of good database design and how to apply them to determine an appropriate set of tables for the Village Library database.

New skills

At the end of this chapter you should be able to explain:

- Why relational databases are preferable to flat databases

- The problems you might encounter in poorly designed databases

- The steps involved in designing a database

- The principles of good database design

New words

In this chapter you will meet the following terms:

- Flat database
- Redundancy
- Modification anomaly
- Multivalue field
- Multipart field

Why not a flat database?

A simple database can consist of a single table. However, most databases consist of a number of related tables. To see why, let's take a look at the problems you might encounter with a flat database and with poorly designed tables.

Flat database
A database consisting of a single table.

The following table contains data about members of a library and the books they have borrowed. You do not need to create this database in order to recognize its pitfalls.

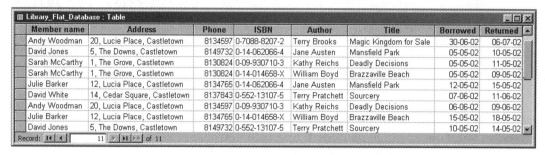

Member name	Address	Phone	ISBN	Author	Title	Borrowed	Returned
Andy Woodman	20, Lucie Place, Castletown	8134597	0-7088-8207-2	Terry Brooks	Magic Kingdom for Sale	30-06-02	06-07-02
David Jones	5, The Downs, Castletown	8149732	0-14-062066-4	Jane Austen	Mansfield Park	05-05-02	10-05-02
Sarah McCarthy	1, The Grove, Castletown	8130824	0-09-930710-3	Kathy Reichs	Deadly Decisions	05-05-02	11-05-02
Sarah McCarthy	1, The Grove, Castletown	8130824	0-14-014658-X	William Boyd	Brazzaville Beach	05-05-02	09-05-02
Julie Barker	12, Lucia Place, Castletown	8134765	0-14-062066-4	Jane Austen	Mansfield Park	12-05-02	15-05-02
David White	14, Cedar Square, Castletown	8137843	0-552-13107-5	Terry Pratchett	Sourcery	07-06-02	11-06-02
Andy Woodman	20, Lucia Place, Castletown	8134597	0-09-930710-3	Kathy Reichs	Deadly Decisions	06-06-02	09-06-02
Julie Barker	12, Lucia Place, Castletown	8134765	0-14-014658-X	William Boyd	Brazzaville Beach	15-05-02	18-05-02
David Jones	5, The Downs, Castletown	8149732	0-552-13107-5	Terry Pratchett	Sourcery	10-05-02	14-05-02

The problems with this table, as with most poorly designed tables, can be summarized as follows:

■ Redundancy

■ Modification anomalies

■ Multivalue fields

■ Multipart fields

Redundancy

Have a look at the records in the table. Every time a member borrows a book, you must enter their name, address and phone number. The table contains each member's details many times.

This is a waste of space and a waste of time. It also increases the likelihood of data entry errors, creating inconsistencies between member details in different records. The unnecessary duplication of data in a database is referred to as *redundancy*.

The table also contains each book's details many times: more wasted space, more inconsistencies, more redundancy.

Redundancy

The unnecessary duplication of data in a database.

Modification anomalies

Member details may change over time. When they do, you must update *every* record containing those details. Otherwise there will be inconsistencies in the database. This is an example of an *update anomaly*.

What happens when you want to add a new book to the database but it hasn't yet been borrowed by a member? The member-related fields will be empty and the primary key will probably be missing or partly missing. So there will be no way to uniquely identify the new record. This is an example of an *insertion anomaly*.

What happens when a member cancels their library subscription and you want to remove them from the database? If you delete all their loan records, you also delete information about the books they have borrowed. And if they are the only member that has borrowed a particular book, you will lose all information about that book. This is an example of a *deletion anomaly*.

Multivalue fields

The table contains a single field for the author of a book. But what about books with multiple authors?

In a single table, you can approach this problem in one of three ways, each with its own problems:

- Include all the authors in the same field, referred to as multivalue field. However, this makes it difficult to work with the data in the field – for example, to search for a single author or to list authors alphabetically.

- Duplicate the entire record for each author, but this considerably increases redundancy and the possibility of inconsistencies.

- Include a separate field for each author. But how many fields should you create? However many you decide, all but one will be empty in most records. In addition, when searching for a particular author you will have to include all the fields in your query.

Multivalue field
A field that contains multiple values for the same data item.

Multipart fields

A multipart field is a field that contains more than one data item. The Library_Flat_Database table contains two typical examples:

- The Member name field contains both the member's first and last names. This makes it difficult to search for or sort members by their last name.

- There is only one address field. If the address contains a street address, a town or city name, and a postal code, it is difficult to manipulate these items separately.

Multipart field
A field that includes more than one data item.

Solution

The solution to multipart fields is to create a separate field for each data item. The solution to redundancy, modification anomalies, and multivalue fields is to separate your data into a number of tables and to define relationships between those tables.

But how do you know what is the correct set of tables? In formal database design theory, you use a process known as *normalization*. This chapter takes a more informal approach that achieves similar results.

Overview of table design

Here are the steps you should follow in order to determine the tables and fields required for a particular database:

1) Determine the purpose of the database.

2) Determine the tasks that you want to accomplish with the database.

3) Determine the subjects of the database and the facts (characteristics) you need to store about each subject.

4) Map the subjects and characteristics to tables and fields.

5) Apply the principles of good database design to the tables and fields.

Database purpose

Formally specifying the purpose of your database provides a focus for your database design and helps you draw up the list of tasks that the database must support.

In the case of the Village Library database, the purpose can be stated as:

> "The purpose of the Village Library database is to maintain the data that is used to support the library service. The database is intended to facilitate staff in cataloguing books, maintaining membership records, and tracking book loans."

Database tasks

Drawing up a list of the major tasks that the database must automate helps you to identify the subjects of the database and the characteristics of those subjects. You can subsequently map these to tables and fields.

In the case of the Village Library database, the tasks include the following:

- Maintain a catalogue of the library's holdings. The specific tasks to be supported include adding new books, removing missing and discarded books, and updating book details.

- Provide facilities for searching the catalogue by author, book, publisher, category, and so on.

- Provide links to author websites.

- Maintain membership records. The specific tasks to be supported include adding new members, removing members, and updating member details.

- Provide facilities for searching the membership records by name, address, and so on.

- Record all loans and returns, including any fines paid for late returns.

- Provide reports on overdue books, books currently on loan, fines paid, borrower activity, the most popular books and book categories, and so on.

- Enforce library lending rules. A member can have a maximum of five books on loan at any one time. The maximum lending period is ten days. Fines for overdue books are imposed at a rate of £0.50 per book per day, but library staff can apply a discount at their own discretion.

Database subjects

The subjects of a database are the people, things, or events about which the database must store data. The characteristics of a subject are the details that describe that subject.

To draw up a list of subjects, take a look at the database purpose and tasks that you have identified and list the subjects mentioned there, as shown below.

Catalogue
Books
Members
Loans
Publishers
Categories
Authors
Returns
Fines
Overdue books
Borrowers

You may intuitively realize that some items in the list are not subjects in their own right. But it is best to review the list methodically.

Are there any duplicates? Catalogue represents the same subject as Books, so one of these can be removed. The same is true of Members and Borrowers.

Does any subject represent a characteristic of another subject rather than a subject in its own right? What about Overdue books, Fines, and Returns? Being overdue is really a characteristic of a loan. The same is true for the return of a book, and for fines relating to late returns. So you can remove these subjects. You can also remove Categories, as a category is a characteristic of a book.

What about Authors and Publishers? Both are characteristics of books. However, if they have characteristics of their own, such as address, phone, and web address, then they are subjects in their own right. Let's leave them in the list for the moment.

Books
Members
Loans
Authors
Publishers

The subject list now includes only Books, Members, Loans, Authors, and Publishers.

Subject characteristics

To identify the characteristics of each subject, look at the list of tasks again and identify the characteristics mentioned there. In a real-world scenario you would find other characteristics by interviewing the library staff and examining the ledgers, reports, and index cards that they currently use.

Assume that the preliminary list of characteristics is as shown below.

Books	Members	Loans	Authors	Publishers
ISBN	Name	ISBN	Name	Name
Title	Address	Title	Web Address	
Author Name	Phone	Author		
Publication Year	Email	Member Name		
Publisher Name		Date Borrowed		
Category		Date Returned		
Date Purchased		Fine Paid		
Cost				

Again review the list methodically:

- Does each characteristic describe the subject under which it is listed and not another subject? Title and Author appear under Loans but they describe a book. So you can remove them from the Loans subject.

- Are there any duplicates?

  - Title and Author Name were duplicated but they have already been removed from the Loans subject.

  - Publisher Name appears under both Books and Publishers. As no other publisher details are required, a separate Publishers subject is unnecessary. So you can remove that subject. A publisher's name now appears only under the Books subject.

– What about ISBN? This is a characteristic of a book. However, it establishes the relationship between a particular loan and a particular book and so must appear under both subjects. Similarly, Member Name establishes the relationship between loans and members, and Author Name establishes the relationship between books and authors.

■ Finally, make sure that no characteristics are missing. For example, does the library require statistics on the gender and age of members? If so you would add these characteristics under Members.

For the moment you can assume that there are no further characteristics to be recorded. So the list of subjects and characteristics now looks as shown below.

Books	Members	Loans	Authors
ISBN	Name	ISBN	Name
Title	Address	Member Name	Web Address
Author Name	Phone	Date Borrowed	
Publication Year	Email	Date Returned	
Publisher Name		Fine Paid	
Category			
Date Purchased			
Cost			

Tables and fields

Each subject of a database is represented by a table in the database. Each characteristic of a subject represents a field in the corresponding table. So the list of subjects and characteristics maps directly to the list of tables and fields for the database.

When naming your tables and fields, follow these simple guidelines:

■ Table and field names should be unique and meaningful.

■ Keep table and field names as short as possible while maintaining their meaningfulness.

■ For tables, use the plural form of the name. For fields, use the singular form of the name.

■ If the same field appears in two tables, give it the same name in each.

With these guidelines in mind, the tables so far determined for the Village Library database might look like those below.

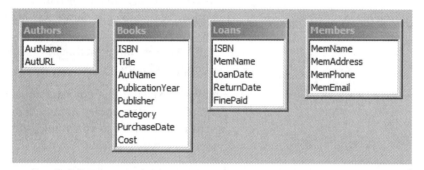

The tables and fields identified here are a good foundation for the Village Library database but they need further refinement, as described in the next section.

Design principles

The principles of good database design can be summarized as follows:

- One table, one subject

- One field, one value

- One table, one primary key

- The key, the whole key, and nothing but the key

One table, one subject

Each table in your database should represent a single subject only. Otherwise, you will have multiple repetitions of the same data in different records. The result: redundancy, inconsistencies, and modification anomalies. The tables identified in the previous section meet this criterion.

You could arrive at the same set of tables by analysing the Library_Flat_Database and eliminating redundancy.

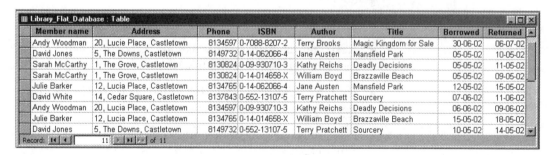

ECDL Advanced Databases

- Whenever Andy Woodman borrows a book, his personal details are duplicated in a new record. To ensure that member details are stored only once, you would create a separate Members table.

- Whenever someone borrows *Sourcery* by Terry Pratchett, the book's ISBN, author and title must be repeated. To ensure that book details are stored only once, you would create a separate Books table.

- If you include an author's website address, then every time someone borrows a book, both the author name and web address must be repeated. To ensure that author details are stored only once, you would create a separate Authors table.

- The Borrowed and Returned dates are the only fields now remaining in the original table. These relate to loans and should be included in a Loans table. This table would also include ISBN and Member name fields so that you can relate the Loans and Books tables and the Loans and Members tables.

From this exercise, you have arrived at the same set of tables as you did by identifying the database subjects and characteristics.

One field, one value

Each field in a table should represent only one data item and should contain only one value for that data item. Otherwise it is difficult to search and sort on values in the field.

There are two examples of *multipart* fields in the Members table: MemName and MemAddress.

- MemName contains both the member's first and last names. This makes it difficult to search and sort on last names. So split the field in two: MemFirstname and MemLastname. And do the same for the AutName field in the Authors table.

- MemAddress contains house numbers, street names and towns. Whether you split this into different fields depends on whether you want to manipulate the different parts of the address separately.

  Let's assume that the library wants to produce statistics on how many members live in each town. In this case, MemTown should be a separate field.

There is one example of a *multivalue* field in the Books table: AutName.

- Books can have more than one author, but including them all in the one field makes it difficult to sort and search on the field.

Resolving this problem involves creating a many-to-many relationship between the Books and Authors tables. You will learn how to do this in Chapter 5. For the moment, leave AutName in the Books table.

The database structure now looks as shown below.

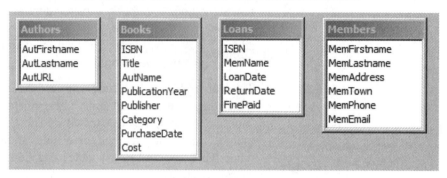

One table, one primary key

Every table must have a primary key that uniquely identifies each record in the table. The key can consist of a single field or a combination of fields (a composite key). If a table has more than one candidate for the primary key, choose the one with the least number of fields.

Let's look at each table in turn. Do any of the fields uniquely identify each record in the table?

- In the Members table, MemLastname is unlikely to be unique, as is the combination of MemFirstname and MemLastname. A combination of MemFirstname, MemLastname and MemAddress may also not be unique, as a parent and child living at the same address could have the same name.

The solution is to add a MemID field and to make it the primary key. In the Loans table, you must then replace the MemName field with the MemID field.

- For the purposes of the case study, we assume that there is never more than one copy of a given book in the library, so that ISBN uniquely identifies a book. Therefore, you can use ISBN as the primary key for the Books table.

ECDL Advanced Databases

- In the Authors table, only the combination of AutFirstname, AutLastname name and AutURL is likely to be unique. But no primary key should include a field that is optional or may be empty, as is the case with AutURL.

  Again, the solution is to add an AutID field and make it the primary key. In the Books table, you must then replace the AutName field with the AutID field.

- In the Loans table, the combination of ISBN and LoanDate is unique for each record. So you can make this the primary key.

The database structure now looks as shown below (the primary key fields are in bold type).

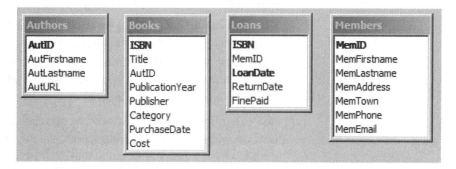

The key, the whole key, and nothing but the key

This phrase summarizes three important attributes of good database design.

- **The key ...** Each field in a table must directly describe the subject of that table, as represented by the primary key.

  For example, a PublisherAddress field should not be included in the Books table, as it describes a publisher and not a book. If you need to record that information, you would create a separate Publishers table.

- **... the whole key ...** When a table has a composite key, each non-key field must depend on the whole key and not just on part of it.

  If the Loans table included a Title field, that field would depend on the value in the ISBN field, but not on the value in the LoanDate field. So it doesn't belong in that table.

- **... and nothing but the key.** Each field in a table must depend on the primary key and on no other field in the table. That is, making a change to data in one non-key field must not require making a change to data in any other non-key field.

For example, if you include a PublisherAddress field in the Books table, then the value of the primary key (ISBN) determines the value of the PublisherAddress field only indirectly. If the value in the Publisher field changes, the value in the PublisherAddress field will also change. So PublisherAddress does not belong in the Books table.

Chapter 2: summary

The aim of good database design is to minimize redundancy and to ensure that each field is directly related to the subject of the table.

When designing a database, you should avoid unnecessary redundancy, multipart and multivalue fields, and modification anomalies.

The first step in designing a database is to establish the purpose of the database and the tasks you want to accomplish with it. From these you can draw up a list of subjects for the database and the characteristics of those subjects. You can then map subjects to tables, and characteristics to fields.

You can refine the tables by checking that each table represents only one subject, that each field represents only one value, that each table has a primary key, and that each field in a table depends on the primary key, the whole key, and nothing but the key.

Chapter 2: quick quiz

Q1	Which of these are problems associated with flat databases?
A.	Redundancy.
B.	Data entry errors.
C.	Modification anomalies.

Q2	True or false – a multivalue field includes more than one value for the same data item.
A.	True.
B.	False.

Q3	True or false – a multipart field includes more than one data item.
A.	True.
B.	False.

Q4	True or false – subjects map to tables and characteristics map to fields.
A.	True.
B.	False.

Q5	Which of these is *not* a principle of good database design?
A.	One table, one subject.
B.	One field, one value.
C.	One value, one key.

Answers

1: All, **2:** A, **3:** A, **4:** A, **5:** C.

Table design: data types, field sizes, field formats

In this chapter

The data type of a field determines the kind of data that can be stored in the field and the operations that can be carried out on that data. The properties of a field determine how data in the field is stored, handled and displayed.

In this chapter you will learn the purpose of each data type and related *Field Size* and *Format* properties.

New skills

At the end of this chapter you should be able to:

- Explain the purpose of each data type

- Apply each data type

- Specify field sizes and formats

- Explain the consequences of changing a field's data type

New words

There are no new terms in this chapter.

Exercise file

In this chapter you will work with the following Access file:

- `Chp3_VillageLibrary_Database`

You will also use the following Word file:

- `MansfieldPark-JaneAusten`

Syllabus reference

In this chapter you will cover the following items of the ECDL Advanced Database syllabus:

- **AM5.1.1.1:** Apply and modify data types such as text, memo, hyperlink, currency, date and time in a field, column.

- **AM5.1.1.2:** Understand the consequences of modifying data types.

About data types

Access supports the following data types:

- Text
- Memo
- Number
- Currency
- Date/Time
- AutoNumber
- Yes/No
- Hyperlink

It is important to choose the appropriate data type for each field when you create it.

Before you enter data in a table, you can change the data type of a field as and when you like. After you have entered data, changing a field's data type has consequences that you must take into account if you do not want to lose data.

Field sizes

Some data types have a *Field Size* property that you can use to set the maximum size for data in a field. Use the smallest possible setting as smaller data sizes can be processed faster and require less memory than larger ones. Users will not be able to enter values larger than the specified field size.

Be careful when reducing the size of a field that already contains data. You will lose data if existing values are larger than those supported by the new field size.

Field formats

Many data types have a *Format* property that you can use to specify how data is displayed and printed. This does not affect how data is stored in a field. For example, you can choose to display dates in any of the following formats:

```
23/05/03

23-May-03

Friday, May 23, 2003
```

For each data type, you can select from a list of predefined formats or you can create your own custom format.

For some predefined Number, Currency and Date/Time formats, Access uses the Regional Settings specified in the Windows Control Panel. The examples used in this book assume that your Regional Settings are set to *English (United Kingdom)*. (See 'Windows Regional Settings' in the Preface for further information.)

Applying data types and field properties

You apply data types to fields in Table Design View. In the Design View window, you use the *Field Name* column to specify the name of a field and you use the *Data Type* column to specify the field's data type.

When you click on a field in the upper part of the Design View window, that field's properties are displayed in the lower part of the window, and you can choose the options you want there.

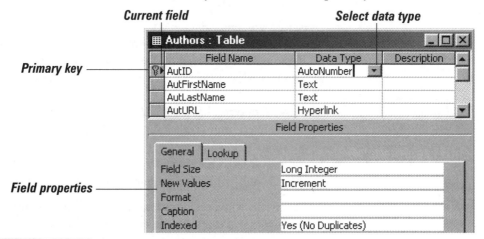

Current field — Select data type — Primary key — Field properties

Text fields

Use a Text data type to store alphanumeric data that does not exceed 255 characters in length. For example, in the Village Library database, a Text data type is appropriate for name, address, ISBN and book title fields.

Use a Text data type also for numbers that are not required in calculations – for example, telephone numbers and postal codes.

The following are all Text fields.

MemFirstname	MemLastname	MemPhon
Andy	White	8134597
David	Jones	8149732

Be aware that in a Text field, numbers are sorted as text strings. If you want to sort them in numeric order, either change the data type to Number or add leading zeros to the number strings to make them all the same length.

Text	Text	Number
1	001	1
10	002	2
100	010	10
13	013	13
2	020	20
20	100	100

Text data type   Text data type   Number data type

Memo fields

Use a Memo data type to store alphanumeric data that is more than 255 characters long. Data in Memo fields can contain tabs and paragraph breaks.

In Datasheet View, you see only a single line of a Memo field at any one time. To view the full contents of the field, click in the field and press **Shift+F2**. This displays the *Zoom* dialog box where you can view and edit the contents of the field. You can use this feature for other field types as well.

Exercise 3.1: Creating a Memo field

In this exercise you will add a Review field to the Books table and set its data type to Memo.

1) Open the starting database for this chapter:

    Chp3_VillageLibrary_Database

2) Open the Books table in Design View. To do this, click on the table in the Database window and click the **Design** button.

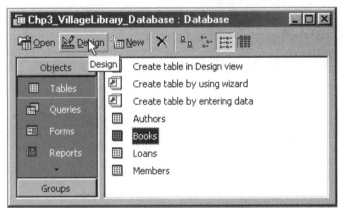

3) Add a new field at the end of the table. Name it Review and select Memo as its data type.

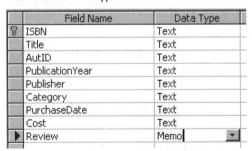

4) Switch to Datasheet View, saving the table as you do.

5) To see how a Memo field works, you need some sample text. To save time, open the Microsoft Access Help Window and copy a few paragraphs of text from there.

6) Click a Review field in the Books table and press **Shift+F2**.

7) When the *Zoom* dialog box appears, paste the copied text into it. Notice that Access preserves the text and paragraph breaks but not the formatting or any graphics.

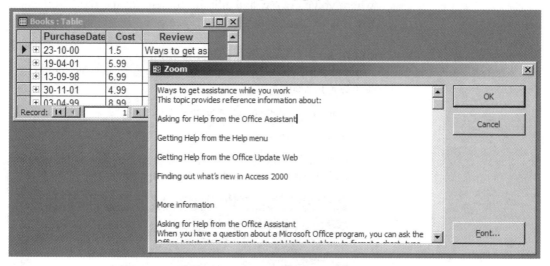

8) Click **OK** to close the *Zoom* dialog box.

9) Now try using the **Arrow** keys to scroll through the field contents. You can see that with any lengthy entry it is much easier to view the data in the *Zoom* dialog box and to edit it there.

10) Press **Shift+F2** again and make some changes to the data.

    You can use standard editing keys such as **Del** and **Backspace**, but to insert a paragraph break you must press **Ctrl+Enter** (pressing **Enter** is the same as clicking **OK**).

11) Click **OK** to save your changes. Then close the Books table.

Number fields

Use a Number data type to store numeric data that is to be used in calculations, except calculations involving currency values.

The following are all examples of Number fields.

Order ID	Quantity	Discount
10248	12	15%
10248	10	20%

Field Size

Use the *Field Size* property to set a specific number type. The options are shown in the following table.

Field Size	Description
Byte	Stores whole numbers from 0 to 255.
Integer	Stores whole numbers from –32,768 to 32,767.
Long Integer	Stores whole numbers from –2,147,483,648 to 2,147,483,647. This is the default size.
Single	Stores numbers from –3.402823E38 to –1.401298E–45 for negative values and from 1.401298E–45 to 3.402823E38 for positive values.
Double	Stores numbers from –1.79769313486231E308 to –4.94065645841247E–324 for negative values and from 1.79769313486231E308 to 4.94065645841247E–324 for positive values.
Replication ID	A special number type relevant only to database replication.
Decimal	Stores numbers from $-10^{28} -1$ through $10^{28} -1$.

When to use a Number data type

You can enter numeric data in Text, Number and Currency fields. How do you decide when to use a Number field and which field size to apply?

Data types for numbers

- If numbers are not going to be used in calculations, you can use the Text data type. Remember, however, that numbers in Text fields sort as text strings (see 'Text fields' above).

- If numbers represent a currency value, use the Currency data type.

- If numbers are going to be used in calculations or need to be sorted in numeric order, use the Number data type.

Number field sizes

- For numbers without fractions, use *Byte*, *Integer* or *Long Integer*, depending on the range of numbers required.

- For values with fractions, use *Single*, *Double* or *Decimal*, depending on the degree of precision required.

Single and *Double* number types can store extremely small and extremely large numbers. However, they use floating-point mathematics and you may encounter small rounding errors when you include them in calculations. If you require a high level of accuracy, and cannot afford even very small rounding errors, use *Decimal* instead, or use a Currency data type (this can store up to 15 digits to the left of the decimal point and up to four digits to the right).

Format

Access provides a number of predefined formats for Number fields. For example, you can choose to include a currency symbol, to include or exclude thousands separators, or to display a number as a percentage.

Exercise 3.2: Applying Number data types

In this exercise you will apply a Number data type to the Books.PublicationYear field so that you can perform calculations on its values. You will also change the field's *Field Size* and *Format* properties.

1) Open the Books table in Design View.

2) Change the *Data Type* setting for the PublicationYear field from *Text* to *Number*.

3) In the *Field Properties* box, you can see that Access sets the field size to *Long Integer* by default. However, no year entered in the Library database will be greater than 32,767 so an *Integer* field size is adequate.

   Click on the *Field Size* property and click the arrow to view the available field sizes. Then select the *Integer* option.

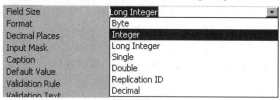

4) Click on the *Format* property and click the arrow to view the available formats.

   You do not want thousands separators, currency symbols or decimal places, so select the *General Number* option. This option does not display decimal places for integers.

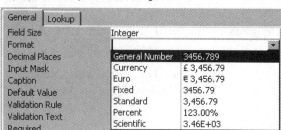

5) For an explanation of all Number formats, press **F1** with the *Format* property still selected. This displays a help topic that explains formats in general. Click the *Number and Currency Data Types* link for information on Number formats specifically. When you have finished, close the Help window.

6) Save the Books table.

Currency fields

Use a Currency data type for monetary values. The default currency symbol displayed depends on your Windows Regional Settings. You can also use a Currency data type for number fields that require a high level of accuracy, with no rounding off during calculations.

Cost
£3.87
£5.99

Exercise 3.3: Applying Currency data types

In this exercise you will apply a Currency data type to the Books.Cost field and select an appropriate *Format* option.

1) Open the Books table in Design View.

2) For the Cost field, change the *Data Type* setting to *Currency*.

3) Notice that the field's *Format* property is automatically set to *Currency*. Click in the property box and click the down arrow to see the display layout of this format.

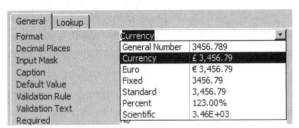

4) Save the Books table.

Date/Time fields

Use a Date/Time data type for dates and times.

By default, Access displays dates and times using the Short Date and Long

LoanDate	ReturnDate
24-May-02	27-05-02

Time settings in your Windows Regional Settings. If a value includes a date only, no time is displayed. If a value includes a time only, no date is displayed.

Exercise 3.4: Applying Date/Time data types

In this exercise you will apply a Date/Time data type to the Books.PurchaseDate field and select an appropriate field format.

1) Open the Books table in Design View.

2) For the PurchaseDate field, change the *Data Type* setting to *Date/Time*.

3) Click on the *Format* property and click the arrow to view the available formats.

4) Select the *Medium Date* format.

Format		
Input Mask	General Date	19-06-94 17:34:23
Caption	Long Date	19 June 1994
Default Value	Medium Date	19-Jun-94
Validation Rule	Short Date	19-06-94
Validation Text	Long Time	17:34:23
Required	Medium Time	05:34
Indexed	Short Time	17:34

5) Close the Books table, saving it as you do.

AutoNumber fields

Use an AutoNumber data type for fields that require unique, consecutive or random numbers. Access generates the numbers automatically. Typically this data type is used for primary key fields such as order numbers, IDs, invoice numbers, and so on.

MemID
000001
000002
000003

By default, Access assigns a *Field Size* property of *Long Integer* and a *New Values* property of *Increment* to AutoNumber fields. These are the most commonly used settings and don't normally need to be changed.

If the same field is included in more than one table, in order to link the two tables, it must have the same data type in both tables. AutoNumber fields are an exception. If a field in one table has an AutoNumber data type, then it must have a Number data type in the linked table and a field size of *Long Integer*.

Note that you cannot include more than one AutoNumber field in a table.

Exercise 3.5: Applying an AutoNumber data type

In this exercise, you will apply an AutoNumber data type to the Authors.AutID field and change the Books.AutID field's data type accordingly.

1) Open the Authors table in Design View.

2) Change the data type of the AutID field to *AutoNumber*. You can see that Access assigns a *Field Size* property of *Long Integer* and a *New Values* property of *Increment* by default. Leave these as they are.

3) Close and save the Authors table.

4) Open the Books table in Design View.

5) AutID is included here as a link to the Authors table. So set the data type to *Number* and the *Field Size* property to *Long Integer*.

6) Close and save the Books table.

Yes/No fields

Use a Yes/No data type for fields that can contain only one of two values.

By default, Access uses a checkbox control for Yes/No fields. However, you can change this to a text box or a combo box if you wish. You can then use the field's *Format* property to specify whether the values display as Yes/No, True/False or On/Off.

FineIssued	Fine
☑	€ 2.50
☐	€ 0.00

FineIssued	Fine
Yes	€ 2.50
No	€ 0.00

Exercise 3.6: Applying a Yes/No data type

In this exercise you will add a FineIssued field to the Loans table and set its data type to Yes/No.

1) Open the Loans table in Design View.

2) Insert a new field before the FinePaid field (click in the row for the FinePaid field and choose **Insert | Rows**). Name the new field FineIssued and set its data type to *Yes/No*.

3) The field's *Format* property is set by default to *Yes/No*. Have a look at the other options available but do not change the current setting.

4) Click on the **Lookup** tab in the *Field Properties* box. Then click the *Display Control* property and open its drop-down list. This lists the types of control that you can use for the field. *Check Box* is the default and most commonly used option, so leave this as it is.

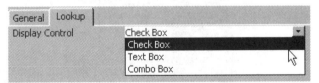

5) Switch to Datasheet View, saving the table as you do. Notice that Access has set the values in your new field to unselected checkboxes by default; this indicates a No value. To change a value, simply click in the checkbox.

6) Close the Loans table.

Hyperlink fields

Use a Hyperlink data type to store hyperlinks to websites, folders and files. Users can then click on the hyperlink to start the relevant application and display the destination of the link.

Exercise 3.7: Applying a Hyperlink data type

In this exercise you will change the data type of the Books.Review field from Memo to Hyperlink.

1) Open the Books table in Design View.

2) Change the Review field's data type to *Hyperlink*.

3) Switch back to Datasheet View, saving the table as you do.

Note that any values already in the Review field are converted to hyperlinks, but the links are invalid and will not work.

Exercise 3.8: Creating a hyperlink to a file

In this exercise you will create a hyperlink to a Word document that contains a review of *Mansfield Park* by Jane Austen.

1) With the Books table in Datasheet View, click in an empty Review field and choose **Insert | Hyperlink**.

   This displays a dialog box where you can browse to the file, folder or web page to which you want to create the link.

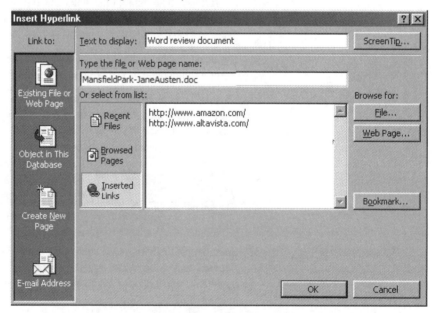

2) In the *Text to display* box, type the text you want to appear in the Hyperlink field in Access. For example:

```
Word review document
```

3) Use the *Browse for: File* option to navigate to the folder to which you copied the contents of the CD that accompanies this book. Then select the following file by double-clicking on it:

`MansfieldPark-JaneAusten`

4) Click **OK**. A hyperlink to the file is now inserted in the Review field.

Review
Word review document

5) Click on the link. This starts Microsoft Word and opens the review document.

6) Close the document, exit Word, and return to Access.

Exercise 3.9: Creating a hyperlink to a web page
In this exercise you will create a hyperlink to a review on a web page.

1) In the Books table, right-click on the link you created in the previous exercise and choose **Hyperlink | Edit Hyperlink** from the pop-up menu. This displays the *Edit Hyperlink* dialog box. Make sure that the *Link to: Existing File or Web Page* option is selected.

2) In the *Text to display* box, replace the existing text with the following:

`Web review`

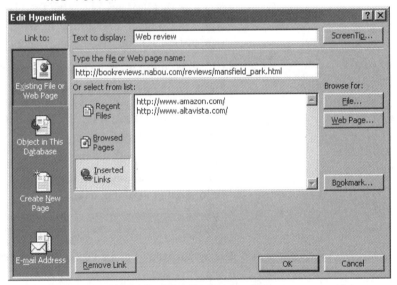

3) Click on the *Browse for: Web Page* option. This starts your web browser.

4) Connect to the Internet and go to the following address:

`http://bookreviews.nabou.com/reviews/mansfield_ park.html`

5) Close your Browser and disconnect. In the *Type the file or Web page name* box, Access automatically enters the address for the last web page you accessed. If it doesn't, you can select the web page from

the list displayed when you click the *Browsed Pages* option in the dialog box.

If you do not have an Internet connection, type the address directly in the *Type the file...* box.

6) Click **OK**. A hyperlink to the web page is now inserted in the Review field.

Review
Web review

7) Click on the link. This starts your web browser. When a connection to the Internet has been established, the web page to which you created the hyperlink is opened.

8) Exit your web browser and disconnect.

9) Return to Access and close the Books table.

Modifying data types

Before you enter data in a table, you can change the data type of a field as and when you like. After you have entered data, however, changing a field's data type may not always be possible or may have consequences that you need to be aware of if you don't want to lose data.

In general, Access can convert any data type to any other data type, provided that data already in the field is valid for the new data type. For example, in exercises in this chapter you changed the data type of fields in the Books and Authors tables without a problem.

However, there are conversions that are not possible or that may cause problems. When a data type modification will result in errors or deletions, Access always displays a warning message and gives you the option of either continuing with or abandoning the conversion.

The following table lists the most common data type conversions and any limitations you need to be aware of if a field already contains data.

From	To	Limitations
Any data type	AutoNumber	Not possible if the field contains values or is part of a relationship.
AutoNumber	Text, Currency, Number	Values may be truncated depending on the new *Field Size* setting.
Text	Memo	None.
Memo	Text	Text longer than 255 characters is truncated. Values may also be truncated depending on the new *Field Size* setting.

Text, Memo	Number, Currency	Text must contain only numbers and valid separators, otherwise it is deleted.
	Date/Time	Text must contain a recognizable date and/or time, otherwise it is deleted.
	Yes/No	Text must contain one the following values only: Yes, No, True, False, On or Off, otherwise it is deleted.
	Hyperlink	Text must contain a valid hyperlink, otherwise the link will not work.
Number	Text, Memo, Currency	Where relevant, make sure that values fit in the new field size.
	Yes/No	Zero and Null convert to No, any other value converts to Yes.
Currency	Text, Memo, Number	Where relevant, make sure that values fit in the new field size.
Date/Time	Text, Memo	None.
Yes/No	Text, Memo	None.
	Number, Currency	Yes converts to −1; No converts to 0.
Hyperlink	Text	Text longer than 255 characters is truncated.
	Memo	None.
	Any other type	Not possible.

Chapter 3: summary

The data type of a field determines the kind of data that can be stored in that field and the operations that can be carried out on the data.

You use a Text data type for alphanumeric data no more than 255 characters long and for numbers that do not require calculations and do not need to be sorted in numeric order. You use a Memo data type for long passages of unformatted text.

You use a Number or Currency data type for numeric data that is to be used in calculations. And you use an AutoNumber data type when you want Access to generate unique, sequential numbers for a field.

You use a Date/Time data type for date fields, a Hyperlink data type to store hyperlinks to websites and files, and a Yes/No data type for fields that have only two possible values.

The properties of a field determine how data in the field is stored, handled, and displayed. You use the *Field Size* property to set the maximum size for data in a field. You use the *Format* property to specify how data is displayed and printed.

Before you enter data in a table, you can change the data type of a field as and when you like. If you change a field's data type after you have entered data, make sure that data already in the field is valid for the new data type; otherwise the data may be lost.

Chapter 3: quick quiz

Q1	True or false – you can apply data types to fields in both Datasheet and Design View.
A.	True.
B. ✓	False.

Q2	To view a field's contents in the *Zoom* dialog you …
A.	Click in the field and press **Ctrl+F2**.
B.	Click in the field and press **Shift+F2**.
C.	Double-click on the field.
D. ✓	Click in the field and choose **View	Zoom**.

Q3	True or false – you use the *Format* property to set the number type (Integer, Decimal, and so on) for a Number field.
A. ✓	True.
B.	False.

Q4	A Yes/No data type is useful for …
A.	Fields that require unique, sequential numbers.
B. ✓	Fields that have only two possible values.
C.	Fields that you want to be able to hide and unhide.
D.	Field that you want to be able to freeze and unfreeze.

Q5	Which data type allows you to store links to Microsoft Word documents in a field?
A.	Memo.
✓ **B.**	Hyperlink.
C.	Text.

Q6	Which data type allows you to store links to web pages in a field?
A.	Memo.
✓ **B.**	Hyperlink.
C.	Text.

Answers

1: B, **2:** B, **3:** B, **4:** B, **5:** B, **6:** B.

4

Table design: advanced field properties

Setting an appropriate data type and field size provides a degree of control over the data that users can enter in a field. For more precise control, and to make data entry easier for users, you can also use lookup fields, input masks, validation rules, default values and required values.

In this chapter you will learn how to create and use these features, which are all field properties.

New skills

At the end of this chapter you should be able to:

- Understand and create lookup fields
- Understand and create input masks
- Understand and create validation rules
- Define default values
- Define required fields

New words

In this chapter you will meet the following terms:

- Lookup field
- Input mask
- Validation rule
- Default value
- Required value

Exercise file

In this chapter you will work with the following Access file:

- Chp4_VillageLibrary_Database

Syllabus reference

In this chapter you will cover the following items of the ECDL Advanced Database syllabus:

- **AM5.1.1.3:** Create and edit a lookup field, column.
- **AM5.1.1.4:** Create and edit a validation rule in a field, column.

- **AM5.1.1.5:** Create and edit an input mask in a field, column.

- **AM5.1.1.6:** Apply and modify default values in a field, column.

- **AM5.1.1.7:** Set a mandatory data field, column.

Lookup fields

A lookup field displays a list of values from which the user selects one to enter in the field. The field can look up its values in a table/query or in a value list that you define when you create the field.

- Use a lookup to another table when the lookup field duplicates values from that table.

    For example, the MemID field in the Loans table refers to MemID values in the Members table. So you could create Loans.MemID as a lookup field that lists members from the Members table and allows users to select a member from the list.

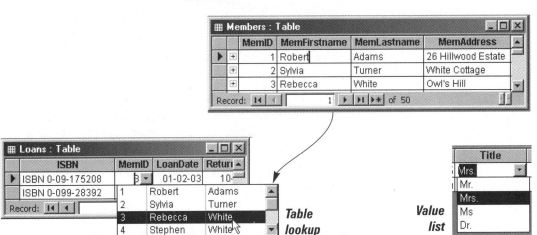

Table lookup

Value list

- Use a value list for fields with a limited set of values that do not change often. For example, a Title field with the options Mr, Mrs, and Ms.

> ### Lookup field
>
> *A field that displays a list from which you select the value to store in the field. The list can look up values either from a table or query or from a fixed value list.*

Access provides a *Lookup Wizard* for creating lookup fields. With the wizard you can either create a fixed value list for the field or specify fields in another table as the list source.

Exercise 4.1: Creating a lookup field with a fixed value list
In this exercise, you will change the Books.Category field to a lookup field and specify a set of values for the lookup list.

1) Open the starting database for this chapter:

    Chp4_VillageLibrary_Database

2) Open the Books table in Design View.

3) Change the data type of the Category field to *Lookup Wizard*. This starts the *Lookup Wizard*.

4) First the wizard prompts you to select the type of lookup field you want to create. Select the second option and click **Next**.

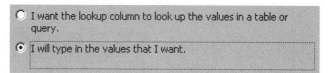

5) The wizard now prompts you for the layout and content of your list.

    You use the *Number of columns* option to specify the number of columns in the list. The default is 1 and is suitable for the category list, so leave this as it is. A single column is displayed in the area below and this is where you enter your list.

    Type the following categories in successive rows of the column, in alphabetical order:

    - Biography
    - Children
    - Computers
    - Cookery
    - Crime
    - Fantasy
    - Fiction
    - Reference
    - Science

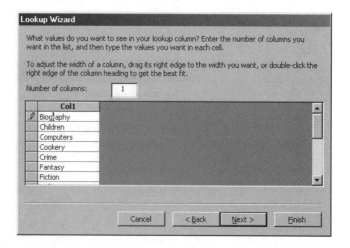

To adjust the column width to fit the longest entry, double-click on the right edge of the column heading. Then click **Next**.

6) When prompted for a name for your lookup field, accept the default (the field name) and click **Finish**.

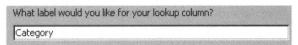

7) Switch to Datasheet View, saving the table as you do.

8) Click in a Category field and click the arrow that appears. This displays the list you have just created.

9) Select a category in the list. This is then entered in the Category field for you.

If you type an entry in the field instead, Access automatically displays the first list item that matches the characters entered.

If you type a value that is not in the list, Access allows the entry and stores the value in the field. However, it doesn't add the value to the list for future lookups.

10) Close the Books table.

If you want to change the list at a later stage, you can use the field's *Row Source* property to add, edit and remove values (see 'Creating and modifying lookup fields manually' below).

Exercise 4.2: Creating a field that looks up values in another table

In this exercise, you will change the Loans.MemID field to a lookup field that looks up values in the Members table.

1) Open the Loans table in Design View.

2) Change the data type of the MemID field to *Lookup Wizard*. This starts the *Lookup Wizard*.

3) In the first page of the wizard, select the first option and click **Next**.

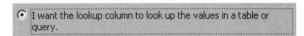

4) The wizard now displays a dialog where you specify the table to which you want to link the lookup field. Select the Members table and click **Next**.

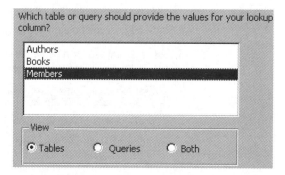

Which table or query should provide the values for your lookup column?

Authors
Books
Members

View
○ Tables   ○ Queries   ○ Both

5) The wizard displays a list of the fields in the Members table and prompts you to select the ones you want to include in the lookup list. Select MemID, MemLastname and MemFirstname.

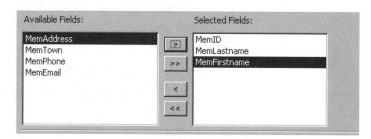

Available Fields:

MemAddress
MemTown
MemPhone
MemEmail

Selected Fields:

MemID
MemLastname
MemFirstname

You need MemID because this is the value you want to enter in records in the Loans table. The other two fields make the list more meaningful. When you have selected the fields, click **Next**.

6) You can now adjust the layout of the columns. Access suggests that you hide the MemID column. However, users will need to be able to differentiate between members with the same first and last names, so deselect the *Hide key column* option.

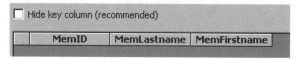

☐ Hide key column (recommended)

	MemID	MemLastname	MemFirstname

You can adjust the width of the columns the same way as you do in a datasheet. Make them just wide enough to fit the ID and name values.

Click **Next** when you have finished.

7) The wizard prompts you to select the field whose value you want to store in the Loans table. Select MemID and click **Next**.

8) The wizard prompts you for a label for the lookup field. This becomes the default name for the field in datasheets and forms. The default is the name of the field you selected in step 7. Leave this as it is and click **Finish**.

9) Save the table when prompted to do so and switch to Datasheet View.

10) Click in a MemID field and click the down arrow to view the lookup list you have just created. Then select a member from the list. Access enters the MemID value in the field for you.

11) Close the Loans table.

If some of the columns in the list are too narrow or too wide for the data they display, you can use the *Column Width* and *List Width* lookup properties to adjust the widths (see 'Creating and modifying lookup fields manually' below).

Basing a lookup field on a query

In the Loans table, it would useful if the ISBN field looked up its values in the Books table. It would be even more useful if the lookup list displayed not only each book's ISBN and title (from the Books table) but also its author's name (from the Authors table), as shown below.

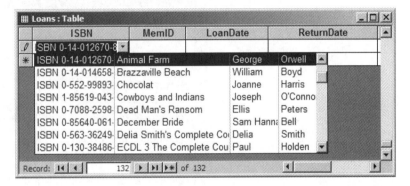

If you want to use the *Lookup Wizard* to create this lookup field, you must first create a query that includes all the fields you want to display, and then base the lookup field on that query. This is because the wizard doesn't allow you to select fields from different tables.

The Chp4_VillageLibrary_Database database includes a suitable query: ISBNLookupField. Open that query now in Design View and take a look at how it is defined. It includes the Books.ISBN, Books.Title, Authors.AutFirstname, and Authors.AutLastname fields, and is sorted by title (in ascending order).

Exercise 4.3: Creating a lookup field based on a query

In this exercise, you will create the ISBN lookup field based on the ISBNLookupField query.

1) Open the Loans table in Design View.

2) Change the data type of the ISBN field to *Lookup Wizard*. This starts the *Lookup Wizard*.

3) In the first page of the wizard, select the first option and click **Next**.

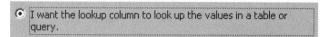

4) In the next page, select the *Queries* option, select the ISBNLookupField query, and then click **Next**.

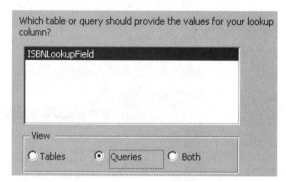

5) When prompted for the fields you want to include in the lookup list, select all the fields and click **Next**.

6) Now adjust the column widths to fit the field contents, as shown below, and click **Next** when you have finished.

7) When prompted for the field whose value you want to store in the Loans table, select ISBN and click **Next**.

8) When prompted for a label for the lookup field, accept the default (which is the field name) and click **Finish**. This returns you to Design View.

9) Save the table and switch to Datasheet View.

10) Click in an ISBN field and click the down arrow to view the lookup list you have just created. Then select a book from the list. Access enters the ISBN value in the field for you.

11) Close the Loans table.

If some of the columns in the list are too narrow or too wide for the data they display, you can use the *Column Width* and *List Width* lookup properties to adjust the widths (see 'Creating and modifying lookup fields manually' below).

Creating and modifying lookup fields manually

In Design View, the **Lookup** tab in the *Field Properties* area displays the properties of a lookup field. The *Lookup Wizard* sets these properties automatically. To change them you can either rerun the wizard or make your changes directly to the properties on the **Lookup** tab.

The lookup properties shown here are those for the MemID lookup field that you created in Exercise 4.2.

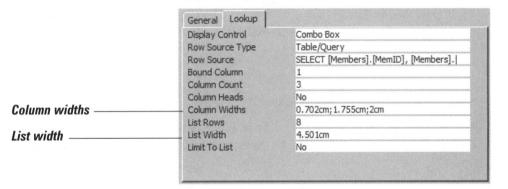

Column widths

List width

General	Lookup
Display Control	Combo Box
Row Source Type	Table/Query
Row Source	SELECT [Members].[MemID], [Members].
Bound Column	1
Column Count	3
Column Heads	No
Column Widths	0.702cm;1.755cm;2cm
List Rows	8
List Width	4.501cm
Limit To List	No

Once you are sufficiently familiar with creating lookup fields you may find it quicker and easier to create them by setting their properties on the **Lookup** tab instead of by using the wizard.

The following table explains each lookup property and the most commonly used options for those properties.

Property	Description
Display Control	Specifies the control to be used for displaying the lookup list.
	Listbox: On forms, the list is always displayed and the values are limited to those in the list.
	Combo box: On forms, the list doesn't display until you open it; so it uses less room than a list box. Also you can allow users to enter values that are not on the list.
Row Source Type	Specifies the type of source for the list values. For example, *Table/Query* or *Value List*.
Row Source	Specifies the source for the values in the lookup field.
	For a *value list*, this specifies the entries in the list. Each entry is enclosed in double quotes and separated from the next entry by a semicolon. For example:
	`"Biography";"Children";"Computers";`
	When the source is one or more *tables/queries*, this property typically takes the form of an SQL SELECT statement that specifies the source tables and fields. For example, if you look at this property for the Loans.MemID field, you will see the following:
	`SELECT [Members].[MemID], [Members].[MemLastname], [Members].[MemFirstname] FROM Members;`
	But you don't need to enter this manually. If the source is a single table and you want to include all its fields in the lookup list, select the table from the property's drop-down list. If the source is multiple tables, or you want to include only selected fields in the lookup list, click the ... button at the right of the property. This starts the *Query Builder* where you can create a query that includes the tables and fields you want to display in the lookup list.

Bound Column	When you include more than one column in a lookup list, Access needs to know which column is bound to the lookup field – that is, which column's data will be stored in the field when you select an item in the list.
	Columns are numbered 1 to *n*, in the order in which they appear in the list. For example, this property is set to 1 for the MemID lookup field, indicating that the value of Members.MemID will be stored in the field.
Column Count	Specifies the number of columns in the lookup list, including hidden columns.
Column Heads	Specifies whether column headings are included in the lookup list. The headings are taken from the field names in the underlying table or query.
Column Widths	Specifies the width of each column in the lookup list, separated by semicolons. For example:
	0 ; 4cm ; 2cm ; 2cm
	You must include a width for each column. Enter 0 to hide a column.
List Rows	Specifies the maximum number of rows to be displayed in the lookup list at any one time.
List Width	Specifies the overall width of the lookup list.
Limit To List	Specifies whether users can enter any value in the field or only those that are included in the list.

What is SQL?

SQL (Structured Query Language) is the standard language used to create and query relational databases. For your convenience, Access provides graphical building tools for tables, queries, forms, and so on. Internally, however, it generates SQL statements to define these database objects.

For ECDL, you do not need to know how to use SQL. However, you will come across it in properties like the Row Source *property for lookup fields and combo box controls, and you can always view the SQL statement that a query uses by displaying the query in SQL View.*

Exercise 4.4: Modifying a fixed value list

In Exercise 4.1 you created a fixed-value lookup list for the Books. Category field. In this exercise, you will change the content and layout of this list.

1) Open the Books table in Design View and display the properties for the Category field.

2) Click the **Lookup** tab and take a look at the lookup properties for the field:

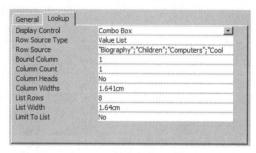

— *Row Source Type*. This specifies that the source for the lookup field is a fixed value list.

— *Row Source*. This specifies the values in the list. Each entry is enclosed in double quotes and separated from the next entry by a semicolon.

— *Column Count*. This specifies that the list has one column.

— *Column Widths*. This specifies the width of the column.

— *List Rows*. This specifies that the list should display eight values at a time.

— *List Width*. This specifies the overall width of the lookup list (in this case, the overall width is the same as the column width).

3) To add an Art category to the list, type the following at the start of the entries in the *Row Source* property:

    "Art";

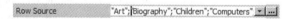

4) Now change the Children category to Children's Literature, as shown here:

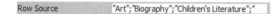

5) The width of the lookup list is now too narrow to show the Children's Literature entry in full, so change the *Column Widths* and *List Width* properties as follows:

6) Save the table and switch to Datasheet View to see the effect of your changes.

Exercise 4.5: Modifying a lookup field that looks up values in another table

In Exercise 4.2 you changed the Loans.MemID field to a lookup field that looks up values in the Members table. The lookup list displays the MemID, MemLastname, and MemFirstname field values for each member. In this exercise you will add the MemTown field to the list.

1) Open the Loans table in Design View and display the properties for the MemID field.

2) Click the **Lookup** tab and take a look at the lookup properties for the field:

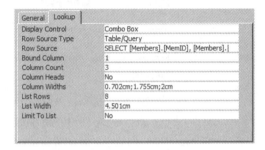

— *Row Source Type*. This specifies that the source for the lookup field is a table.

— *Row Source*. This consists of an SQL statement that specifies the source table and fields for the lookup list.

— *Bound Column*. This specifies which value should be stored in the Loans.MemID field when users select an entry in the lookup list. In this case it is the value in the first column (that is, the MemID).

— *Column Count*. This specifies that the list comprises three columns.

— *Column Widths*. This specifies the width of each column.

3) Click the *Row Source* property and then click the ![...] button at the right of the property. This starts the *Query Builder*, which displays the SQL statement as a query.

4) In the *Query Builder* window, add the MemTown field to the query design grid. To do this, double-click the MemTown field in the field list in the upper part of the window.

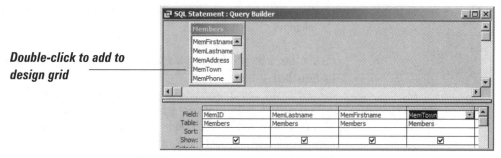

Double-click to add to design grid

5) Close the *Query Builder* window. When prompted to confirm your changes, click **Yes**. This updates the SQL statement in the *Row Source* property.

6) The lookup list now comprises four columns, so update the *Column Count* property as follows:

| Column Count | 4 |

7) Enter a width for the new column in the *Column Widths* property, as follows:

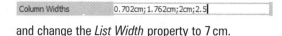

| Column Widths | 0.702cm;1.762cm;2cm;2.5| |

and change the *List Width* property to 7 cm.

8) Save the table and switch to Datasheet View to see the effect of your changes.

Input masks

An input mask is a template that specifies an exact pattern for data entered in a field and controls the type of data that can be entered at each position in the pattern. It makes data entry easier for users and helps to ensure entry of valid data.

Typically, an input mask consists of a combination of fixed characters (such as parentheses around telephone codes) and blank spaces where users fill in the field data.

For example, the telephone number input mask below enters the parentheses for you and requires entry of exactly three digits between the parentheses and seven digits after the parentheses.

Input mask ———
— **Valid value**

Input masks are most commonly used for Text and Date/Time fields but are also available for Number and Currency fields. Here are just some of the ways in which they can aid and control data entry:

- Automatically enter and display characters common to all entries in a field. For example, parentheses around telephone codes, date separators, and fixed text such as ISBN or SSN.

- Restrict the type of data that can be entered in a field. For example, input could be restricted to digits only or to a fixed pattern of digits and letters, as might be required for user IDs or social security numbers.

- Control the number of characters that can be entered in a field. For example, input of a credit card number could be restricted to exactly sixteen digits.

- Convert between uppercase and lowercase characters. For example, the input mask for a first name field could convert the first letter to uppercase and all others to lowercase, regardless of how they are entered.

Text, Date/Time, Number and Currency fields all have an *Input Mask* property, which you use to create input masks. A wizard is available for creating Text and Date/Time input masks.

> **Input mask**
>
> *A template that assists data entry and controls the type, number, and pattern of characters that can be entered in a field.*

Input mask examples

The Books table includes two examples of input masks. These illustrate how input masks work. Open the Books table in Datasheet View and take a look at the following fields:

- **PublicationYear:** This has an input mask that restricts entries to exactly four digits. When you click in an empty field, four underline characters (_) are displayed to indicate where you enter the digits.

  You cannot enter letters, you cannot enter more than four digits, and if you exit the field with fewer than four digits entered, Access displays a warning message that forces you to input the correct number. Try it and see!

  (Note that if you enter a value in a *new* record without entering an ISBN value, which is the primary key, Access displays an error message when you try to move to a different record or to close the table. If this happens, click the **Undo** button to undo your entry and then continue normally.)

- **PurchaseDate:** This has an input mask that forces input of dates in Short Date format (for example, 28-01-02) and automatically enters the separators for you. The template appears when you click in an empty PurchaseDate field.

  Access rejects any input other than numbers and forces input of exactly two numbers each for day, month and year. Again, try it and see!

Creating an input mask with the wizard

The *Input Mask Wizard* offers predefined input masks for dates, phone numbers and postal codes, and allows you to modify these to your own requirements. It is available only for Text and Date/Time fields.

Exercise 4.6: Creating an input mask with the *Input Mask Wizard*

In this exercise you will use the *Input Mask Wizard* to create an input mask for the Members.MemPhone field.

1) Open the Members table in Design View and display the field properties for the MemPhone field.

2) Click the *Input Mask* property and click the ... button that appears. This starts the *Input Mask Wizard*.

3) The first page of the wizard displays a list of predefined input masks. Select the *Phone Number* option and click **Next**.

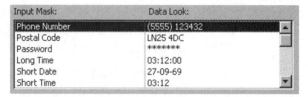

4) The second page of the wizard allows you to modify the selected mask and to select a placeholder character – that is, the character that indicates where data can or must be entered. The default is an underscore (_). Leave this as it is and click **Next**.

5) The third page of the wizard offers the option of storing the field data with or without any fixed characters. Again accept the default and click **Finish**.

6) Access now automatically inserts the input mask definition in the *Input Mask* property box. Ignore this for the moment and switch to Datasheet View, saving the table as you do.

7) Try entering some data in the MemPhone field. You will find that Access accepts any of the values shown here (spaces were entered where blanks are shown).

MemPhone
(　) 3456677
(　) 12345612
(1234) 233 1234

Input mask definitions

Now that you've seen how input masks work and how you can create them with a wizard, let's take a look at how input masks are defined.

Open the Members table in Design View and take a look at the *Input Mask* property for the MemPhone field. The property contains a string of characters as shown here. This is the *input mask definition*.

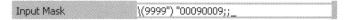

Input Mask   \(9999") "00090009;;_

The definition has three sections, separated by semicolons. The last two sections specify whether fixed display characters are stored with the field data and which character is displayed for blanks in the input mask. These sections are optional and can usually be omitted. By default, Access doesn't store display characters with a field's data and it uses an underscore (_) as the placeholder character.

The first section of the input mask definition is the input mask string. This uses special characters to specify the type of data that can be entered at each position in the mask and whether entry is optional or mandatory.

For example, in the input mask for the MemPhone field, '9' indicates that you can enter a digit or a space, but that entry is optional. A '0' indicates that you can enter a digit (0–9) only and that entry is mandatory. So users can enter up to four digits between the parentheses in the input mask and from 6 to 8 digits after the parentheses.

Input mask characters

Here is a list of the special characters that you can use to create an input mask.

Note that leaving a position blank is not the same as entering a space character in it. The two may look the same when you are entering data but they are handled differently by input masks. Blank positions are omitted when the data is saved, while space characters are saved with the data.

Character	Meaning
0	A digit (0–9) must be entered at this position.
9	An entry is optional, but if entered it must be a digit (0–9) or a space character.
#	An entry is optional, but if entered it must be a digit (0–9), a space character, or a plus or minus sign.
L	A letter (A–Z, a–z) must be entered at this position.
?	An entry is optional, but if entered it must be a letter (A–Z, a–z).
A	A letter (A–Z, a–z) or digit (0–9) must be entered at this position.
a	An entry is optional, but if entered it must be a letter (A–Z, a–z) or digit (0–9).
&	Any character or a space character. Entry is mandatory.
C	Any character or a space character. Entry is optional.
.	Decimal placeholder. The actual character used depends on your Windows Regional Settings.
,	Thousands separator. The actual character used depends on your Windows Regional Settings.
:;-/	Date and time separators. The actual character used depends on your Windows Regional Settings.
<	Converts all following characters to lowercase.
>	Converts all following characters to uppercase.

!	Characters typed into the mask fill it from left to right, but when you exit the field, the characters are shifted to the right side of the mask.
	
	For example, if you type 1234567 into the following input masks, the results are displayed as follows:
	
	`!(999) 9999999    (  ) 1234567`
	`(999) 9999999     (123) 4567`

Character	Meaning
\	Displays the next character as a literal character. This is used to display as a literal character any of the special characters listed in this table. For example, to display A you would enter \A.
	Characters that are not special input mask characters are automatically recognized as literals by Access and do not need to be specifically identified as such. However, when Access saves an input mask it automatically inserts the '\' character before a single literal character.
"literal"	Displays the enclosed characters as literal characters. This is used to display strings of special characters as literals. For example, to display CALL as a literal string, you could enter \C\A\L\L, but it is easier to enter "CALL".
	Strings that do not include special characters do not need to be enclosed by double quotes. However, when Access saves an input mask it automatically inserts double quotes around literal strings.

Input mask definition examples

Here is a list of input mask strings with examples of valid values for those masks.

Definition	Value examples
0000	1234 4562
(000) 0000000	(021) 2347654
(999) 9999999!	(021) 2347654 ( ) 1234567
>L0L 0L0	Z2Y 1C3
AAA-AAA	123-xyz XyZ-354
000-999	123-456 123-45 123-
>L<?????????	Judith Robbie Jennifer

Modifying an input mask

To modify an input mask, you make the required changes to the input mask string in the *Input Mask* property.

Exercise 4.7: Modifying an input mask

In this exercise you will modify the MemPhone input mask so that users must enter a three-digit area code followed by a seven-digit phone number.

1) Open the Members table in Design View and display the field properties for the MemPhone field.

2) Change the input mask string to:

```
\(000") "0000000;;_
```

3) Switch to Datasheet View, saving the table as you do.

   You will now find that you *must* enter three digits between the parentheses, and seven digits after them. Spaces will not be accepted.

Creating an input mask manually

To create an input mask manually, you enter the input mask definition string directly in the *Input Mask* property.

Exercise 4.8: Creating an input mask manually

In this exercise you will create an input mask for the ISBN field in the Books table.

1) Open the Books table in Design View, and display the properties for the ISBN field.

2) Enter the following input mask definition string in the *Input Mask* property:

```
ISBN &&&&&&&&&&&A
```

An ISBN always consists of ten digits preceded by the letters ISBN. The ten digits are divided into four parts, separated by hyphens or spaces. The number of digits in the first three parts varies but the total number is always nine. The final part contains a single digit or X. For example:

ISBN 0-14-014658-X   ISBN 0-099-28392-1   ISBN 1-85702-712-4

The input mask you have just specified requires entry of 13 characters in total. The first 12 can be any combination of numbers and hyphens; the last character can be either a digit or a letter. Access enters the letters ISBN automatically.

3) Switch to Datasheet View, saving the table as you do.

4) Enter the following values in the ISBN field by typing the characters shown:

To get this ISBN value …	Type …
ISBN 0-14-014658-X	0-14-014658-X
ISBN 0-099-28392-1	0-099-28392-1

5) Save and close the Books table.

Field validation rules

While input masks provide control over the type and number of characters entered in a field, field validation rules set limits or conditions on the values that you can enter. For example, an input mask could specify that input must be three digits, and a validation rule could then specify that the values entered must be between 100 and 200.

Field validation rules are enforced when you add or edit data in a field. Access checks the new value against the rule when you attempt to leave the field. If the value breaks the rule, Access displays a warning message and you must then either change the value to one that is acceptable or use the **Undo** command to undo your entry.

Field validation rule
A rule that sets limits or conditions on the values that you can enter in a field.

Creating field validation rules

A validation rule is specified as an expression that consists of a combination of operators (for example, +, >, =), literal values (for example, 123.5, 23/1/03, "Hello"), field names, and functions.

Validation rule expressions follow the same rules, and use the same operators and functions, as expressions used in queries, forms, and reports. For full details, see Appendix A.

You enter a validation rule expression in the *Validation Rule* property of a field. And in the *Validation Text* property, you enter the error message to be displayed when the rule is broken.

Open the Books table in Design View and take a look at the *Validation Rule* and *Validation Text* properties for the PublicationYear field.

Validation Rule	>1900
Validation Text	Publication year must be later than 1900

The validation rule states that any value entered into the field must be greater than 1900. Try entering years like 1812 or 1899 in the field and see what happens!

To create a validation rule you can use the Expression Builder tool or you can enter the validation rule expression directly in the *Validation Rule* property. The Expression Builder is not explained here. If you want to try it out for yourself, you can open it by clicking on the *Validation Rule* property box and clicking the ⋯ button.

Exercise 4.9: Creating a field validation rule

In this exercise you will add a validation rule to the Books.PurchaseDate field. The rule will ensure that dates entered in the field cannot be later than the current date.

1) Open the Books table in Design View and display the field properties for the PurchaseDate field.

2) Type the following expression in the *Validation Rule* property:

   <=Date()

   Date() is a function that returns the current date.

3) Type the following message in the *Validation Text* property: A book's purchase date must be the current date or earlier.

4) Switch to Datasheet View, saving the table as you do.

5) The following message is displayed, warning you that existing data in the PurchaseDate field may break the validation rule and asking whether you want to test the data. Click **No**.

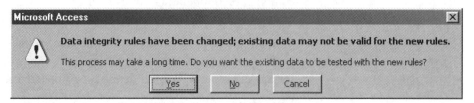

6) Now try entering various dates in the PurchaseDate field and see what happens.

Modifying field validation rules

You modify a field validation rule by making the required changes to the expression in the *Validation Rule* property.

Exercise 4.10: Modifying a field validation rule

In this exercise you will modify the validation rule for the Books.PublicationYear field so that the field accepts only year values greater than 1900 and less than 2050.

1) Open the Books table in Design View and display the properties for the PublicationYear field.

2) Change the expression in the *Validation Rule* property to the following:

   >1900 And <2050

3) Change the message in the *Validation Text* property to read as follows:

   Publication year must be later than 1900 and earlier than 2050.

4) Switch to Datasheet View, saving the table as you do.

   A message is displayed, warning you that existing data in the table may break the new validation rule and asking whether you want to test the data. Click **No**.

5) Now try entering years like 2051 or 2075 in the PublicationYear field and see what happens.

Validation rule examples

The following table shows various field validation rule expressions and their meaning.

Note that text strings in expressions must be enclosed by double quotes (for example "Hello") and dates must be enclosed by hash (#) symbols (for example, #21-01-03#).

Rule	Explanation
>0	Value must be greater than zero.
>=0 And <=100	Value must be in range 0 to 100.
=0 Or >100	Value must be either 0 or greater than 100.
>=#01/01/02#	Value must be a date equal to or later than 1 January, 2002.
Between 1 And 100	Value must be in the range 1 to 100.
In ("Mr", "Mrs", "Ms")	Value must be one of those listed.
=Date()	Only today's date is valid in the field. For example, this would be a useful validation rule for the Loans.LoanDate field.
>=Date()+30	Value must be a date 30 days or more in the future.

Default values

A default value is a value that Access automatically enters in a field when you create a new record. Where the same value is frequently entered in a field, having a default value speeds up data entry considerably. If the default value is not appropriate, you can simply overwrite it.

For example, if most books in the library are in the Fiction category, you could make Fiction the default value for the Books.Category field. Or if most members live in Castletown, you could make that the default value for the Members.MemTown field.

> **Default value**
>
> *A value that is automatically entered in a field when you create a new record.*

Creating default values

The default value for a field can be any valid value for that field. You enter the expression for the default value in the field's *Default Value* property.

When including a text string in a default value expression, enclose it in double quotes (for example "Fiction"). When specifying a date, enclose it with hash (#) symbols (for example, #21-01-03#).

Note that when you create a Number field, Access automatically assigns a default value of 0. If this is not appropriate, simply delete it from the *Default Value* property.

When you create a Yes/No field, Access automatically defaults the value to *No* when you add a new record. This is usually the appropriate default value and so there is no need to change it.

Exercise 4.11: Creating a default value

In this exercise, you will set a default value for the Loans.LoanDate field.

1) Open the Loans table in Design View and display the field properties for the LoanDate field.

2) Type the following in the *Default Value* property:

| Default Value | Date() | ... |

3) Switch to Datasheet View, saving the table as you do.

4) Add a new record to the table and you will see that the current date is automatically entered in the LoanDate field.

5) Close the table.

Note that defining a default value for a field has no effect on existing records. It you want to enter the default value in an existing record, click on the relevant field and press **Ctrl+Alt+Spacebar**.

Default value examples

Here are some further examples of default values.

Expression	Default field value
"Castletown"	Castletown
Date()	Today's date
Now()	The current date and time
Date()+10	Today's date plus 10
"Fiction"	Fiction
10	10

Required values

All fields, other than AutoNumber fields, have a *Required* property that specifies whether or not the field is mandatory and must contain a value.

In most tables, there are fields where it doesn't matter if a value is entered or not – for example, Members.MemEmail and Authors.AutURL. And there are other fields that must contain a value if a record is to be meaningful – for example, Books.Title.

To force entry of a value in a field, you set the field's *Required* property to *Yes*. When you then create a new record, Access will not allow you to save the record until you have entered a value in the field.

> **Required field**
>
> *A field in which it is mandatory to enter a value.*

Exercise 4.12: Creating a required value

In this exercise, you will define the Books.Title field as a required field.

1) Open the Books table in Design View and display the field properties for the Title field.

2) Click on the *Required* property and select *Yes*.

Required	Yes
Allow Zero Length	Yes
Indexed	No

3) Save the table. The following message is displayed.

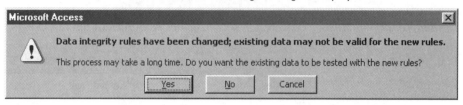

Microsoft Access

⚠ **Data integrity rules have been changed; existing data may not be valid for the new rules.**

This process may take a long time. Do you want the existing data to be tested with the new rules?

[Yes]   [No]   [Cancel]

This warns you that there may be existing records where there is no value in the Title field. It also gives you the option of checking whether this is so.

4) Click **No** to save the table without checking existing records and then switch to Datasheet View.

5) Add a new record to the table, leaving the Title field blank. When you move the focus from the new record, Access displays a message warning you that you must enter a value in the Title field. You can then either enter a value or use the **Undo** command to remove the new record.

6) Close Chp4_VillageLibrary_Database.

Chapter 4: summary

A *lookup field* displays a list of values from which the user selects one to enter in the field. The field can look up its values in a table or query or in a fixed value list. You can use the *Lookup Wizard* to create either type of lookup field.

An *input mask* is a template that specifies an exact pattern for data entered in a field and controls the type of data that can be entered at each position in the pattern. It makes data entry easier for users and helps to ensure entry of valid data. You enter the input mask definition for a field in the *Input Mask* property for that field.

A *field validation rule* set limits or conditions on the values that you can enter in a field. The rule is enforced when you add or edit data in the field. You enter the validation rule for a field in the *Validation Rule* property for that field.

A *default value* is a value that Access automatically enters in a field when you add a new record. Where the same value is frequently entered in a particular field, having a default value makes data entry much easier and quicker. You enter the default value for a field in the *Default Value* property for that field.

A *required field* is one in which it is mandatory to enter a value. You use a field's *Required* property to make it a required field.

Chapter 4: quick quiz

Q1	True or false – a lookup field can look up values in more than one table.
A.	True.
✓ B.	False.

Q2	True or false – with the *Lookup Wizard* you can base a lookup field on either a table or a query.
A.	True.
✓ B.	False.

Q3	Which of the following input masks specifies mandatory entry of exactly four digits?
A.	9999
B.	0000
C.	&&&&
✓ D.	####

Q4	Which of these validation rules requires dates entered to be in the year 2000?
A.	In "2000"
B.	Year = 2000
C.	Between #01/01/2000# And #31/12/2000#
✓ D.	>= #01/01/2000# And <= #31/12/2000#

Q5	Which of the following validation rules restricts a field's values to Mr, Mrs or Ms?
✓ A.	In ("Mr", "Mrs", "Ms")
B.	"Mr" Or "Mrs" Or "Ms"
C.	="Mr" Or ="Mrs" Or ="Ms"

Q6	Which of these default value expressions enters today's date automatically in a date field?
A.	Date = (Today)
B.	Date(Today)
C.	Date()
D.	#99/99/99#

(✓ marked next to B.)

Answers

1: A, **2:** A, **3:** B, **4:** C and D, **5:** All, **6:** C.

5

Table design: relationships

In this chapter

When working with multiple tables, you need to tell Access how to bring together data from different tables so that you can retrieve meaningful information. You do this by defining relationships between the tables.

In this chapter you will learn how to define relationships and how to apply referential integrity to those relationships.

New skills

At the end of this chapter you should be able to:

- Understand and create a one-to-one and a one-to-many relationship
- Understand and resolve a many-to-many relationship
- Understand and apply referential integrity

New words

In this chapter you will meet the following terms:

- One-to-one relationship
- One-to-many relationship
- Many-to-many relationship
- Referential integrity

Exercise file

In this chapter you will work with the following Access database file:

- Chp5_VillageLibrary_Database

Syllabus reference

In this chapter you will cover the following items of the ECDL Advanced Database syllabus:

- **AM5.1.2.1:** Understand the basis for creating a valid relationship.
- **AM5.1.2.2:** Create, modify one-to-one and one-to-many relationships between tables.

- **AM5.1.2.3:** Understand and modify a many-to-many relationship between tables.

- **AM5.1.2.5:** Apply and use referential integrity.

- **AM5.1.2.6:** Apply automatic deletion of related records.

What is a valid relationship?

The purpose of creating a relationship between two tables is to enable Access to combine related records from the tables. For a valid relationship:

- The two tables must have a common field, so that Access can match values in those fields when joining the tables.

- The common fields must have the same data type; in the case of Number fields, they must also have the same field size.

  AutoNumber fields are an exception to this rule. If a field has an AutoNumber data type in one table, it must have a Number data type and a field size of *Long Integer* in the other table.

- Both fields usually have the same name.

- One of the fields is typically a primary key field and the related field is then referred to as a foreign key field.

In the example here, a relationship has been created between the Books and Authors tables based on their common AutID fields. AutID is the primary key field of the Authors table and is a foreign key field in the Books table.

The relationship enables Access to retrieve, for example, a list of book titles and their authors. To do this, it looks for a matching AutID value in the Authors table for each book in the Books table.

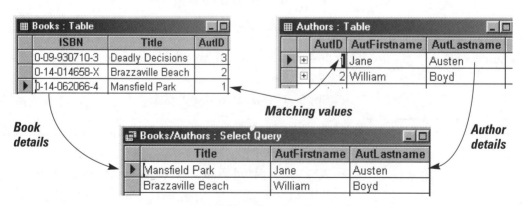

Book and author details

Relationship types

Relational databases support three types of relationship:

- One-to-one

- One-to-many

- Many-to-many

One-to-one

This is an unusual relationship type. Each record in one table can have no more than one matching record in the other table, and, typically, the two tables have the same primary key, as in the example here.

Books : Table						
ISBN	**Title**	**AutID**	**Publica**	**PublisherName**	**Category**
▶ 0-09-930710-3	Deadly Decisions	3	2001	Arrow Books Ltd	Crime
0-14-014658-X	Brazzaville Beach	2	1991	Penguin Group	Crime
0-14-062066-4	Mansfield Park	1	1994	Penguin Group	Fiction
0-552-13107-5	Sourcery	4	1989	Transworld Ltd.	Fantasy
0-7088-8207-2	Magic Kingdom for	5	1986	Futura Publications	Fantasy

BooksConfidential : Table		
ISBN	**PurchaseDate**	**Cost**
▶ 0-09-930710-3	24-08-01	€9.65
0-14-014658-X	23-06-00	€6.99
0-14-062066-4	23-06-00	€3.87
0-552-13107-5	23-06-00	€5.99
0-7088-8207-2	23-06-00	€6.42

The Books and BooksConfidential tables have a one-to-one relationship based on common ISBN fields. Each record in one table has no more than one matching record in the other table.

So why not merge the two tables? In this case, the library does not want members to have access to purchasing information. So the PurchaseDate and Cost fields have been moved to a separate table that members can't access.

The requirement to keep some information confidential is the most common reason for creating a one-to-one relationship. Another is to separate out data that is accessed infrequently. This speeds up access to the main table.

> **One-to-one relationship**
>
> *A relationship in which each record in one table can have no more than one matching record in the other table.*

One-to-many

This is by far the most common relationship type. Each record in one table can have many matching records in the second table, while records in the second table can have only one matching record in the first table.

In the Village Library database, the relationships between the Books and Loans tables and between the Members and Loans tables are examples of one-to-many relationships.

Let's take a look at the Loans and Members tables.

Loans : Table			
ISBN	**MemID**	**LoanDate**	**ReturnDate**
▶ ISBN 0-130-98983-5	1	04-06-01	13-06-01
ISBN 0-130-98984-3	1	04-06-01	13-06-01
ISBN 0-571-20408-2	1		
ISBN 1-862-30063-1	1		
ISBN 0-130-38486-0	1		
ISBN 0-563-36249-9	2		
ISBN 0-552-99893-1	3		
ISBN 0-14-062066-4	3		

Members : Table				
MemID	**MemFirstname**	**MemLastname**	**MemAddress**	**MemTown**
1	Robert	Adams	26 Hillwood Estate	Burnford
2	Sylvia	Turner	White Cottage	Belmount
3	Rebecca	White	Owl's Hill	Belmount
4	Stephen	White	Owl's Hill	Belmount
▶ 5	Linda	White	Owl's Hill	Belmount

Each member can have many books out on loan, but each loan involves only one member. So the relationship between the two tables is one-to-many, based on a common MemID field. MemID is a primary key field in the Members table and a foreign key field in the Loans table.

If you want to view a list of the books currently out on loan, with details of their borrowers, Access can retrieve the borrower details for each loan by finding the record in the Members table that has the same MemID value as the MemID field in the loan record.

One-to-many relationship

A relationship in which each record in the first table can have many matching records in the second table. But each record in the second table can have only one matching record in the first table.

Many-to-many

A many-to-many relationship is one in which each record in the first table can have one or more related records in the second table and each record in the second table can have one or more related records in the first table.

So far in this book we've treated the Authors and Books tables as if they had a one-to-many relationship. In reality, however, they have a many-to-many relationship – each author can have many books, and each book can have many authors.

One book, many authors　　　***One author, many books***

Access does not support this type of relationship directly. A direct relationship between Books and Authors would involve, for example, including multiple records for some books in the Books table, one for each author of those books. The result? Redundancy, inconsistencies and wasted space.

Instead, you create a linking (or junction) table that matches books to authors using both their primary key fields, as shown below:

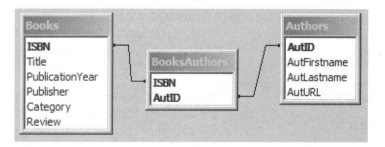

Instead of an unwieldy many-to-many relationship, you now have two standard one-to-many relationships, one between Books and the linking table, and one between Authors and the linking table. And Access can bring together information from Books and Authors indirectly, by using the linking table as an intermediary.

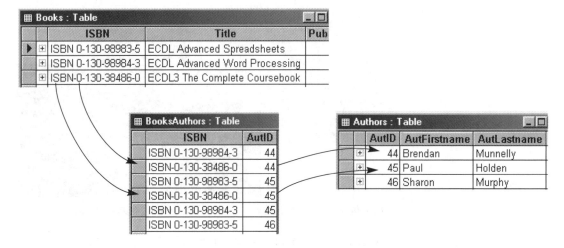

ISBN and AutID are foreign key fields in the BooksAuthors table. Neither field is limited to unique values in the table and so neither can act as its primary key. Instead, you can use a combination of ISBN and AutID, as each combination of these fields will be unique.

> ### Many-to-many relationship
>
> *A relationship in which each record in the first table can have many matching records in the second table. And each record in the second table can have many matching records in the first table.*

Primary tables

When two tables are related, one is referred to as the *primary table*, the other simply as the related table. The primary table is the one whose primary key is used as the linking field.

So, in a one-to-many relationship, the table on the 'one' side of the relationship is always the primary table. In a one-to-one relationship, either table can be the primary table. You make the choice when you create the relationship.

Which table is the primary table of a relationship is important when you enforce referential integrity for the relationship and allow cascading deletes and updates (see 'Referential integrity' below).

The Relationships window

You use Access's Relationships window to create, edit and view relationships.

Access's sample Northwind database includes a variety of tables with relationships already defined, so we'll use it to explore the Relationships window. Open that database now and then open its Relationships window.

Opening the Relationships window

To open the Relationships window, close any open tables, and then:

- Choose **Tools | Relationships**, or
- Click the **Relationships** button in the Access toolbar.

Provided that you haven't previously made any changes to the layout in Northwind's Relationships window, it should look as shown below.

Table ————

Field list ————

Join line ————

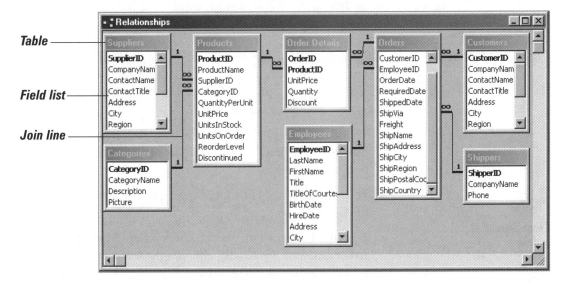

Understanding the Relationships window

In the Relationships window, you can display some or all of the tables in your database and the relationships between them:

- **Tables.** Each table is displayed with its field list. Primary key fields are displayed in bold type.

- **Relationships.** A relationship between two tables is represented by a join line between the two related fields.

- **Relationship types.** One-to-many relationships are indicated by a '1' at the 'one' end of the join line, and an infinity (∞) symbol at the 'many' end of the line. One-to-one relationships are indicated by a '1' at both ends.

When you open the Relationships window, a **Relationships** menu is added to the Access menu bar, and a number of buttons are added to the Access toolbar. Options are provided for:

- Organizing the layout of tables in the window. See 'Organizing the layout' below.

- Creating, editing and deleting relationships. See 'Creating and editing relationships' below.

A well-designed layout, like the Northwind example, clearly illustrates the structure of a database and makes it easy to understand the relationships between tables. Which tables you choose to display or not display in the layout affects only the layout here in the Relationships window; it does not affect the database in any way.

Organizing the layout

Initially, the Relationships window for a new database is empty. You can add and remove tables in various ways, as outlined here. Try out each option in Northwind's Relationships window, but do *not* save your new layout.

- To hide a table, click on it and choose **Relationships | Hide Table** or right-click on it and choose **Hide Table** from the pop-up menu.

Clear Layout button

- To clear the entire layout, click the **Clear Layout** button on the toolbar.

Show All button

- To add all tables to the layout, choose **Relationships | Show All** or click the **Show All** button on the toolbar. This works only for tables for which relationships have been defined.

Show Table button

- To add selected tables to the layout, choose **Relationships | Show Table** or click the **Show Table** button on the toolbar. This displays the *Show Table* dialog box, which lists all your database tables. Double-click on each table you want to add to the layout and click **Close** when finished.

Access automatically arranges tables in rows across the layout, positioning each table that you add in the next available space. This can result in a confusing network of join lines. If you want to move a table you can do so by clicking on its title bar and dragging it to its new location.

You can save the current layout at any time by choosing **File | Save** or clicking the **Save** button on the toolbar. Whenever you open the Relationships window, the last saved layout is always displayed.

Creating and editing relationships

Provided that you have designed your tables appropriately, creating and editing relationships in the Relationships window is very straightforward:

- To create a relationship between two tables, drag the primary key field from the primary table to the related field in the other table.

- To edit a relationship, double-click on the relevant join line and make your selections in the *Edit Relationships* dialog box.

- To delete a relationship, right-click on the relevant join line and choose **Delete** from the pop-up menu.

Exercise 5.1: Creating and editing relationships

In this exercise you will create all the relationships required by the Village Library database.

1) Open the starting database for this chapter:

   Chp5_VillageLibrary_Database

2) Open the Relationships window and add all the database tables to the layout. Arrange them as shown here.

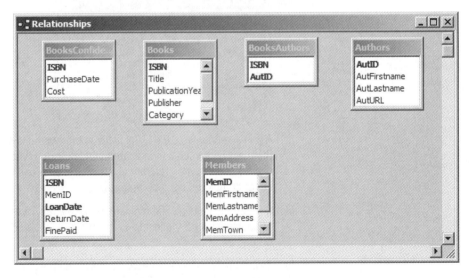

3) To create the one-to-one relationship between Books and BooksConfidential, drag the ISBN field from the Books table to the ISBN field in the BooksConfidential table.

   The *Edit Relationships* dialog box is now displayed. This lists the fields on which the relationship is based and indicates the type of relationship that will be created.

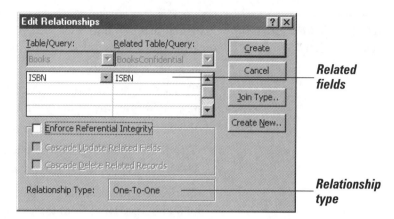

Related fields

Relationship type

Access determines the relationship type automatically. It creates a one-to-one relationship if both fields are primary keys; it creates a one-to-many relationship if only one is a primary key. In the Books/BooksConfidential relationship, the Books table becomes the primary table because it is the table whose primary key you dragged to the other table.

4) For the moment, ignore the other options in the dialog box and click **Create** to create the relationship.

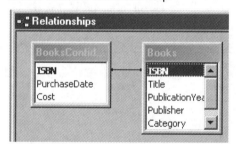

A join line now links the ISBN fields in the two tables. Notice that there are no symbols to indicate the relationship type – these are displayed only when referential integrity is enforced (see 'Referential integrity' below). Let's do that now.

5) Click on the join line and choose **Relationships | Edit Relationship**, or double-click on the join line. This redisplays the *Edit Relationships* dialog box.

6) Select the *Enforce Referential Integrity* option and click **OK**. The join line now indicates the relationship type.

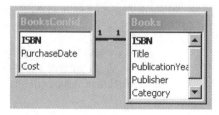

7) Now create the relationship between Books and BooksAuthors by dragging the ISBN field from the Books table to the ISBN field in BooksAuthors.

8) In the **Edit Relationships** dialog box, Access correctly identifies the relationship type as one-to-many. Select the *Enforce Referential Integrity* option and click **Create**.

9) Now create the following relationships, selecting the *Enforce Referential Integrity* option in each case:

Tables	Type	Related fields
Authors and BooksAuthors	one-to-many	AutID
Books and Loans	one-to-many	ISBN
Members and Loans	one-to-many	MemID

The Relationships window should now look similar to that shown here:

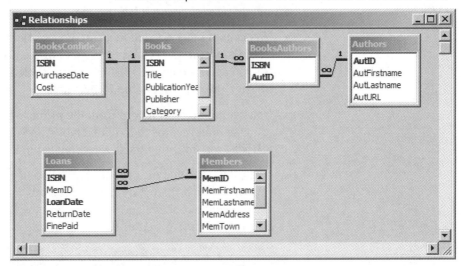

10) Close the Relationships window, saving the current layout as you do.

Referential integrity

You've seen how the relationship between the Books and BooksAuthors tables is based on including the primary key of the Books table (ISBN) as a foreign key in the BooksAuthors table.

To ensure consistency between the two tables, each ISBN value in BooksAuthors must have a matching value in the Books table – that is, it must point to a Books record that exists. If this is true, then the relationship has *referential integrity*.

Without referential integrity, the BooksAuthors table could have 'dangling' references that point nowhere, as shown below.

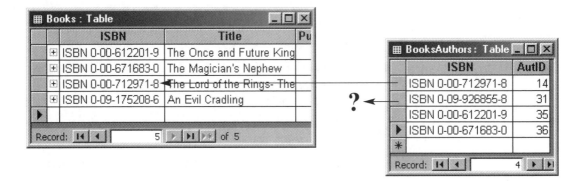

This would happen, for example, if you delete a Books record that is referenced by a record in the BooksAuthors table.

Referential integrity restrictions

When referential integrity is enforced, Access applies the following restrictions to relationships:

- You cannot enter a value in a foreign key field if that value doesn't exist in the primary key field of the primary table. So you cannot enter an ISBN value in BooksAuthors if it doesn't already exist in the Books table.

- You cannot delete a record from the primary table if there are matching records in a related table. So you cannot delete a Books record if that book is referenced in BooksAuthors.

- You cannot change the primary key value of a record in the primary table if there are matching records in a related table. So you cannot change an ISBN value in the Books table if that value is referenced in BooksAuthors.

> **Referential integrity**
>
> *A set of rules that ensures that the relationships between records in related tables are valid, and that you do not accidentally delete or change related data.*

Enforcing referential integrity

To enforce referential integrity in Access, you select the *Enforce Referential Integrity* option when creating or editing relationships between tables. You did this when you created the relationships in Exercise 5.1.

Overriding referential integrity restrictions

When you select the *Enforce Referential Integrity* option, two further options became available: *Cascade Update Related Fields* and *Cascade Delete Related Records*.

These allow you to perform the actions restricted by referential integrity but ensure that Access takes automatic action to prevent inconsistencies.

- **Cascade Update Related Fields.** When this is selected, if you change a primary key value in the primary table, Access automatically changes any matching values in related records.

- **Cascade Delete Related Records.** When this is selected, if you delete a record in the primary table, Access automatically deletes all matching records in the related table.

Note that cascades work in one direction only – changes to the primary table are automatically applied to the related table but not vice versa.

It is a good idea to enforce referential integrity for all relationships. However, enabling the *Cascade* options may result in Access automatically deleting or changing many records, so you should do so only after careful thought.

For example, let's suppose that both *Cascade* options have been enabled for all relationships in the Village Library database. These are some of the consequences:

- When you delete a record in the Books table, Access also deletes all records in the BooksConfidential, BooksAuthors, and Loans tables that have the same ISBN.

- When you update an ISBN value in the Books table, Access automatically updates any instances of that ISBN in the BooksConfidential, BooksAuthors, and Loans tables.

- When you delete a record in the Members table, Access also deletes all records in the Loans table that have the same MemID.

Exercise 5.2: Using the *Cascade Delete Related Records* option

In this exercise you will enable the *Cascade Delete Related Records* option for some relationships and see what happens when you delete a record.

1) Open the Relationships window for the Chp5_VillageLibrary_Database database.

2) Double-click on the join line between the Books and BooksConfidential tables to display the *Edit Relationships* dialog box.

3) Select the *Cascade Delete Related Records* option and click **OK**.

4) When a table is the primary table in multiple relationships, you normally set the same referential integrity options for all the relationships. So repeat steps 2 and 3 for the other relationships involving the Books table – that is, Books and BooksAuthors, and Books and Loans.

5) Close the Relationships window.

6) Open the Books table and delete a record. Access displays a message similar to the following.

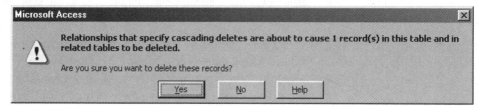

This informs you that deleting the record will cause records in related tables to be automatically deleted.

7) Click **Yes**. Access now deletes the Books record and all related records in the BooksConfidential, BooksAuthors, and Loans tables.

Remember that changes to a primary table cascade down to related tables but not vice versa. To demonstrate this, open the Loans table and delete a record. This time Access prompts you to confirm the deletion and deletes only the selected record.

Chapter 5: summary

Defining a *relationship* between two tables enables Access to combine records from the two tables. The two tables must have a common field with the same data type (AutoNumber fields are an exception).

In a *one-to-one relationship*, each record in one table has no more than one matching record in the other table. In a *one-to-many relationship*, each record in the primary table can have many matching records in the related table, but records in the related table can have only one matching record in the primary table.

In a *many-to-many relationship*, each record in one table can have many matching records in the second table and vice versa. For this type of relationship, you create a linking table that contains the primary key fields from the two tables. You then create a one-to-many relationship between each of the two tables and the linking table.

You use the *Relationships window* to create and edit relationships. To create a relationship, simply drag the primary key field from the primary table to the related field in the other table.

Referential integrity ensures that foreign key values in a related table always have matching values in the primary key field of the primary table. This prevents records in the related table from including foreign keys that point to nonexistent records.

Chapter 5: quick quiz

Q1	For a valid relationship between two tables, which of the following statements must be true?
A.	The two tables must have a common field with shared values.
B.	The two tables must have the same number and types of fields.
C.	The fields that the two tables have in common must have the same Format properties.
D.	The fields that the two tables have in common must have the same data type, unless one is an AutoNumber field.

(check mark next to A.)

Q2	To create a relationship in the Relationships window, you …
A.	Choose **Relationships | Create Relationship** and then drag the primary key field from one table to the related field in the other table.
B.	Select the two fields on which the relationship is to be based and choose **Relationships | Create Relationship**.
C.	Choose **Relationships | New**, select the two tables to be related, select the related fields in the two tables, and click **OK**.
D.	Drag the primary key field from the primary table to the related foreign key field in the other table.

(check mark next to D.)

Q3	How does Access know which type of relationship you want to create between two tables?
A.	You select the relationship type from the **Relationships** menu.
B.	You select the relationship type in the *Edit Relationships* dialog box.
C.	You select the relationship type by using the **Relationship Type** button on the toolbar.
✓ D.	Access automatically creates a one-to-one relationship if both fields on which the relationship is based are primary key fields. And it automatically creates a one-to-many relationship if only one is a primary key.

Q4	True or false – when you enforce referential integrity for a relationship, you cannot delete a record in the primary table if there is a matching record in the related table.
✓ A.	True.
B.	False.

Q5	True or false – when you select the *Cascade Delete Related Records* option for a relationship, you cannot delete a record from the primary table if there is a matching record in the related table.
A.	True.
✓ B.	False.

Q6	Which of these options do you select if you want Access to automatically update the primary key value on the 'one' side of a relationship when you change it on the 'many' side?
A.	Cascade Update Related Fields.
B.	Cascade Update Related Records.
C.	Cascade Update Related Tables.
✓ D.	Cascade Delete Related Records.

Answers

1: A and D, 2: D, 3: D, 4: A, 5: B, 6: None.

Table design: joins

When a relationship has been defined between two tables, you can use a query to combine records from the tables based on values in their common fields. This operation is referred to as a *join*.

In this chapter you will learn about the different types of joins that you can use and how you apply them to relationships.

New skills

At the end of this chapter you should be able to:

- Understand and apply the different join types
- Create a query based on a self join
- Set the default join type for a relationship
- Override the default join type in a query
- Define relationships in a query

New words

In this chapter you will meet the following terms:

- Inner join
- Left outer join
- Right outer join
- Self join

Exercise file

In this chapter you will work with the following Access database file:

- `Chp6_VillageLibrary_Database`

Syllabus reference

In this chapter you will cover the following items of the ECDL Advanced Database syllabus:

- **AM5.1.2.4**: Apply inner, outer, and self joins.
- **AM5.1.2.7**: Relate/join data when designing queries.

Join types

The operation of combining records from two tables is referred to as a join. By default, when you run a query involving two tables, Access checks the values in the related fields, combines the records with matching values, and then returns only those records. This is one type of join – an inner join – but it is not the only type you can use.

In this section we will look at the following join types:

- Inner join
- Left outer join
- Right outer join
- Self join

To help you understand the different join types, the Chp6_VillageLibrary_Database database includes queries that use each type. Open the database now and take a look at the contents of the Members and Loans tables.

- The Members table contains records for 24 members, not all of whom have borrowed books.
- The Loans table contains records for 22 loans, some representing different books borrowed by the same member. It also contains two records where the MemID value does not have a matching record in the Members table (remember that this is possible only when referential integrity is not enforced).

In the following sections we will look at how different join types affect the results of queries run on these tables.

> **Join**
>
> *The process of combining records from two tables.*

Inner joins

An *inner join* is Access's default join type and the one with which you are probably most familiar. In this case, a query returns only records that have matching values in their related fields. It omits unmatched values in both tables.

The InnerJoin query in the Chp6_VillageLibrary_Database database performs an inner join on the Members and Loans tables. Open the database and run that query now.

The query combines all records with matching MemID values in the Loans and Members tables. There are 20 records in the Loans table with matching records in the Members table, so the query returns 20 records. It ignores the two records in the

Loans table that have no matching record in the Members table, and ignores all records in the Members table that have no matching record in the Loans table.

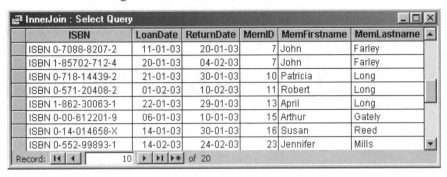

Left outer joins

A *left outer join* is one in which a query returns *all* records from the primary table but only matching records from the related table.

The LeftOuterJoin query performs a left outer join on the Members and Loans tables. Run that query now and take a look at the records it returns.

The query combines all records with matching MemID values in the Loans and Members tables. It also returns all records from the Members table (the primary table) that do not have matching records in the Loans table. In these records the fields from the Loans table are blank. The query ignores the two records in the Loans table that have no matching record in the Members table.

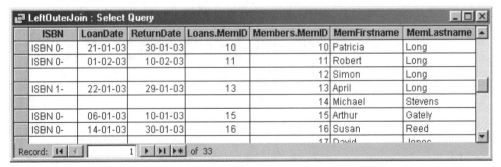

Right outer joins

A *right outer join* is one in which a query returns *all* records from the related table but only matching records from the primary table.

The RightOuterJoin query performs a right outer join on the Members and Loans tables. Run that query now and take a look at the records it returns.

The query combines all records with matching MemID values in the Loans and Members tables. It also returns the two records from the Loans table that do not have matching records in the Members table. In these records the fields from the Members table are blank. The query ignores records in the Members table that do not have matching records in the Loans table.

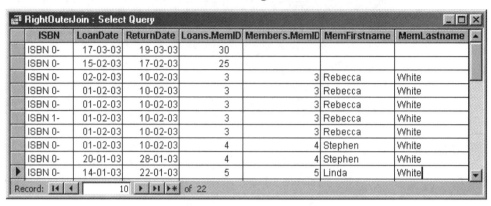

Self joins

A *self join* is one in which a table is joined to itself. This is useful, for example, when you want to find records that have the same values in one or more fields in the same table.

The SelfJoin query performs a self join on the Members table. Run that query now and take a look at the records it returns.

The query returns a list of all members who reside at the same address as another member. You will learn how to create this query later in the chapter.

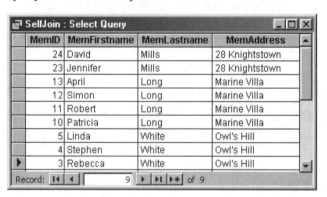

Setting a default join type

When you create a relationship between two tables, Access applies an inner join as the default join type for the relationship. When you create a query on the two tables, this is the join type that is used by default.

You can change the default join type for any relationship in the Relationships window. You can also override the default join type in a query.

Exercise 6.1: Setting the default join type for a relationship

In this exercise you will change the default join type for the Books and Loans relationship.

1) Open the Relationships window for the Chp6_VillageLibrary_Database database.

2) Double-click on the join line linking the Books and Loans tables. This displays the *Edit Relationships* dialog box.

3) Click the **Join Type** button. This displays the *Join Properties* dialog box, which describes each of the available join types.

4) Select option *2*, which applies a left outer join, and click **OK**.

> ○ 1: Only include rows where the joined fields from both tables are equal.
>
> ◉ 2: Include ALL records from 'Books' and only those records from 'Loans' where the joined fields are equal.
>
> ○ 3: Include ALL records from 'Loans' and only those records from 'Books' where the joined fields are equal.

5) When returned to the *Edit Relationships* dialog box, click **OK** again.

6) Close the Relationships window.

The default join type for the Books and Loans tables is now a left outer join. Any queries you subsequently create on those tables will, by default, return all records from the Books table but only matching records from the Loans table.

Setting a join type in a query

Whatever the default join type defined for a relationship, you can override it when you create a query in Design View.

Exercise 6.2: Setting a join type in a query

The default join type for the Books and Loans relationship is now a left outer join. In this exercise you will create a query that overrides this default and joins the tables with an inner join instead.

1) Open a new query in Design View. To do this, click *Queries* in the *Objects* list in the Database window and then double-click the *Create query in Design view* option.

2) When prompted for the tables you want to include in the query, select Books and Loans. To do this, double-click on each of these tables in the list displayed and then click **Close**.

   Both tables are now displayed in the *Field List* area of the Query Design window, with a join line representing the relationship between them.

3) Add the following fields to the query design grid, in the order shown:

   – Books.ISBN

   – Books.Title

   – Loans.MemID

   – Loans.LoanDate

   – Loans.ReturnDate

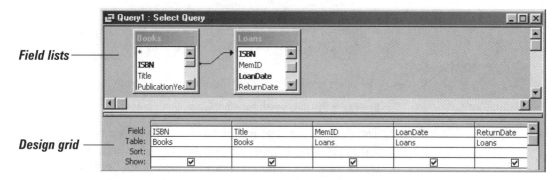

Field lists

Design grid

You can do this by using any of the following methods:

– Drag the field from the field list to an empty column in the design grid.

– Double-click the field in the field list. This adds the field to the next empty column in the design grid.

– Click in a *Field* cell in the design grid, click the arrow at the right of the cell, and then select a field from the list displayed.

Run button

4) Run the query by choosing **Query | Run** or by clicking the **Run** button on the toolbar. Then take a look at the results.

There are many books in the Books table that have never been borrowed and so have no matching record in the Loans table. Because the default join for the two tables is a left outer join, all records in the Books table are listed anyway, with the fields from Loans left blank where there is no matching record.

5) Switch back to Design View.

6) Right-click on the join line between the tables and choose **Join Properties** from the pop-up menu, or double-click on the join line.

7) In the *Join Properties* dialog box, change the join type from option *2* to option *1* (an inner join) and click **OK**.

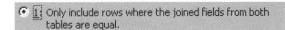

8) Now run the query again. This time only the records with matching ISBN values in both tables are displayed.

9) Save the query with the name BooksLoans and then close it.

Note that the default join type for the Books and Loans relationship remains a left outer join. When you set a join type in a query, it applies only to that query.

Creating self joins

A self join is not one of the join types offered in the *Join Properties* dialog box. A self join is actually a one-to-one relationship between two instances of the same table and must be set up manually.

Exercise 6.3: Creating a self join
In this exercise you will create the HouseMates query, which is a version of the SelfJoin query described in 'Self joins' above. The query returns a list of all members who reside at the same address as another member, as shown here.

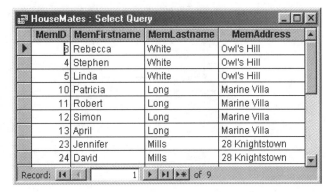

1) Open a new query in Design View. When prompted for the tables you want to include in the query, select Members twice. Two instances of the table are displayed – the second is named Members_1.

2) No relationship has been defined between these tables. However, Access allows you to relate tables in a query in the same way as you create a relationship in the Relationships window.

   In the case of the HouseMates query, you want to compare the Address fields in the two tables, so drag the Members.MemAddress field to the Members_1.MemAddress field. A join line now links the tables. By default, the join type is an inner join.

3) Add the following fields to the design grid and set a sort order of *Ascending* for the Members.MemID field.

   - Members.MemID

   - Members_1.MemID

   - Members.MemFirstname

   - Members.MemLastname

   - Members.MemAddress

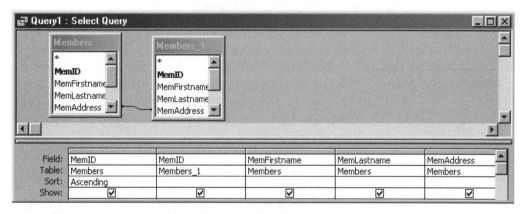

4) Run the query and take a look at the records it returns.

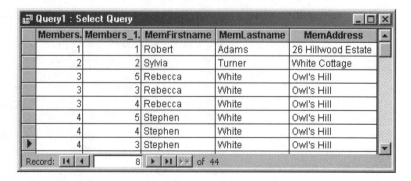

As the two tables are joined on their Address fields, Access joins *every* record in Members to *every* record in Members_1 with a matching address value.

- Every record in Members has a duplicate record in Members_1, so Access displays a record for each of these combinations, showing that each member lives at the same address as himself or herself! The record for Robert Adams is an example.

- Some members share the same address, so Access also displays a record for each of these combinations. For example, the fifth record displayed joins the record for Rebecca White in the Members table to the record for Stephen White in the Members_1 table, and the eighth record joins the record for Stephen White in the Members table to the record for Rebecca White in the Members_1 table.

5) Switch back to Design View. You are now going to refine the query so that it excludes all members that don't share an address with another member and displays a single record for each member that does.

6) To exclude records that join members to themselves, enter the following expression in the *Criteria* row for the Members.MemID field:

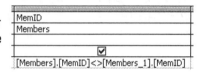

```
Members.MemID <> Members_1.MemID
```

This tells Access to return only records where the MemID value in the Members table is *not* equal to the MemID value in the Members_1 table – that is, to omit records that have the same MemID value in both tables.

7) Run the query and you will see that the results are now limited to members that share an address with other members. Then switch back to Design View.

8) Now you want limit the results to a single record for each member that shares an address with another member.

The properties of a query include a *Unique Values* property. This omits duplicates from the query results – a duplicate being a record that displays the same values as another record in all its fields. While the MemID fields from both tables are included in the results, there are no duplicates. However, if you remove Members_1.MemID, all records for the same member will display the same values in all fields. You can then use *Unique Values* to remove the duplicates.

So delete the Members_1.MemID field from the design grid by clicking its column selector and then pressing the **Delete** key. This affects only which fields the query displays, and not which records it displays. You can verify this by running the query.

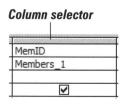

9) Now set the *Unique Values* property to *Yes*.

To do this, right-click on a blank part of the field list area in the Query Design window and choose **Properties** from the pop-up menu. This displays the *Query Properties* dialog box. Select *Yes* in the drop-down list for the *Unique Values* property and then close the dialog box.

10) Run the query again. The results should be the same as those shown at the start of the exercise. At a glance you can see how many and which members live together at Owl's Hill or Marine Villa.

11) Save the query with the name HouseMates and then close it.

Defining relationships in a query

In the previous exercise, you were able to join the Members and Members_1 tables even though you had not previously defined a relationship between the tables.

This is possible for any two tables that share a field with the same or a compatible data type. To create the join simply drag the join field from one table to the related field in the other table.

It is important to know that you cannot apply Referential Integrity to tables related in this way, and that the relationship applies only to the query in which it was created. To define a permanent relationship between two tables you must use the Relationships window.

Chapter 6: summary

You can use a query to combine records from two related tables based on values in their common fields. This operation is referred to as a *join*. With an *inner join*, a query returns only records that have matching values in their related fields. With a *left outer join*, a query returns all records from the primary table, but only matching records from the related table. With a *right outer join*, a query returns all records from the related table, but only matching records from the primary table. With a *self join*, you combine records from two instances of the same table.

You set the *default join type* for a relationship when you create or edit that relationship in the Relationships window. You can then override this default join type for individual queries. You can also join tables in a query even if no relationship has been defined between them.

Chapter 6: quick quiz

Q1	In a query, which join type returns all records from the primary table but only matching records from the related table?
A.	Inner join.
B.	Left outer join.
C.	Right outer join.

Q2	In a query, which join type returns all records from the related table but only matching records from the primary table?
A.	Inner join.
B.	Left outer join.
C.	Right outer join.

Q3	Where do you set the default join type for a relationship?
A.	In the *Join Properties* dialog box when creating a query.
B.	In the *Edit Relationships* dialog box when creating a relationship in the Relationships window.
C.	In the *Join Properties* dialog box when creating a relationship in the Relationships window.

Q4	True or false – you can join two tables in a query even when no relationship has been created between the tables.
A.	True.
B.	False.

Q5	True or false – you can create a permanent relationship between two tables by joining them in a query.
A.	True.
B.	False.

Q6	Which of the following must be true in order to join two tables in a query?
A.	The related fields must have the same name.
B.	The related fields must have the same data type.
C.	The related fields must have the same or a compatible data type.

Answers

1: B, **2**: C, **3**: C, **4**: A, **5**: B, **6**: C.

7

Query design: action queries

Any queries you have used so far in this book relate to retrieving records for viewing or updating. This type of query is known as a *select query*.

In this chapter, you will learn about another query type – the action query – which you can use to copy, delete and modify multiple records at a time.

New skills

At the end of this chapter you should be able to:

- Create and use an update query
- Create and use a make-table query
- Create and use an append query
- Create and use a delete query

New words

In this chapter you will meet the following terms:

- Action query
- Update query
- Make-table query
- Append query
- Delete query

Exercise file

In this chapter you will work with the following Access file:

- Chp7_VillageLibrary_Database

Syllabus reference

In this chapter you will cover the following items of the ECDL Advanced Database Syllabus:

- **AM5.2.1.1**: Create and use a query to update data in a table.
- **AM5.2.1.2**: Create and use a query to delete records in a table.

- **AM5.2.1.3**: Create and use a query to save selected information as a table.

- **AM5.2.1.4**: Append records to a table using a query.

What is an action query?

If you need to copy, change, or delete a small number of records in a table it is easy enough to find those records in Datasheet View and make the changes manually. However, if you want to modify a large group of records, it is usually quicker and easier to use an action query.

There are four types of action query:

- **Update query**. Makes changes to values in a group of records from one or more tables.

- **Make-table query**. Creates a new table from data in one or more existing tables.

- **Append query**. Copies a group of records from one or more tables and appends them to the end of another table.

- **Delete query**. Deletes a group of records from one or more tables.

Access uses a different icon for each query type, as shown below. This means that you always know what type of action a query will perform before you run it.

Append query	⊕!
Delete query	✗!
Make-table query	▤!
Select query	▦
Update query	✐!

> **Action query**
>
> *A query that copies or changes groups of records from one or more tables.*

Safeguarding your data

When you use an action query to modify records, in most cases you cannot then undo the changes. There are two methods you can use to ensure that you do not make unwanted and irreversible changes to your data.

- You can preview the records that will be modified by the action query and then decide whether or not you want to proceed with the action.

- You can make a copy of the table you want to modify before running the action query. If you need to undo the changes, you can then simply delete the modified table and rename the copy with the name of the original table.

In a real-life scenario, it is always advisable to make backup copies of your tables before running any action query other than a make-table query.

Update queries

You use an update query when you want to make global changes to data in one or more tables. Typical uses include:

- Updating all instances of a particular value in a field – for example, changing all instances of Yes to No, or changing all instances of a publisher's name.

- Updating all values in a field based on a mathematical expression – for example, updating all prices by 10%, or updating all prices less than £10 by 5% and all prices over £10 by 7%.

- Updating the values in one field based on the values in another field – for example, updating the Category value for all books by a particular author, or reducing the unit price of a product where the quantity ordered is greater than ten.

Creating an update query

In the following exercises, you will create update queries to update all instances of a particular value in a field and to update the values in one field based on values in another field.

Exercise 7.1: Creating a query to globally update a particular value

In this exercise you will create an update query to change all instances of the publisher name 'Penguin Books' to 'Penguin'.

1) Open the starting database for this chapter:

   Chp7_VillageLibrary_Database

2) Open a new query in Design View. When prompted for the tables you want to include in the query, select Books.

3) As the Publisher field is the one you want to update, add that field to the design grid.

**Query Type
button**

4) By default, Access assumes that you want to create a select query. To specify an update query instead, choose **Update Query** in the **Query** menu or in the list displayed when you click the arrow next to the **Query Type** button on the Access toolbar. An *Update To* row is now added to the design grid. This is where you specify the new value for a field.

5) To specify that you want to update all instances of 'Penguin Books' in the Publisher field, type the following in the *Criteria* row for the field:

Penguin Books

6) To specify 'Penguin' as the new value, type that value in the *Update To* row.

7) Now run the query. Access warns you that you are about to update a number of records and that you cannot undo the changes. Click **Yes**.

Field:	Publisher
Table:	Books
Update To:	"Penguin"
Criteria:	"Penguin Books"
or:	

8) Save the query under the name PublisherUpdate and then close it.

You can now open the Books table and review the changes.

Exercise 7.2: Creating a query to update values in one field based on values in another field
In this exercise you will create an update query to change the Category value for all books written by J.K. Rowling.

1) Open a new query in Design View. When prompted for the tables you want to include in the query, add Books, BooksAuthors and Authors.

   You add the Books table because you want to update records in that table. You add Authors because you want to use a value in that table to select the records to be updated. Finally, you add BooksAuthors because this is the linking table between Books and Authors.

2) Add the Books.Category and Authors.AutLastname fields to the design grid.

3) Change the query type to an update query.

4) Type 'Rowling' in the *Criteria* row for the AutLastname field. This specifies that you want to update all records where the author's last name is 'Rowling'.

5) Type 'Fantasy' in the *Update To* row for the Category field. This specifies that you want to change the Category value to 'Fantasy' for all records that match the query criteria.

6) Run the query. Access warns you that you are about to update three records. Click **Yes**.

7) Close the query without saving it.

You can now open the Books table and review the changes. The category value for the 'Harry Potter' books has been updated to 'Fantasy'.

Make-table queries

You use a make-table query to create a new table from existing records in one or more tables. Typical uses include:

- Making backup copies of tables.

- Creating an archive table to store records no longer needed in the active table.

- Creating a table that contains selected fields from one or more tables.

- Creating a table containing summary data from one or more tables.

Creating a make-table query

The Village Library periodically removes old records from the Loans table and moves them to an archive table.

In the following exercise, you will use a make-table query to create the archive table and add the first batch of records to it. In later exercises, you will use a delete query to delete the archived records from the Loans table, and you will use an append query to add another batch of records to the new table.

Exercise 7.3: Using a make-table query to create an archive table

1) Open a new query in Design View. When prompted for the tables you want to include in the query, select Loans.

2) Add to the design grid the fields you want to include in the new table. In the case of the LoansArchive table, you want to include all fields from the Loans table, so add each in turn to the design grid.

3) Change the query type to a make-table query. When prompted for the name of the new table, enter LoansArchive, and click **OK**.

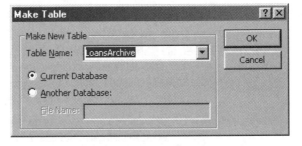

By default the new table is created in the current database.

4) Now you need to specify the criteria for selecting the records you want to add to the archive table. To do this, you enter an expression in the *Criteria* row for the ReturnDate field. For example:

`<Date()-90`	Selects all records where the return date is more than 90 days ago.
`<=#31-12-01#`	Selects all records where the return date is 31 Dec 2001 or earlier.
`>=#01-01-02# And <=#31-03-02#`	Selects all records where the return date is between 1 Jan 2002 and 31 March 2002 (inclusive).

In a real-world scenario, you would probably choose the first example. You could then save the query and run it at the end of every quarter. For the purposes of this exercise, however, use the second example.

5) Run the query. Access warns you that you are about to paste three records into a new table. Click **Yes**.

6) Close the query without saving it.

The LoansArchive table is now listed in Tables view in the Database window. If you open the table, you will see that it has the same structure as the Loans table and currently contains three records.

Exercise 7.4: Creating a new table with selected fields from an existing table

In the Chp7_VillageLibrary_Database database, book costs and purchase dates are included in the Books table and not in a separate BooksConfidential table. In this exercise, you will use a make-table query to create the BooksConfidential table.

1) Open a new query in Design View. When prompted for the tables you want to include in the query, select Books.

2) Add to the design grid the fields you want to include in the new table – that is, ISBN, PurchaseDate and Cost.

3) Change the query type to a make-table query.

4) When prompted for the name of the new table, enter BooksConfidential, and click **OK**.

5) Run the query. Access warns you that you are about to paste a particular number of records into a new table. Click **Yes**.

6) Close the query without saving it.

The BooksConfidential table is now listed in Tables view in the Database window. If you open it, you will see that it contains complete copies of the ISBN, PurchaseDate and Cost fields from the Books tables.

Note that when you create a table with a make-table query, the new table is not assigned a primary key. You must do this manually.

Append queries

You use an append query to copy selected records from one or more tables and insert them into another table. Typical uses include:

■ Copying records from an active table to an archive table.

■ Importing data from an external source.

■ Exporting data to an external destination.

■ Copying records from one or more tables to a table that contains selected fields from those tables.

Creating an append query

Exercise 7.5: Creating an append query

In a previous exercise, you created an archive table for storing old records from the Loans table. In this exercise, you will copy more records from the Loans table to the LoansArchive table.

1) Open a new query in Design View. When prompted for the tables you want to include in the query, select Loans.

2) Add each field in the Loans table to the design grid.

3) Change the query type to an append query.

4) When prompted for the name of the destination table for the records, select LoansArchive from the *Table Name* drop-down list and click **OK**.

   An *Append To* row is now added to the design grid. You use this to specify the name of the destination field for each source field in the design grid. For fields with the same names in the source and destination tables, Access automatically fills in the *Append To* value. For those that don't, you must enter the *Append To* value manually.

Field:	ISBN	MemID	LoanDate	ReturnDate	FinePaid
Table:	Loans	Loans	Loans	Loans	Loans
Sort:					
Append To:	ISBN	MemID	LoanDate	ReturnDate	FinePaid

5) Enter the following expression in the *Criteria* row for the ReturnDate field:

`>=#01-01-02# And <=#31-12-02#`

This selects all records where the return date is in the year 2002.

6) Run the query. When prompted to confirm the append operation, click **Yes**.

7) Save the query with the name AppendArchiveLoans and then close it.

If you open the LoansArchive table now you will see that a number of new records have been added from the Loans table.

Appending records with AutoNumber fields

When an AutoNumber field is involved in an append operation, you can choose to copy its values from the original table to the destination table, or to have Access automatically create new AutoNumber values in the destination table.

- To copy the AutoNumber values from the original table, include the AutoNumber field in the design grid for the append query.

- If you want Access to automatically create AutoNumber values in the destination table, omit the AutoNumber field from the design grid.

Delete queries

You use a delete query to delete a group of records from one or more tables. With this type of query you always delete entire records, not just selected fields.

Remember that if you have enabled referential integrity for a relationship, but not cascade deletes, you will not be able to delete records from the primary table if there are matching records in the related table. In such a case, you must delete the records from the related table first, and only then delete the records from the primary table.

If you have enabled relational integrity and also the *Cascade Delete Related Records* option, Access allows you to delete records from the primary table, even if there are matching records in the related table, as it automatically deletes those matching records as well.

Exercise 7.6: Creating a delete query

In previous exercises, you copied records from the Loans table to an archive table. In this exercise, you will use a delete query to remove the archived records from the Loans table.

1) Open a new query in Design View. When prompted for the tables you want to include in the query, select Loans.

2) For a delete query, the only fields you *must* include in the design grid are those for which you want to set selection criteria. So add the ReturnDate field to the design grid. You need this to specify the criteria for selecting the records to be deleted.

3) Change the query type to a delete query. A *Delete* row is added to the design grid. Access automatically fills the appropriate values for this row.

4) In previous exercises, you archived all records with a return date of 31-12-02 or older. To select these records for deletion, enter the following expression in the *Criteria* row for the ReturnDate field:

    <=#31-12-02#

    This selects all records where the return date is 31 December 2002 or earlier.

5) Run the query. When prompted to confirm the delete operation, click **Yes**.

6) Save the query with the name DeleteArchivedLoans and then close it.

If you now open the Loans table you will see that all records with a return date of 31 December 2002 or earlier have been removed.

Chapter 7: summary

Action queries enable you to copy, delete, or update groups of records from one or more tables. It is always advisable to make backup copies of your tables before running action queries on them.

An *update query* makes global changes to data in one or more tables. A *make-table* query creates a new table from selected data in one or more tables. An *append query* copies a group of records from one or more tables and appends them to the end of another table. A *delete query* deletes a group of records from one or more tables.

You specify the type of query you are creating by choosing an option on the **Query** menu or by selecting an option from the list displayed when you click the arrow next to the **Query Type** button on the Access toolbar.

Q1	Which type of query would you use to increase all prices in the Books table by 10%?
A.	An append query.
B.	An update query.
C.	A change values query.
D.	A make-table query.

Q2	True or false – with an update query, you can change the name of the publisher for all books written by a particular author.
A.	True.
B.	False.

Q3	True or false – with a make-table query you can create a table that combines records from the Books and Authors table.
A.	True.
B.	False.

Q4	Which type of query would you use to copy records from one table to another existing table?
A.	An append query.
B.	An update query.
C.	A make-table query.

Q5	How do you tell Access which records to delete with a delete query?
A.	Use the **Select Records** option on the **Query** menu.
B.	Use the *Show* checkbox in the design grid.
C.	Enter selection criteria in the *Criteria* row in the design grid.
D.	Enter selection criteria in the *Delete* row in the design grid.

Answers   **1**: B, **2**: A, **3**: A, **4**: A, **5**: C.

Query design: total queries

In this chapter

There are many types of calculations that you can perform in a query. In this chapter you will be introduced to the various types, and you will learn how to use Access's aggregate functions to summarize field values.

New skills

At the end of this chapter you should be able to:

- Calculate totals (sums, averages, and so on) for all records in a table

- Calculate totals for groups of records

- Use wildcards in queries

- Create and use a crosstab query

- Use logical operators in query criteria

New words

In this chapter you will meet the following terms:

- Aggregate function

- Wildcard

- Crosstab query

Exercise file

In this chapter you will work with the following Access file:

- Chp8_VillageLibrary_Database

Syllabus reference

In this chapter you will cover the following items of the ECDL Advanced Database Syllabus:

- **AM5.2.2.1**: Group information in a query.

- **AM5.2.2.2**: Use functions in a query: sum, count, average, max, min.

- **AM5.2.2.3:** Use a crosstab query.

- **AM5.2.2.4:** Use wildcards in a query.

- **AM5.2.2.5:** Use arithmetic, logical expressions in a query.

About query calculations

There are three types of calculations that you can perform in a query:

- You can use Access's aggregate functions to summarize field values. For example, you could calculate the total cost of books in the village library, or the total cost of books in each category.

- You can create a field that displays the result of calculations on other fields. For example, a FineDue field in the Loans table could calculate the default fine for overdue books – multiply the number of days each book is overdue by the daily fine amount.

- You can use calculations as criteria for selecting which records a query displays or performs an action on. For example, you could tell a query to return only records for late returns – subtract the LoanDate from the ReturnDate and return only records where the result is greater than 10.

You will learn about the latter two calculation types in Chapter 9.

About aggregate functions

Access provides a number of aggregate or 'totals' functions that you can use to summarize field values. The following table shows the ones you need to know for ECDL.

Function	Description
Sum	Returns the sum of the values in a field.
	This works with Number, Date/Time, Currency and AutoNumber data types.
Avg	Returns the average of the values in a field.
	This works with Number, Date/Time, Currency and AutoNumber data types.
Min	Returns the minimum value in a field.
	This works with Text, Number, Date/Time, Currency and AutoNumber data types.
Max	Returns the maximum value in a field.
	This works with Text, Number, Date/Time, Currency and AutoNumber data types.
Count	Returns a count of the number of values in a field.
	This works with Text, Memo, Number, Date/Time, Currency, AutoNumber, Yes/No and OLE Object data types.

About total queries

A total query uses aggregate functions to calculate summary field values for all records or for groups of records returned by the query.

This following query counts the number of books in the Books table and calculates their total cost, and their average, maximum and minimum prices.

CountOfISBN	SumOfCost	AvgOfCost	MinOfCost	MaxOfCost
56	£ 439.77	£ 7.85	£ 1.50	£ 24.80

And the following query groups the books by publisher. It then counts the number of books by each publisher, together with the total cost of those books, and their average, maximum and minimum prices.

Publisher	SumOfCost	AvgOfCost	MinOfCost	MaxOfCost	CountOfISBN
Pearson Education Ltd	£ 48.97	£ 16.32	£ 12.99	£ 18.99	3
Penguin Books	£ 91.12	£ 7.59	£ 4.15	£ 24.80	12
Picador	£ 17.45	£ 5.82	£ 5.55	£ 5.95	3
Puffin Books	£ 6.98	£ 3.49	£ 2.99	£ 3.99	2

If you open the BooksCostPerPublisher query in Design View, you will see how this query was created.

In a total query, a *Total* row is added to the query design grid, and it is here that you specify the fields by which you want to group the records and the type of calculation you want to perform on each field. A drop-down list provides all the available options.

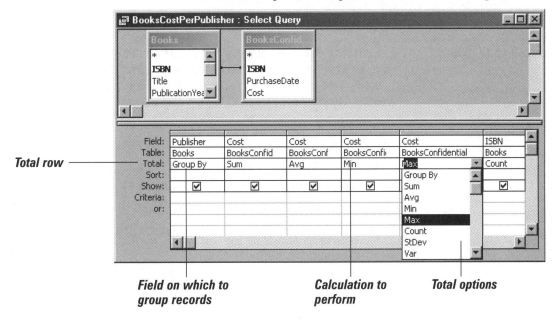

Total row

Field on which to group records

Calculation to perform

Total options

The only fields you need to include in the query are:

- The field(s) by which you want to group the results – BooksCostPerPublisher uses the Publisher field.

- The fields on which you want to perform calculations – BooksCostPerPublisher includes the Books.ISBN field, for counting the number of records per publisher, and four instances of the BooksConfidential.Cost field, so that several calculations can be performed on that field.

- The fields you want to use for setting selection criteria – see 'Using criteria in total queries' below.

If you switch to Datasheet View, you will see that, for the fields that perform calculations, Access automatically combines the function and field name to identify the column. But you can specify your own column names if you wish.

Total query

A query that calculates summary values for all records or for groups of records in tables/queries.

Creating total queries

You can create total queries with the *Simple Query Wizard* or in Query Design View. Using the wizard, however, has limitations:

- You can calculate totals only for Number fields.

- You cannot specify selection criteria for the query.

Totalling all records

Exercise 8.1: Calculating totals for all records in a query

In this exercise, you will create a query that displays the total number of books in the library and calculates totals for various fields in the BooksConfidential table.

1) Open the starting database for this chapter:

   Chp8_VillageLibrary_Database

2) Open a new query in Design View. When prompted for the tables you want to include in the query, select Books and BooksConfidential.

3) Add to the design grid all the fields on which you wish to perform calculations. To perform more than one calculation on a field, add an instance of the field for each calculation. For this exercise add the following fields:

   - Books.ISBN (to calculate the total number of books).

   - Two instances of BooksConfidential.Cost (to calculate the total and average cost of books).

   - Two instances of BooksConfidential.PurchaseDate (to calculate the earliest and latest dates on which books were purchased).

Totals button

4) Click the **Totals** button on the Query Design toolbar. This adds the *Total* row to the design grid.

5) By default, Access sets the *Total* row to *Group By* for all fields. Instead, select a calculation for each field, as shown here:

Field:	ISBN ▾	Cost	Cost	PurchaseDate	PurchaseDate
Table:	Books	BooksConfidential	BooksConfidential	BooksConfidential	BooksConfidential
Total:	Count	Sum	Avg	Min	Max
Sort:					

6) Save the query with the name BookTotals and then close it.

You can now open the query in Datasheet View and see the results, which should be similar to those shown here.

CountOfISBN	SumOfCost	AvgOfCost	MinOfPurchaseDate	MaxOfPurchaseDate
56	£ 439.77	£ 7.85	24-02-98	16-03-03

- **CountOfISBN.** The number of records in the Books table.

- **SumOfCost.** The sum total of the values in the Cost field.

- **AvgOfCost.** The average of the values in the Cost field.

- **MinOfPurchaseDate.** The earliest date in the PurchaseDate field.

- **MaxOfPurchaseDate.** The latest date in the PurchaseDate field.

Why include the Books table in the query when you could use BooksConfidential.ISBN to count the books? Well, it is possible that some books would not have a record in BooksConfidential – for example, if they were donated and so had no PurchaseDate or Cost values. Using Books.ISBN to count the books covers this possibility.

Renaming fields in a query

In the previous exercise, Access automatically generated names for the calculated fields – a combination of the function name and field name. You can change these to more meaningful names in Design View.

In the *Field* row in the design grid, type the new name to the left of the field name, followed by a colon (:).

Field:	Number of Books: ISBN	Total Cost: Cost	Average Price: Cost	First Purchase: PurchaseDate	Last Purchase: PurchaseDate
Table:	Books	BooksConfidential	BooksConfidential	BooksConfidential	BooksConfidential
Total:	Count	Sum	Avg	Min	Max
Sort:					
Show:	☑	☑	☑	☑	☑

Design View

Datasheet View

Number of Books	Total Cost	Average Price	First Purchase	Last Purchase
56	£ 439.77	£ 7.85	24-02-98	16-03-03

Note that this changes only the name used as the column heading in Datasheet View. It does not change the actual field name.

Totalling groups of records   When totalling values, you will often want to see the totals for particular groups of records instead of for the entire table. For example, you might want the total cost of books for each publisher or for each book category.

To calculate totals for groups of records, you select the *Group By* option in the *Total* row for the field(s) on which you wish to group the records. When you group records by more than one field, Access groups records by values in the leftmost field(s) first.

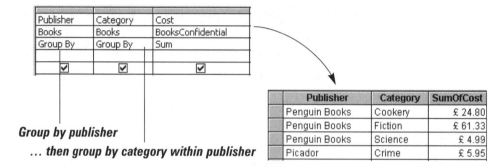

Group by publisher
... then group by category within publisher

Publisher	Category	SumOfCost
Penguin Books	Cookery	£ 24.80
Penguin Books	Fiction	£ 61.33
Penguin Books	Science	£ 4.99
Picador	Crime	£ 5.95

Exercise 8.2: Calculating totals for groups of records

In this exercise, you will create a query that displays the total number of books in each book category and the total, average, minimum and maximum cost of books in each category.

1) Open a new query in Design View. When prompted for the tables you want to include in the query, select Books and BooksConfidential.

2) Add the following fields to the design grid, in the order listed:

   – Books.Category (to group the records).

   – Books.ISBN (to count the records).

   – Four instances of BooksConfidential.Cost (to calculate the cost totals).

3) Click the **Totals** button to add the *Total* row to the design grid.

4) Rename the fields, and select a *Total* option for each field, as shown here:

Field:	Category	Quantity: ISBN	Total Cost: Cost	Avg Cost: Cost	Min Cost: Cost	Max Cost: Cost
Table:	Books	Books	BooksConfidential	BooksConfidential	BooksConfidential	BooksConfidential
Total:	Group By	Count	Sum	Avg	Min	Max
Sort:						
Show:	☑	☑	☑	☑	☑	☑

5) Save the query with the name BookCategoryTotals.

You can now run the query to see the results, which should be similar to those shown here.

Category	Quantity	Total Cost	Avg Cost	Min Cost	Max Cost
Biography	1	£ 12.75	£ 12.75	£ 12.75	£ 12.75
Children	6	£ 40.90	£ 6.82	£ 2.99	£ 18.99
Computers	3	£ 48.97	£ 16.32	£ 12.99	£ 18.99
Cookery	3	£ 48.78	£ 16.26	£ 5.99	£ 24.80
Crime	7	£ 33.93	£ 4.85	£ 2.09	£ 8.99
Fantasy	6	£ 36.74	£ 6.12	£ 4.99	£ 7.50
Fiction	25	£ 163.87	£ 6.55	£ 1.50	£ 13.60
Reference	1	£ 14.95	£ 14.95	£ 14.95	£ 14.95
Science	4	£ 38.88	£ 9.72	£ 4.99	£ 12.50

The Category column lists each book category. The Quantity field displays the number of books in each category. The remaining fields calculate totals for the cost of books in each category.

Using criteria in total queries

You can use criteria in total queries for three different purposes:

- To limit the records on which calculations are performed – for example, to calculate totals only for books that cost less than £20.

- To limit the groups on which calculations are performed – for example, to calculate totals only for Fiction, Fantasy and Crime books.

- To limit the records displayed based on the calculation results – for example, to display only groups where the total book cost is greater than £30.

Using multiple criteria

You enter selection criteria for a query in the *Criteria* and *Or* rows in the design grid. Criteria entered on different rows are combined using logical Or – that is, a record is selected if it satisfies *any* of the criteria. Criteria entered on the same row, but for different fields, are combined using logical And – that is, a record is selected only if it satisfies *all* the criteria.

You can, if you wish, combine different criteria in a single *Criteria* cell by including the logical operators in the criteria expression.

- Both the following examples select books published in 2000 by Penguin Books.

Field:	PublicationYear	Publisher
Table:	Books	Books
Sort:		
Show:	✔	✔
Criteria:	2000	"Penguin Books"
or:		

Field:	PublicationYear
Table:	Books
Sort:	
Show:	✔
Criteria:	2000 And [Publisher]="Penguin Books"

- This example selects books that are published either in 2000 or by Penguin Books or both.

Field:	PublicationYear	Publisher
Table:	Books	Books
Sort:		
Show:	☑	☑
Criteria:	2000	
or:		"Penguin Books"

- Both the following examples select books that are published in 2000 by either Puffin Books or Penguin Books.

Field:	PublicationYear	Publisher
Table:	Books	Books
Sort:		
Show:	☑	☑
Criteria:	2000	"Puffin Books"
or:	2000	"Penguin Books"

Field:	PublicationYear	Publisher
Table:	Books	Books
Sort:		
Show:	☑	☑
Criteria:	2000	"Penguin Books" Or "Puffin Books"

Limiting the records included in calculations

To limit the records on which a total calculation is performed:

1) Add to the design grid the field for which you wish to specify criteria. If you are also calculating a total for this field, you must add a second instance of the field for the calculation.

2) Select *Where* in the *Total* row for the field.

3) Enter your criteria for the field.

For example, when calculating totals for BooksConfidential.Cost, the criterion shown here specifies that only records where the cost is less than £20 are to be included in the calculation. To see this query in action, run the LimitRecords query.

Field:	Category	Cost	Cost
Table:	Books	BooksConfidential	BooksConfidential
Total:	Group By	Sum	Where
Sort:			
Show:	☑	☑	☐
Criteria:			<20

Before grouping or totalling, Access retrieves only books that cost less than £20

Note that Access always hides fields that have their *Total* row set to *Where*.

Limiting the groups on which calculations are performed

To limit the groups on which calculations are performed, you enter your selection criteria in the *Criteria* row(s) for the field(s) that define the groups.

For example, when grouping books by category and calculating total costs for each category, the criteria shown here specify that the calculations are to be performed only on the Fiction, Crime and Fantasy groups. To see this query in action, run the LimitGroups query.

Field:	Category		Cost	Cost
Table:	Books		BooksCo	BooksCo
Total:	Group By		Sum	Where
Sort:				
Show:		☑	☑	☐
Criteria:	"Fiction" Or "Crime" Or "Fantasy"			<20

Before totalling the cost, Access limits the groups to be totalled

Limiting the results to be displayed

To limit the records displayed by the query to those where a calculation result matches certain criteria, specify the criteria in the field that contains the calculation.

For example, when grouping books by category and calculating total costs for each category, the criteria shown here specify that the query is to return only those categories where the total cost is more than £50. To see this query in action, run the LimitResults query.

Field:	Category		Cost	Cost
Table:	Books		BooksConfi	BooksConfi
Total:	Group By		Sum	Where
Sort:				
Show:		☑	☑	☐
Criteria:	"Fiction" Or "Crime" Or "Fantasy"		>50|	<20

After totalling the cost, Access returns only groups for which the total cost is over £50

Exercise 8.3: Specifying criteria for a total query

In this exercise, you will create a query that groups books by publisher, and for each publisher calculates the total cost of books in the 1990s. The query limits the results to publishers for which the total cost is more than £15.

1) Open a new query in Design View. When prompted for the tables you want to include in the query, select Books and BooksConfidential.

2) Add the following fields to the design grid in the order listed:

   – Books.Publisher (to group the selected records).

   – BooksConfidential.PurchaseDate (to select books bought in the 1990s).

   – BooksConfidential.Cost (to calculate the totals and specify the criteria those totals must satisfy).

3) Click the **Totals** button to add the *Total* row to the design grid.

4) Select *Where* in the *Total* row for the PurchaseDate field and enter the following criteria expression for that field:

   Between #01-01-90# And #31-12-99#

5) Select *Group By* in the *Total* row for the Publisher field.

6) Select *Sum* in the *Total* row for the Cost field and enter the following criteria expression for that field:

   >15

Field:	Publisher	PurchaseDate	Cost
Table:	Books	BooksConfidential	BooksConfidential
Total:	Group By	Where	Sum
Sort:			
Show:	☑	☐	☑
Criteria:		Between #01-01-90# And #31-12-99#	>15

7) Save the query with the name BookPublisherTotals.

You can now run the query to see the results, which should be similar to those shown here.

Publisher	SumOfCost
BBC Books	£ 17.99
Fourth Estate	£ 16.60
Penguin Books	£ 45.20
▶ Virgin Publishing	£ 18.99

The Publisher column lists the Publishers for which the total cost of books bought in the 1990s was more than £15, and the SumOfCost column lists the total cost of those books for each publisher.

Using wildcards in queries

A wildcard character is a special character that takes the place of one or more other characters in a literal value.

You can use wildcards in query criteria to select values that match particular patterns of characters instead of specifying the values individually. For example, to select Publishers whose name begins with 'P', you could specify "P*" instead of "Penguin Books" Or "Puffin Books" Or "Picador". . ., and so on.

Wildcard

A special character that represents one or more other characters in a literal value.

Appendix A lists and explains the available wildcard characters. The following table presents some examples of using wildcard characters in query criteria.

Note that query criteria that include wildcard characters must be enclosed by double quotes, even when the values are numbers or dates. In addition, Access automatically adds the Like operator to criteria with wildcard characters (see Appendix A for details).

ECDL Advanced Databases

Field	Criteria	Result
Publisher	Like "P*"	Selects publishers whose name begins with the letter 'P'.
Publisher	Like "*Books"	Selects publishers whose name ends with the word 'Books'.
Publisher	Like "P[eu]*"	Selects publishers whose name begins with 'Pe' or 'Pu'. For example, Penguin Books and Puffin Books.
Publisher	Like "P[!eu]*"	Selects publishers whose name begins with 'P' and whose second letter is neither 'e' nor 'u'. For example, Picador.
Title	Like "*Potter*"	Selects titles that include the word 'Potter'. This would include the Harry Potter books and also 'From Potter's Field'.
PublicationYear	Like "200?"	Selects publication years from 2000 to 2009.
Cost	Like "*.99"	Selects cost values with 99 after the decimal point.
Cost	Like "*.9?"	Selects cost values with 90, 91, 92, and so on after the decimal point.
PurchaseDate	Like "??-??-0?"	Selects purchase dates in the years 2000 to 2009.

Note that you can use wildcard characters in any query, not just total queries.

About crosstab queries

A crosstab query is a special type of query that calculates totals for records that are grouped on more than one field and displays the results in a compact, spreadsheet-like format. For example, you could use a crosstab query to display the total number of books by category for each publisher.

Category groups

Publisher	Children	Computers	Cookery	Crime	Fiction
Minerva					1
Pearson Education Ltd		3			
Penguin Books			1		10
Picador				1	2

Publisher groups

Total for a particular publisher and category

The Publisher groups are displayed as row headings, the Category groups as column headings, and the totals are displayed in the intersection cells for each publisher and category.

You can use a standard total query to display the same data, as illustrated by the BooksByPublisherAndCategory query. If you run this query, you will get results similar to those shown here.

In this case, both the Publisher and Category groups are displayed as row headings, with a separate record for each Publisher/Category combination. In this format, it is more

Publisher	Category	Count
Pearson Education Ltd	Compute	3
Penguin Books	Cookery	1
Penguin Books	Fiction	10
Penguin Books	Science	1
Picador	Crime	1
Picador	Fiction	2
Puffin Books	Children	2

difficult to compare the totals than it is in the corresponding crosstab query (CrosstabBooksByPublisherAndCategory).

The disadvantages of a crosstab query are that you can calculate only one total in the query and you cannot sort the results on the total values.

Crosstab query

A query that calculates totals for records that are grouped on more than one field and displays the results in a spreadsheet-like format.

Creating a crosstab query

You can create a crosstab query in Query Design View or by using the *Crosstab Query Wizard*. To include fields from more than one table when using the wizard, you must first create a query containing those fields and then use that query as the basis for the crosstab query.

Exercise 8.4: Using the *Crosstab Query Wizard*

In this exercise you will create a crosstab query that groups books by publisher and category and calculates the total cost of books for each combination.

1) Click *Queries* in the *Objects* list in the Database window, click the **New** button on the window's toolbar, select the *Crosstab Query Wizard* option, and click **OK**.

2) When prompted for the table or query on which to base the new query, choose the PublisherCategoryCost query and then click **Next**.

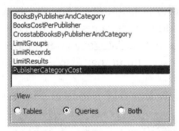

The PublisherCategoryCost query contains the Books.Publisher, Books.Category and BooksConfidential.Cost fields.

3) When prompted for the field whose values you want to use as row headings, select Publisher and click **Next**.

Note that the Sample in the lower part of each wizard window illustrates the result of your selection in that window.

4) When prompted for the field whose values you want to use as column headings, select Category and click **Next**.

5) When prompted for the calculation you want to perform, select *Sum*.

On the same page of the wizard, you are asked whether you want to summarize each row. The default is 'Yes', so

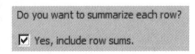

leave this as it is. The results will include an overall total for each publisher, as well as category totals. Click **Next**.

6) Finally, accept the default name for the query and click **Finish**.

The records displayed by the query should be similar to those shown here:

Publisher	Total Of Cost	Biography	Children	Computers	Cookery	Crime	Fantasy	Fiction	
Anchor	£ 9.45							£ 9.45	
Arrow	£ 8.99					£ 8.99			
BBC Books	£ 17.99				£ 17.99				
Black Swan	£ 14.98							£ 14.98	
Blackstaff Press	£ 5.50							£ 5.50	
Bloomsbury	£ 24.43					£ 5.99	£ 18.44		
Collins	£ 14.48		£ 5.99				£ 6.99	£ 1.50	
Corgi Books	£ 5.99						£ 5.99		

The individual publishers are displayed as row headings on the left side of the datasheet. The categories are displayed as column headings. The intersection cell for each Publisher and Category displays the total cost of books for that Publisher/Category combination. In addition, there is a Total Of Cost column that displays a grand total for each publisher.

Using Query Design View   Now let's take a look at your crosstab query in Design View.

Field:	Publisher	Category	Cost	Total Of Cost: Cost
Table:	PublisherCategoryC	PublisherCategoryC	PublisherCategoryC	PublisherCategoryC
Total:	Group By	Group By	Sum	Sum
Crosstab:	Row Heading	Column Heading	Value	Row Heading
Sort:				
Criteria:				

The design grid includes a *Crosstab* row where you specify which fields contain the row headings, the column headings, and the calculated totals.

Note that you can include more than one row heading. In this example, the second row heading calculates the total cost of books from each publisher.

Exercise 8.5: Creating a crosstab query in Design View

In this exercise you will create a crosstab query that displays the number of books in each category that were purchased on a particular date.

1) Open a new query in Design View. When prompted for the tables to include in the query, select Books and BooksConfidential.

2) Add the following fields to the design grid, in the order listed:

   – BooksConfidential.PurchaseDate (to form the row headings).

   – Books.Category (to form the column headings).

   – BooksConfidential.ISBN (to count the records).

3) Choose **Query | Crosstab Query** to specify the query type. Both a *Total* row and a *Crosstab* row are added to the design grid.

4) For the field whose values you want displayed as row headings – PurchaseDate – select the *Row Heading* option in the *Crosstab* row. You must also select *Group By* in the *Total* row for this field.

5) For the field whose values you want displayed as column headings – Category – select the *Column Heading* option in the *Crosstab* row. You must also select *Group By* in the *Total* row for this field.

6) For the field whose values you want to total – ISBN – select the *Value* option in the *Crosstab* row and select the type of total you want to calculate in the *Total* row. Select *Count*.

Field:	PurchaseDate	Category	ISBN
Table:	BooksConfidential	Books	BooksConfidential
Total:	Group By	Group By	Count
Crosstab:	Row Heading	Column Heading	Value
Sort:			

7) Save the query with the name PurchaseDateCategoryCrosstab.

You can now run the query to see the results, which should be similar to those shown here.

PurchaseDate	Biography	Children	Computers	Cookery	Crime	Fantasy	Fiction	Reference	Science
24-02-98						1	4		
13-09-98		1		2	1	1	2		
03-04-99					1		4		1
07-07-99	3				1		3		1
01-05-00	1				2		3		
23-10-00				1	1		3		
19-04-01	1					1	3		

The individual purchase dates are displayed as row headings down the left side of the datasheet. The book categories are displayed as column headings. The intersection cell for each PurchaseDate/Category combination displays the number of books in that category that were purchased on that date.

Using criteria in crosstab queries

You can specify selection criteria for a crosstab query in the same way you do for other total queries. See 'Using criteria in total queries' above.

- To limit the records on which the total calculation is performed:

  1) Add to the design grid the field for which you wish to specify criteria.

  2) Select *Where* in the field's *Total* row.

  3) Enter your criteria for the field.

- To limit the row headings for which the calculation is performed, enter your criteria in the *Criteria* row for the field with *Row Heading* in its *Crosstab* row. For example, to include only purchase dates in the twenty-first century, enter the following expression in the PurchaseDate field's *Criteria* row:

  >=#01-01-00#

- To limit the column headings for which the calculation is performed, enter your criteria in the *Criteria* row for the field with *Column Heading* in its *Crosstab* row. For example, to include only the Fantasy and Fiction categories in the query, enter the following expression in the Category field's *Criteria* row:

```
Like "F*"
```

Chapter 8: summary

A *total query* uses functions such as Sum, Avg, Count, Max and Min to calculate and display summary field values. You can calculate totals for all records or for groups of records.

You can create total queries with the *Simple Query Wizard* or in Query Design View. In Design View you use the *Total* row options to specify the fields by which you want to group your records and the type of total calculation you want to perform for each field.

You use selection criteria in a total query to limit the records on which a total calculation is performed, to limit the groups on which it is performed, and to limit the results to be displayed.

A *crosstab query* calculates totals for records that are grouped on more than one field and displays the results in a compact, spreadsheet-like format. One group forms the row headings, another the column headings, and the total value for each row/column combination is displayed in the intersection cell for that row/column. You can specify criteria for crosstab queries in the same way you do for standard queries.

A *wildcard character* is a special character that represents one or more other characters in a literal value. You can use wildcards in query criteria to select values that match particular patterns of characters instead of specifying the values individually.

Chapter 8: quick quiz

Q1	Which of these total functions counts the number of values in a field?
A.	Sum.
B.	Max.
C.	Count.

Q2	True or false – with the *Simple Query Wizard* you can calculate totals for all records or for groups of records in a table/query.
A.	True.
B.	False.

Q3	You can specify criteria in a total query to ...
A.	Display only records where the calculation result satisfies certain criteria.
B.	Exclude certain records from the calculations.
C.	Calculate totals for certain groups only.

Q4	Which of these expressions selects all books that contain 'The' in the title?
A.	Like "*The".
B.	Like "The*".
C.	Like "*The*.
D.	Like "?The?".

Q5	True or false – you can use a single crosstab query to calculate the average and maximum cost of books for each publisher/category combination.
A.	True.
B.	False.

Q6 Which of the following query definitions calculates the total cost of books for each publisher by purchase date?

A.

Field:	PurchaseDate	Publisher	Cost
Table:	BooksConfidential	Books	BooksConfidential
Total:	Group By	Group By	Sum
Crosstab:	Row Heading	Column Heading	Value

B.

Field:	PurchaseDate	Publisher	Cost
Table:	BooksConfidential	Books	BooksConfidential
Total:	Group By	Group By	Sum
Crosstab:	Column Heading	Row Heading	Value

C.

Field:	PurchaseDate	Publisher	Cost
Table:	BooksConfidential	Books	BooksConfidential
Total:	Group By	Group By	Sum
Crosstab:	Row Heading	Row Heading	Value

Answers   **1**: C, **2**: A, **3**: All, **4**: C, **5**: B, **6**: A and B.

9

Query design: custom calculations

In this chapter

In the previous chapter you learned how to use Access's predefined aggregate functions to summarize field values in queries. In this chapter you will learn how to use your own custom calculations to define query criteria and to create calculated fields.

New skills

At the end of this chapter you should be able to:

- Use calculations in query criteria
- Create calculated fields
- Use aggregate functions in calculated fields

New words

In this chapter you will meet the following term:

- Calculated field

Exercise file

In this chapter you will work with the following Access file:

- Chp9_VillageLibrary_Database

Syllabus reference

In this chapter you will cover the following items of the ECDL Advanced Database Syllabus:

- **AM5.2.2.2**: Use functions in a query: sum, count, average, max, min.
- **AM5.2.2.5**: Use arithmetic, logical expressions in a query.

About custom calculations

A custom calculation uses arithmetic and/or logical expressions to perform calculations on values in one or more fields. You can use them to create new, calculated fields in a query – for example, DueDate (LoanDate plus 10) or FineDue (DaysOverdue multiplied by daily fine amount). You can also use custom calculations to specify query selection criteria.

The expressions can include one or more of the following operators (see Appendix A for more details):

- Arithmetic operators – that is, +, -, *, /.

- Aggregate functions – for example, Sum(), Avg() and Max().

- Logical functions – for example, IIf().

The values on which calculations are performed can be any of the following (see Appendix A for more details):

- Literal values – for example, 100, 2.5, 0.75.

- Field identifiers – for example, [Cost] and [ReturnDate].

The following table shows some examples of custom calculations.

Expression	Result
[Quantity] * [UnitPrice]	Calculates the total cost of an order by multiplying the unit price by the quantity ordered.
[DeliveryCharge]+ ([Quantity] * [UnitPrice])	Calculates the invoice amount by adding the delivery charge to the order value.
[Quantity]*[UnitPrice]*.95	Discounts the order amount by 5%.
Sum([Quantity]*[UnitPrice])	In a query grouped by customer, calculates the total value of each customer's orders.
([Bonus]/([Wages]+[Bonus]))* 100	Where total pay is the sum of wages and bonus, this calculates what percentage the bonus is of the total pay.
<Date()-30	As a query criterion, selects records where the date is more than 30 days earlier than the current date.
<#01/04/03# -30	As a query criterion, selects records where the date is more than 30 days earlier than 1 April 2003.

Note that field names must be enclosed within square brackets and expressions being evaluated by a function must be enclosed within parentheses. You also use parentheses to indicate the evaluation order of expressions.

Calculations as query criteria

You can use calculations as criteria for determining which records a query displays or performs an action on. The following exercise provides two examples.

Exercise 9.1: Using calculations in query criteria

In this exercise you will create a query that retrieves records for books that were returned late.

1) Open the starting database for this chapter:

   Chp9_VillageLibrary_Database

2) Open a new query in Design View. When prompted for the tables to include in the query, select Loans and Members.

3) Add the following fields to the design grid, in the order listed:

   – Loans.ISBN

   – Loans.LoanDate

   – Loans.ReturnDate

   – Members.MemLastname

   – Members.MemFirstname

4) In the *Criteria* row for the ReturnDate field, type the following:

   >[LoanDate]+10

Field:	ISBN	LoanDate	ReturnDate	MemLastname	MemFirstname
Table:	Loans	Loans	Loans	Members	Members
Sort:					
Show:	☑	☑	☑	☑	☑
Criteria:			>[LoanDate]+10		

This limits the records retrieved to those where the return date is more than 10 days later than the loan date.

5) Switch to Datasheet View to confirm that the correct records have been retrieved.

ISBN	LoanDate	ReturnDate	MemLastname	MemFirstname
ISBN 0-00-671683-0	02-11-02	16-11-02	Long	April
ISBN 0-14-023171-4	19-11-02	01-12-02	Chase	Paul
ISBN 0-14-012670-8	19-11-02	01-12-02	Chase	Paul
ISBN 0-7088-8207-2	19-03-03	04-04-03	Mills	David
ISBN 0-14-023171-4	24-05-03	12-06-03	Woods	Richard
ISBN 0-14-012670-8	07-02-03	25-02-03	Worth	Richard
ISBN 0-14-014658-X	14-01-03	30-01-03	Reed	Susan

Only books returned late are listed

6) Switch back to Design View and replace the criteria expression with:

   [ReturnDate]-[LoanDate]>10

7) Switch to Datasheet View again and you will see that the results are the same.

8) Close the query without saving it.

Calculated fields

A calculated field is a query field that displays the result of a calculation on other fields in the query. For example, a calculated field named DueDate could calculate the due return date for a book by using the following expression:

`[LoanDate]+10`

You create a calculated field by entering the field name and the required expression in the *Field*

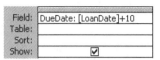

row of a blank column in the design grid. The example shown here creates the DueDate field.

Calculated fields are not stored in a database table. Instead Access reruns the calculation each time you run the query. To include calculated fields in a form or report, you can base the form or report on a query that contains those fields.

Calculated fields in the Village Library database

When library staff are processing book returns, they need to check if the books are overdue and to issue an appropriate fine if this is the case. This involves calculating the number of days that a book is overdue and then multiplying the result by the daily fine amount (£0.50).

Creating a query that includes the following fields would greatly facilitate this process.

Field	Description
DueDate	Members can borrow books for up to ten days. This calculated field displays the due date for borrowed books.
DaysOut	This calculated field displays the number of days that a book has been out on loan.
DaysOverdue	This calculated field displays the number of days by which a book is overdue (if any).
FineDue	The fine for overdue books is £0.50. This calculated field displays the amount due by multiplying the number of days overdue by 0.50.
FinePaid	Library staff have discretion to reduce fines in certain cases, so they must enter the actual amount paid manually in a table field where it can be stored for later analysis. FinePaid is that field.
Discount	This calculated field displays the percentage (if any) by which a fine was discounted.

The DueDate, DaysOut, FineDue and Discount fields involve straightforward calculations, as shown below.

Field	Expression
DueDate	[LoanDate]+10
DaysOut	[ReturnDate]-[LoanDate]
FineDue	[DaysOverdue]*0.5
Discount	(([FineDue]-[FinePaid])/[FineDue])*100

Calculating DaysOverdue, however, is more complicated, and requires use of the IIf() function.

Note that these calculations ignore books that have not yet been returned. You will learn how to deal with these in Chapter 10.

The IIf() function

For an overdue book, you can calculate DaysOverdue by subtracting 10 from DaysOut. For a book returned early or on time, however, this calculation returns a negative value, when what we want displayed is either zero or a blank field.

Basically we want Access to evaluate the result of the calculation before displaying it. Then if the result is greater than zero we want to display it, and if the result is zero or a negative value, we want to leave the field blank.

DaysOut	DaysOverdue
12	2
6	

Access provides the IIf() (or Immediate If) function to handle this type of situation – that is, to display one of two possible results depending on the evaluation of an expression. The IIf() function takes three arguments (that is, elements to which the function applies). Its syntax is:

```
IIf(expression, value_if_true, value_if_false)
```

where *expression* is the expression to be evaluated, *value_if_true* is the value to be displayed if the expression evaluates to true, and *value_if_false* is the value to be displayed if the expression evaluates to false.

In the case of the DaysOverdue field, we can use any of the following expressions to achieve the desired result:

```
IIf([DaysOut]>10,[DaysOut]-10,Null)
```

```
IIf([DaysOut]-10>0,[DaysOut]-10,Null)
```

```
IIf([ReturnDate]-[LoanDate]>10,[ReturnDate]-
[LoanDate]-10,Null)
```

The first example is the shortest and quickest. Access checks whether or not DaysOut is greater than ten (that is, whether the book is overdue). If it is, it calculates and displays the number of days overdue by subtracting ten from DaysOut. If it is not, it leaves the field blank.

Note that Null is a special value that indicates a blank field (see 'Null values' in Chapter 10). If you want DaysOverdue to display zero instead of Null, you would replace Null with 0 in the above expressions.

Creating calculated fields

You create a calculated field in a query by entering the field name and the required expression in the *Field* row of a blank column in the design grid.

Exercise 9.2: Creating calculated fields

In this exercise, you will create all the calculated fields described in 'Calculated fields in the Village Library database' above.

1) Open a new query in Design View. When prompted for the tables to include in the query, select Loans.

2) Add all fields from the table to the design grid.

3) Specify a sort order of *Descending* for the FinePaid field.

4) To create the DueDate field, insert a new column between the LoanDate and ReturnDate fields (click in the ReturnDate column and choose **Insert | Columns**). Then enter the following in the *Field* row of the new column:

   ```
   DueDate:[LoanDate]+10
   ```

   You can enter the expression directly in the *Field* cell, or you can display the *Zoom* dialog box and enter it there. The *Zoom* dialog box is the more flexible option, especially when entering or editing long expressions. To display the dialog box, click in the *Field* cell and press **Shift+F2**. When finished, close the dialog by clicking **OK**.

5) To create the DaysOut field, insert a new column after the ReturnDate field and enter the following in its *Field* row:

   ```
   DaysOut:[ReturnDate]-[LoanDate]
   ```

6) To create the DaysOverdue field, insert a new column after the DaysOut field and enter the following in its *Field* row:

   ```
   DaysOverdue:IIf([DaysOut]>10,[DaysOut]-10,Null)
   ```

7) To create the FineDue field, insert a new column after the DaysOverdue field and enter the following in its *Field* row:

```
FineDue:[DaysOverdue]*0.5
```

8) To create the Discount field, insert a new column after the FinePaid field and enter the following in its *Field* row:

```
Discount:(([FineDue]-[FinePaid])/[FineDue])*100
```

Field:	DueDate: [LoanDate]+10	ReturnDate	DaysOut: [ReturnDate]-[LoanDate]	DaysOverdue: IIf([DaysOut]>10,[DaysOut]-10,Null)
Table:		Loans		

9) Save the query with the name LoansExtended.

You can now run the query and see the results, which should be similar to those shown here. If you are prompted to enter a parameter instead, you have probably misspelled the name of a field in one of your calculations and should return to Design View and correct the mistake.

ISBN	MemID	LoanDate	DueDate	ReturnDate	DaysOut	DaysOverdue	FineDue	FinePaid	Discount
ISBN 0-1	39	07-02-03	17-02-03	25-02-03	18	8	4	£ 4.00	0
ISBN 0-1	28	24-05-03	03-06-03	12-06-03	19	9	4.5	£ 4.00	11.11111111
ISBN 0-1	16	14-01-03	24-01-03	30-01-03	16	6	3	£ 3.00	0
ISBN 0-7	24	19-03-03	29-03-03	04-04-03	16	6	3	£ 3.00	0
ISBN 0-1	23	14-04-03	24-04-03	30-04-03	16	6	3	£ 2.50	16.66666667
ISBN 0-3	43	21-01-03	31-01-03	05-02-03	15	5	2.5	£ 2.50	0
ISBN 0-1	26	30-01-03	09-02-03	13-02-03	14	4	2	£ 2.00	0

The calculated fields should be displaying the correct calculated values. However, you need to adjust the formatting of the FineDue and Discount fields. You will do this in the next exercise.

Changing calculated field properties

When you include a table field in a query, it inherits the properties defined for it in the table – for example, Format, Decimal Places and Input Mask. With a calculated field, however, there is no table field from which to inherit properties. Instead you can set the field's properties by using the **Properties** button on the *Query Design* toolbar. You can also use this option to change a table field's properties – the changes apply only to the query in which they are made.

Exercise 9.3: Changing calculated field properties
In this exercise, you will change the format of the FineDue field to Currency, and you will change the format of the Discount field to Percent.

1) Open the LoansExtended query in Design View.

Properties button

2) Click in the FineDue column and click the **Properties** button on the toolbar. This displays the *Field Properties* dialog box.

ECDL Advanced Databases

3) Select the *Currency* option in the *Format* property.

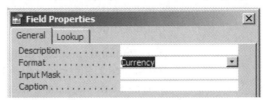

4) Click in the Discount column. That field's properties are now displayed in the *Field Properties* dialog box. Select *Percent* in the *Format* property.

5) When you apply a *Percent* format to a field, Access multiplies values in the field by 100 and appends a percent sign (%). The expression you used to create the Discount field also multiplies the values by 100. To avoid multiplying by 100 twice, change the expression to:

```
Discount:([FineDue]-[FinePaid])/[FineDue]
```

6) Save the query and then switch to Datasheet View to see the result of your changes. Both FineDue and Discount values are now more appropriately formatted.

FineDue	FinePaid	Discount
£ 4.00	£ 4.00	0.00%
£ 4.50	£ 4.00	11.11%
£ 3.00	£ 3.00	0.00%
£ 3.00	£ 3.00	0.00%

You could refine the Discount field still further by hiding all zero discount values. To do this you would change the field expression to:

```
Discount:IIf((([FineDue]-[FinePaid])=0,Null,
(([FineDue]-[FinePaid])/[FineDue]))
```

Sorting, totalling and defining criteria for calculated fields

Once you have set up the fields you want to include in a query, there are several design grid options that you can use to control the query output:

- **Sort**. You can use the *Sort* options to sort the records on one or more fields.

- **Show**. You can use the *Show* row to specify which fields to show or hide in the results.

- **Total**. You use the *Total* options to summarize the records.

- **Criteria**. You can enter selection criteria to limit the records that the query displays.

All these options are available for calculated fields, but with limitations:

- You cannot sort or specify criteria for calculated fields that reference another calculated field. For example, you can sort and specify criteria for DueDate but not DaysOverdue.

- You cannot hide a calculated field if it is referenced by another calculated field. For example, you can hide Discount but not FineDue.

- You cannot total a calculated field if it references another calculated field or includes the IIf() function. For example, you can calculate the minimum and maximum dates in DueDate but you cannot calculate the average value in DaysOverdue.

These appear to be serious limitations but there is a simple solution. Instead of specifying your sort orders, criteria, and so on in the original query, create a new query based on the original query and specify your sort orders, criteria and totalling requirements in this new query.

The SummaryOverdueBooks query provides an example of this type of query. If you open this query in Design View, you will see how it is defined.

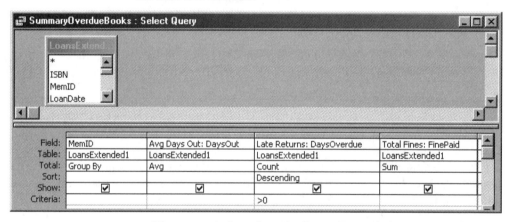

- The query is based on the LoansExtended1 query, which is a predefined version of your LoansExtended query.

- For each member, it calculates the average number of days they have had any books out on loan, the number of times that they have returned books late, and the total fines they have paid.

- It then groups records by MemID and limits the results to members who have returned books late on one or more occasions.

- The results are sorted by DaysOverdue in descending order.

If you run the query, the results should resemble those shown below.

MemID	Avg Days Out	Late Returns	Total Fines
9	8.75	2	£ 2.00
32	9.83	2	£ 2.00
23	9.00	1	£ 2.50
7	9.50	1	£ 2.00

Note that when you base a new query on an existing query, calculated fields in the new query do not inherit the properties set for those fields in the original query. You must reset them in the new query.

Using aggregate functions in calculated fields

The expression for a calculated field can include aggregate functions such as Sum() and Avg(). For example, the following calculated field returns the average daily fine paid for overdue books.

```
Daily Fine:Avg([FinePaid]/[DaysOverdue])
```

When calculated fields contain aggregate functions, you must display the *Total* row in the design grid and select *Expression* as the *Total* option for those fields. If there are other calculated fields in the query you must then select *Expression* in their *Total* rows also; you can leave the *Total* setting for non-calculated fields as *Group By*. This is not necessary if the calculated field(s) are the only fields in the query.

Field:	ISBN	MemID	LoanDate	ReturnDate	DaysOut: [ReturnDate]-[LoanDate]	FinePaid	Daily Fine: Avg([FinePaid]/[DaysOverdue])
Table:	Loans	Loans	Loans	Loans		Loans	
Total:	Group By	Group By	Group By	Group By	Expression	Group By	Expression
Sort:						Descending	
Show:	☑	☑	☑	☑	☑	☑	☑

Chapter 9: summary

Custom calculations in a query use arithmetic and logical expressions to perform calculations on values in one or more fields. You can use them to create new, calculated fields and to specify record selection criteria.

A *calculated field* is a query field that displays the result of a calculation on other fields in the query. You create a calculated field by entering the field name and the required expression in the *Field* row of a blank column in the query design grid. The field name must be immediately followed by a colon (:). You can change the properties of a calculated field in the same way you change the properties of other fields in a query – use the **Properties** button on the *Query Design* toolbar.

Calculated fields are not stored in a database table. Instead Access reruns the calculation each time you run the query.

You can use the IIf() function in a calculated field when you want Access to display different results depending on whether a particular condition is true or false. You can also use aggregate functions in a calculated field.

You can sort, total, and specify criteria for calculated fields, but there are limitations. When you want to perform these operations on calculated fields, it is often preferable to create the calculated fields in one query and then specify the sort orders, criteria, and total calculations in another query that is based on the original query.

Chapter 9: quick quiz

Q1	True or false – a calculated field can include more than one calculation.
A.	True.
B.	False.

Q2	Which of the following are valid calculated fields?
A.	DaysOverdue:[ReturnDate]-[LoanDate]>10
B.	DaysOverdue:[DaysOut]>10
C.	DaysOverdue:[DaysOut]-10

Q3	Which of these calculated fields displays Yes if a book was returned late and No if it was not?
A.	Overdue:IIf([DaysOut]>10,"No","Yes")
B.	Overdue:IIf([ReturnDate]-[LoanDate]>10, "Yes","No")
C.	Overdue:IIf([DaysOut]>10,"Yes","No")

Q4	For which of these calculated fields can you specify selection criteria?
A.	`DaysOut:[ReturnDate]-[LoanDate]`
B.	`DaysOverdue:[ReturnDate]-[DueDate]`
C.	`Overdue:IIf([ReturnDate]-[LoanDate]>10,` `"Yes","No")`
D.	`Overdue:IIf([DaysOut]>10,"Yes","No")`

Q5	True or false – the following is a valid calculated field: `AvgDaysOut:Avg([ReturnDate]-[LoanDate])`
A.	True.
B.	False.

Q6	True or false – you can sort and specify criteria for any calculated field in a query.
A.	True.
B.	False.

Answers

1: A, **2**: C, **3**: B and C, **4**: A and C, **5**: A, **6**: B.

10 Query design: refining queries

In this chapter

In this chapter you will learn various ways in which you can refine your queries and control their output.

New skills

At the end of this chapter you should be able to:

- Understand and use Null values
- Show and hide duplicate records and values
- Find unmatched records and values
- Display the highest or lowest range of values in a field
- Create and use parameter queries

New words

In this chapter you will meet the following terms:

- Null
- Duplicate record
- Unique record
- Unmatched record
- Top values
- Parameter query

Exercise file

In this chapter you will work with the following Access file:

- Chp10_VillageLibrary_Database

Syllabus reference

In this chapter you will cover the following items of the ECDL Advanced Database syllabus:

- **AM5.2.3.1**: Show duplicates.
- **AM5.2.3.2**: Show unmatched values.
- **AM5.2.3.3**: Show highest, lowest range of values in a query.
- **AM5.2.3.4**: Allow query input from a data prompt (parameter query).
- **AM5.2.3.5**: Refining queries using Null and NOT values.

Null values

Null is a special value that indicates missing or unknown data, or a field to which data is not applicable. Access automatically enters a Null value when you leave a field blank.

DueDate	ReturnDate	DaysOut	DaysOverdue	FineDue
05-12-02	01-12-02	6		
13-07-03				
29-11-02	01-12-02	12	2	£ 1.00
24-04-03	19-04-03	5		

All blank fields here contain Null values

Missing   Unknown   Not applicable

Primary key fields cannot contain Null values and you can prevent other fields from accepting Null values by setting their *Required* property to Yes (see 'Required values' in Chapter 4).

You can use Null values in query criteria and calculated field expressions by entering the keyword **Null**. But Nulls have some special properties that can affect your query results.

- You cannot use the equal to (=) and not equal to (<>) operators with the Null keyword. For example, [ReturnDate]=Null is not a valid expression. Instead you must use the Is Null and Is Not Null operators or the IsNull() function (see below).

- Aggregate functions ignore Null values. For example, the result of an Avg() calculation is based only on fields with non-Null values. To include Null values in this type of calculation, you must first convert the Null values to zeros (see 'Nz() function' below).

  To include Null values when counting records, you can use Count(*) instead of Count().

- Expressions that include arithmetic operators (+, -, *, /) always return a Null value if any of the fields in the expression contain a Null value.

  For example, [OrderAmount]+[Freight] returns Null if there is no freight charge. To prevent this happening you can convert all Null values in the Freight field to zeros before performing the calculation (see 'Nz() function' below).

- When you use the criteria expression Like "*" for a field, the query does *not* return records that contain Nulls in that field.

> **Null**
>
> *A special value (displayed as a blank field) that indicates missing or unknown data, or a field to which data is not applicable.*

Is Null and Is Not Null operators

Is Null and Is Not Null are comparison operators that mean 'is equal to Null' and 'is not equal to Null' respectively.

Specifying Is Null as the selection criteria for a field returns all records where that field contains a Null value; specifying Is Not Null returns all records where the field does not contain a Null value.

For example, the BooksOnLoan query in Chp10_VillageLibrary_Database lists the books that are currently out on loan. If you open the query in Design View, you will see that the Is Null operator has been entered as the criteria for the

Field:	ISBN	Title	ReturnDate
Table:	Loans	Books	Loans
Sort:			
Show:	☑	☑	☐
Criteria:			Is Null

ReturnDate field. This tells Access to display only records where the ReturnDate field is empty – that is, books that have been borrowed but not yet returned.

IsNull() function

IsNull() is a function that tests whether a value is Null. It is typically used in calculated fields in combination with the IIf() function.

Remember that the IIf() function returns one of two possible results depending on the evaluation of an expression. You can use the IsNull() function as the expression and so display one result if a field is Null and a different result if the field contains a non-Null value.

For example, take an InvoiceAmount field that is calculated as the sum of OrderAmount and Freight:

```
InvoiceAmount:[OrderAmount]+[Freight]
```

If no freight is being charged on an order, this calculation evaluates to Null because the freight value is Null. One way to overcome this problem is to use this expression instead:

```
InvoiceAmount:IIf(IsNull([Freight]),[OrderAmount],
[OrderAmount]+[Freight])
```

The IsNull([Freight]) expression tests whether the Freight value is Null. If it is, then the IIf() function returns the OrderAmount value. If it is not, then the IIf() function returns the sum of OrderAmount and Freight.

Exercise 10.1: Using the IsNull() function in calculated fields

In this exercise you will modify the LoansExtended query to include a new field: Overdue. This is a Yes/No field that indicates whether or not a book is overdue. Then you will change the expression in the DaysOverdue field so that it can handle books that have not yet been returned.

1) Open the LoansExtended query in Design View.

2) Take a look at the expression for the DaysOverdue field:

```
DaysOverdue:IIf([DaysOut]>10,[DaysOut]-10,Null)
```

If a book is overdue, the field displays the number of days that it is overdue. If a book is not overdue, the field displays Null. So to create an Overdue field that indicates whether or not a book is overdue, you can use the following expression:

```
Overdue:IIf(IsNull([DaysOverdue]),"No","Yes")
```

3) Add a new column to the left of the DaysOverdue column, and create the Overdue field by using the above expression.

4) Save the query and then run it.

DueDate	ReturnDate	DaysOut	Overdue	DaysOverdue
29-11-02	01-12-02	12	Yes	2
29-11-02	01-12-02	12	Yes	2
13-03-03	14-03-03	11	Yes	1
23-07-03			No	

Notice that 'No' has been entered for all books that have not yet been returned, even if they are overdue.

Why? Because DaysOut is calculated by subtracting LoanDate from ReturnDate. For fields with no return date, this calculation returns Null, and this Null carries through to the DaysOut, DaysOverdue and Overdue fields, resulting in a 'No' value in the latter.

5) You need to modify the query to address this problem. Switch back to Design View and take a look at the expression in the DaysOut field.

```
DaysOut:[ReturnDate]-[LoanDate]
```

This calculates the number of days out, but only for books that have a ReturnDate value. For books that have not yet been returned, the calculation should be:

```
Date()-[LoanDate]
```

To enable the DaysOut field to handle both calculations, you need an IsNull() function to test whether ReturnDate is Null and an IIf() function so that one calculation is performed when ReturnDate is Null and the other is performed when ReturnDate is not Null. The appropriate expression is:

```
DaysOut:IIf(IsNull([ReturnDate]),Date()-
[LoanDate],[ReturnDate]-[LoanDate])
```

6) Replace the current definition of the DaysOut field with the new one shown above.

7) Save the query and then run it to see the result of your changes.

DueDate	ReturnDate	DaysOut	Overdue	DaysOverdue	FineDue
11-07-03		20	Yes	10	£ 5.00
11-07-03		20	Yes	10	£ 5.00
01-07-03	27-06-03	6	No		
11-07-03		20	Yes	10	£ 5.00

This time books that have not yet been returned are included in all the calculations. When a book is returned and a return date entered, the query will recalculate the calculated fields for that record.

Note that when you run the query, the results differ from those shown above. This is because, for books not yet returned, the value of DaysOut depends on the value returned by Date(), which is always the current date.

Nz() function

Expressions that include arithmetic operators always return Null if one of the fields in the expression contains a Null value. In a previous example, the following expression was used in an InvoiceAmount field to overcome the problem of Null freight values:

```
InvoiceAmount:IIf(IsNull([Freight]),[OrderAmount],
[OrderAmount]+[Freight])
```

But there is a shorter way to achieve the same result. This involves using the Nz() function.

The Nz() (or Null to Zero) function converts Null values to zeros before performing a calculation, so the results will never be Null. The syntax for the function is as follows:

```
Nz(expression,value_if_null)
```

where *expression* is the field or expression you want converted when it evaluates to Null and *value_if_null* is the value (typically 0) to which you want to convert Null values.

In the case of the InvoiceAmount field, you can use the following expression to overcome the problem of Null Freight values:

```
InvoiceAmount:[OrderAmount]+Nz([Freight],0)
```

Now when Freight contains a Null value, the Null is converted to zero before Freight is added to OrderAmount. This produces the desired result without having to use the IIf() function.

Duplicate records and values

Duplicate records are records that contain identical values in all their fields. Unique records are records that contain different values in at least one field.

By definition, values in the primary key field of a table must be unique, so a table with a primary key will contain only unique records. However, a query may return duplicate records if it doesn't include the primary keys of the tables on which it is based.

For example, this query here displays the MemLastname and MemTown fields from the Members table. Because some members share the same last name and address, the results include several duplicate records.

Turner	Belmount
White	Belmount
White	Belmount
White	Belmount
Woods	Newtown
Worth	Castletown
Worth	Castletown

Access provides the following features for working with duplicate records:

- *Find Duplicates Query Wizard*

- *Unique Values* property

- *Unique Records* property

Find Duplicates Query Wizard

The *Find Duplicates Query Wizard* enables you to find duplicate records in a table or query. You can use it to find entire duplicate records in a table. However, you are more likely to use it to find records that share the same value(s) in one or more fields. For example:

- Find all library members who live at the same address. In Chapter 6, you used a self join in a query to find this information. Using the *Find Duplicates Query Wizard* is a much simpler option.

- Find all books that have been borrowed more than once.

- Find all books that have been borrowed more than once by the same member.

- Find all books in a particular category that have been borrowed more than once.

To include fields from more than one table in the query, you must first create a query that includes those fields and then base the *Find Duplicates Query* on that query.

Exercise 10.2: Finding duplicate values in table fields

In this exercise you will create a query that lists all books that have been borrowed more than once.

1) Click the *Queries* option in the *Objects* list in the Database window, click the **New** button on the window's toolbar, select the *Find Duplicates Query Wizard* option, and click **OK**.

2) When prompted for the table or query in which you wish to search for duplicate field values, choose the Loans table and click **Next**.

3) When prompted for the field(s) that you want to check for duplicate values, choose ISBN and click **Next**.

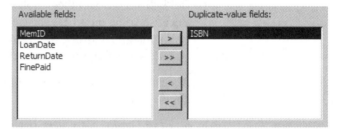

4) The wizard than asks you whether you want to include additional fields in the query, other than the ones with duplicate values:

   - If you don't select a field here, the query results will group records that have duplicate values in the field(s) specified in step 3 and display the number of duplicates in each group.

   - If you do select additional fields, the query results will display the records individually.

For this exercise, you don't need additional fields, so just click **Next**.

5) When prompted to name the query, enter DuplicateLoanISBNs and click **Finish**.

ISBN Field	NumberOfDups
ISBN 0-00-6122	5
ISBN 0-00-7129	2
ISBN 0-099-283	4
ISBN 0-130-384	2

The query results display the ISBN value for each book that has been borrowed more than once and the number of times each of those books has been borrowed.

To see how the query works, switch to Design View. Notice that the design grid includes three instances of Loans. ISBN:

Field:	ISBN Field: ISBN	NumberOfDups: ISBN	ISBN
Table:	Loans	Loans	Loans
Total:	First	Count	Group By
Sort:			
Show:	☑	☑	☐
Criteria:		>1	

- **ISBN.** This instance is used to group records in the Loans table by ISBN value.

- **NumberOfDups.** This instance is used to count the number of records in each ISBN group and to limit the query results to those groups where the count is greater than one.

- **ISBN Field.** This instance is used to retrieve and display the ISBN value from the first record in each group.

To find all books that have been borrowed more than once by the same member, you would follow exactly the same procedure but select the MemID field as well as the ISBN field in step 3 of Exercise 10.2. The results would be similar to those shown here.

ISBN Field	MemID Field	NumberOfDups
ISBN 0-14-0390	41	2
ISBN 0-85640-0	32	2

Exercise 10.3: Including additional fields in a Find Duplicates Query

In this exercise you will create a query that lists all addresses where more than one member lives and the names of those members.

1) Start the *Find Duplicates Query Wizard*.

2) When prompted for the table or query in which you wish to search for duplicate field values, choose the Members table and click **Next**.

3) When prompted for the field(s) that you want to check for duplicate values, choose MemAddress and then click **Next**.

4) When prompted to select additional fields, choose MemFirstname and MemLastname and then click **Next**.

5) When prompted for a name for the query, enter DuplicateMemAddresses, and click **Finish**.

The query results display all addresses that are shared by more than one member and the names of those members. The following is an extract from those results.

MemAddress	MemFirstname	MemLastname
21 West Drive	Annabel	Worth
21 West Drive	Richard	Worth
28 Knightstown	David	Mills
28 Knightstown	Jennifer	Mills
Halfway House	Rodney	Black
Halfway House	Judith	Gibbs

To see how the query works, switch to Design View. In this case, a *subquery* is used to achieve the desired results. A subquery is a select query that is contained within another select query. You do not need to know about subqueries for ECDL.

By default, Access queries display all records retrieved by a query, including duplicates. If you want to omit duplicates, use one of the following query properties:

- **Unique Values**. Omits records with duplicate values in all fields displayed by the query, even if those records refer to different records in the underlying data source.

  For example, this query here is designed to show the range of book categories published by each publisher. The initial results include many duplicate records, representing individual books that share the same publisher and category. But if you set the *Unique Values* property, the query omits all but one of the records with duplicate values in the displayed fields.

Publisher	Category
Pearson Education Ltd	Computers
Pearson Education Ltd	Computers
Pearson Education Ltd	Computers
Penguin Books	Fiction
Penguin Books	Fiction
Penguin Books	Cookery
Penguin Books	Fiction
Penguin Books	Fiction

Publisher	Category
Pearson Education Ltd	Computers
~~Pearson Education Ltd~~	~~Computers~~
~~Pearson Education Ltd~~	~~Computers~~
Penguin Books	Fiction
~~Penguin Books~~	~~Fiction~~
Penguin Books	Cookery
~~Penguin Books~~	~~Fiction~~
~~Penguin Books~~	~~Fiction~~

Unique Values not used   *Unique Values used*

- **Unique Records**. Omits duplicates that represent the same record in the underlying data sources of a query. This property has an effect only when a query is based on more than one table and only if it displays fields from some, *but not all*, of those tables.

  For example, the following query is designed to list books that have been borrowed at least once. The initial results include many duplicates, representing books that have been borrowed many times. But if you set the *Unique Records* property, the query omits all but one of the duplicates that represent the same book.

ISBN	Title
ISBN 0-14-062010-9	Emma
ISBN 0-14-062010-9	Emma
ISBN 0-297-81410-9	The Man in the Ice
ISBN 0-297-81410-9	The Man in the Ice
ISBN 0-09-175208-6	An Evil Cradling
ISBN 0-552-13107-5	Sourcery
ISBN 0-552-13107-5	Sourcery

ISBN	Title
ISBN 0-14-062010-9	Emma
~~ISBN 0-14-062010-9~~	~~Emma~~
ISBN 0-297-81410-9	The Man in the Ice
~~ISBN 0-297-81410-9~~	~~The Man in the Ice~~
ISBN 0-09-175208-6	An Evil Cradling
ISBN 0-552-13107-5	Sourcery
~~ISBN 0-552-13107-5~~	~~Sourcery~~

Unique Records not used   *Unique Records used*

Unique Values and *Unique Records* are mutually exclusive options. For most queries to which *Unique Records* is applicable, using *Unique Values* produces the same results, but with one difference – queries that use *Unique Records* are updateable, while queries that use *Unique Values* are not.

What is an updateable query?

An updateable query is one that allows you to edit the records it returns. The changes are applied to the underlying table(s).

In general, single-table queries are updateable, as are multi-table queries based on tables with one-to-one relationships. Multi-table queries based on tables with one-to-many relationships are usually updateable but there are restrictions.

No query is updateable if it groups records, contains an aggregate function, or uses the Unique Values *property.*

Exercise 10.4: Using *Unique Records* and *Unique Values*

The UniqueValuesRecords query displays the publisher and category for all books that have been borrowed at least once. In this exercise, you will apply the *Unique Records* and *Unique Values* properties to see the different results that are returned by the query in each case.

1) Open the UniqueValuesRecords query in Design View.

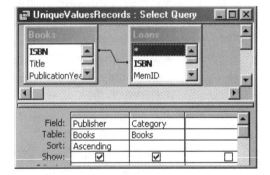

As you can see, the query includes the Books and Loans tables, related by an inner join on their ISBN fields. So the query compares values in the two ISBN fields and returns a record for each match found. For each record returned it then displays the Publisher and Category values.

2) Run the query and you will see that 131 records are displayed, including many duplicates. Basically, the query returns publisher and category details for each book loan. Some duplicates represent different books that have the same publisher and category. Others represent separate loans of the same book.

For example, a computer book from Pearson Education has been borrowed on five occasions. But we don't know whether these records represent the same or different books.

Publisher	Category
Pearson Education Ltd	Computers
Pearson Education Ltd	Computers
Pearson Education Ltd	Computers
Pearson Education Ltd	Computers
Pearson Education Ltd	Computers

3) Now let's see what effect the *Unique Values* and *Unique Records* properties have on the query. Switch back to Design View and open the *Query Properties* dialog box (click a blank part of the field list area and click the **Properties** button in the toolbar).

4) Select the *Yes* option in the *Unique Records* property.

5) Run the query. Only 46 records are now displayed, but there are still some duplicates. So which duplicates have been omitted?

Remember that *Unique Records* omits duplicates that represent the same record in the underlying data source. So, in this query all duplicates that represent the same book are omitted. For example, the results now include three records for computer books published by Pearson Education. This indicates that three *different* computer books from that publisher have been borrowed at some time.

Publisher	Category
Pearson Education Ltd	Computers
Pearson Education Ltd	Computers
Pearson Education Ltd	Computers

6) Now switch back to Design View and set the *Unique Values* property to *Yes* (Access automatically sets the *Unique Records* property to *No* when you do this).

7) Run the query again. This time only 30 records are displayed and there are no duplicates.

Publisher	Category
Minerva	Fiction
Pearson Education Ltd	Computers
Penguin Books	Cookery

Remember that *Unique Values* omits all but one of the records that have duplicate values in the displayed fields – that is, all records with the same publisher and category values. So the results include only one record for computer books by Pearson Education. This indicates that at least one computer book by that publisher has been borrowed at some time.

8) Close the query, saving it as you do.

Unmatched records

Most multi-table queries display results based on matching values in related tables. If, instead, you want to find the records in one table that have *no* matching records in another table, you can use the *Find Unmatched Query Wizard*. For example:

- Find all books that have never been borrowed.

- Find all members that have never borrowed a book.

- Find all books that were not borrowed in a particular time period.

Using the Find Unmatched Query Wizard

Exercise 10.5: Finding unmatched records

In this exercise you will use the *Find Unmatched Query Wizard* to create a query that lists the books that have never been borrowed.

1) Click the *Queries* option in the *Objects* list in the Database window, click the **New** button on the window's toolbar, select the *Find Unmatched Records Query Wizard* option, and click **OK**.

2) The first page of the wizard prompts you for the table that contains the unmatched records you want to view. You are looking for records in the Books table that have no matching records in the Loans table, so select the Books table and click **Next**.

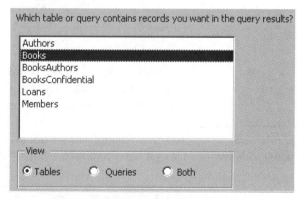

3) The second page prompts you for the related table. You are looking for books that have no entries in the Loans table, so select the Loans table and click **Next**.

4) The third page prompts you to select the field on which the two tables are joined. Select the ISBN field in both lists and click the <=> button. Then click **Next**.

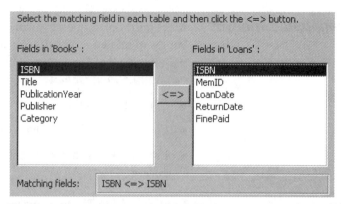

Select the matching field in each table and then click the <=> button.

Fields in 'Books' :

ISBN
Title
PublicationYear
Publisher
Category

<=>

Fields in 'Loans' :

ISBN
MemID
LoanDate
ReturnDate
FinePaid

Matching fields: ISBN <=> ISBN

5)   The fourth page prompts you for the fields that you want to display in the query results. Select ISBN, Title and Category and then click **Next**.

6)   When prompted to name the query, enter BooksWithoutLoans and click **Finish**.

ISBN	Title	Category
ISBN 0-7171-1738-3	A Simply Delicious Christmas	Cookery
ISBN 0-283-06145-6	New Guide to the Planets	Science
ISBN 0-600-30451-5	The Adventurous Four	Children
ISBN 0-7548-0731-2	The New Guide to Cat Care	Referenci
ISBN 0-09-926855-8	Music & Silence	Fiction
ISBN 0-7088-2639-3	The Devil's Novice	Crime
ISBN 0-552-99702-1	A Walk in the Woods	Fiction
ISBN 0-451-16776-7	Feeling Good: The New Mood Ther	Science
ISBN 0-099-93072-0	Fatal Voyage	Crime
ISBN 0-14-012389-X	Love in the Time of Cholera	Fiction

The query results list all records in the Books table for which there are no matching records in the Loans table – that is, all books that have never been borrowed.

Unmatched Records queries in Design View

To see how the BooksWithoutLoans query works, open it in Design View and take a look at it there.

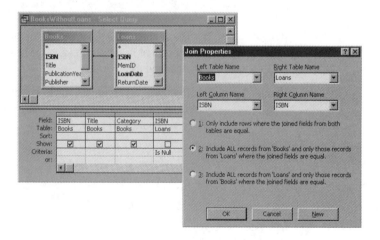

ECDL Advanced Databases

- Notice that the Books and Loans tables have been joined with a left outer join (option 2) so that the query returns all records from the Books table but only matching records from the Loans table. For books with no matching records in the Loans table, the fields from the Loans table will be blank – that is, they will contain a Null value. (See 'Left outer joins' in Chapter 6.)

- The records that have Null values in their Loan fields are the ones you are interested in, as they represent books that have never been borrowed. So, to limit the results to just those records, the query includes the Loans.ISBN field in the design grid and specifies Is Null as its selection criterion.

With the *Find Unmatched Records Wizard* you can't display fields from more than one table. For example, in the previous exercise, you couldn't include the author name in the query results. If you want to do this, you can use either of the following methods:

- Create a query that contains all the fields you want to display and base the BooksWithoutLoans query on that query, as shown here.

Query ——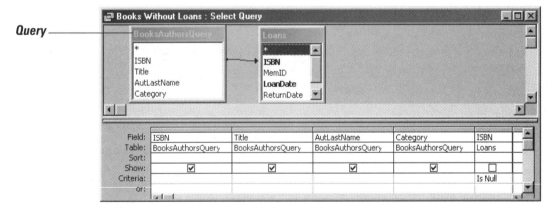

- Create the BooksWithoutLoans query as you did in Exercise 10.5 and then modify it in Design View, as shown here.

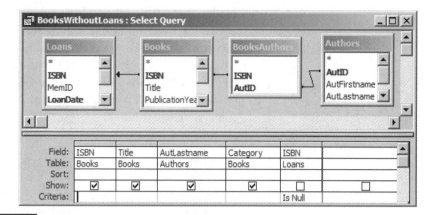

Unmatched values

Earlier in this chapter you learnt that you can use the Is Not Null operator in query criteria to exclude all records that contain a Null value in a particular field. To exclude records based on specific non-Null values you use the Not operator instead.

For example, to retrieve all books *not* published by Penguin Books, you would specify the following criterion for the Publisher field:

```
Not "Penguin Books"
```

The following table shows some examples of the Not operator in query criteria.

Field	Criteria	Result
Publisher	Not "P*"	Selects records where the publisher name does not begin with 'P'.
PublicationYear	Not 20??	Selects publication years that are not in the range 2000 to 2099.
ReturnDate	Not ([LoanDate]+10))	Selects return dates that are not the same as the due date.
Category	Not("Fiction" Or "Fantasy")	Selects all categories except Fiction and Fantasy.

Highest and lowest values

You can use a query's *Top Values* property to display a particular number or percentage of the records retrieved by the query – for example, to display only the first ten records retrieved. This property is particularly useful when used with sorted fields.

For example, if you set a descending sort order for the BooksConfidential.Cost field in a query, the most expensive books are displayed first in the results. If you also set the *Top Values* property to three, the query displays only the three most expensive books. If you specify an ascending sort order instead, the query displays the three cheapest books.

Books in descending order of cost

ISBN	Title	Cost
ISBN 0-718-14439-2	The Return of the Naked Chef	£ 24.80
ISBN 0-130-38486-0	ECDL 3 The Complete Courseboo	£ 18.99
ISBN 1-85613-666-3	A Children's Treasury of Milligan	£ 18.99
ISBN 0-563-36249-9	Delia Smith's Complete Cookery C	£ 17.99
ISBN 0-130-98984-3	ECDL Advanced Word Processing	£ 16.99
ISBN 0-7548-0731-2	The New Guide to Cat Care	£ 14.95
ISBN 0-571-20408-2	The History of the Kelly Gang	£ 13.60
ISBN 0-130-98983-5	ECDL Advanced Spreadsheets	£ 12.99
ISBN 0-09-175208-6	An Evil Cradling	£ 12.75
ISBN 0-297-81410-9	The Man in the Ice	£ 12.50

ISBN	Title	Cost
ISBN 0-718-14439-2	The Return of the Naked Chef	£ 24.80
ISBN 0-130-38486-0	ECDL 3 The Complete Courseboo	£ 18.99
ISBN 1-85613-666-3	A Children's Treasury of Milligan	£ 18.99

Top three records only

You can set the *Top Values* property in a query's property sheet or by using the *Top Values* box on the *Query Design* toolbar.

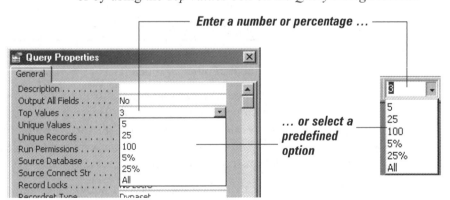

Exercise 10.6: Using the *Top Values* property

In this exercise you will create a query that displays the five most popular books in the library. You will do this by counting the number of times each book has been borrowed, sorting on this value in descending order, and limiting the results to five records.

1) Open a new query in Design View. When prompted for the tables to include in the query, select Loans and Books.

2) Add the following fields to the design grid, in the order listed here:

   – Loans.ISBN (to group all loans of the same book)

   – Books.Title

   – Loans.ISBN (to count the number of records in each group)

3) Change the name of the second instance of the ISBN field to Total Loans.

4) Click the **Totals** button in the *Query Design* toolbar to display the *Total* row in the design grid.

5) Select *Count* as the *Total* option for the Total Loans field and select *Descending* as its *Sort* option. Your query should now look like this:

Field:	ISBN	Title	Total Loans: ISBN
Table:	Loans	Books	Loans
Total:	Group By	Group By	Count
Sort:			Descending
Show:	☑	☑	☑

6) Set the query's *Top Values* property by typing 5 in the *Top Values* box on the *Query Design* toolbar and pressing **Enter**.

7) Save the query with the name TopFiveBooks and then run it.

ISBN	Title	Total Loans
ISBN 0-552-99893-1	Chocolat	8
ISBN 0-330-28414-2	The Name of the Rose	7
ISBN 0-7475-3007-6	Snow Falling On Cedars	7
ISBN 1-85702-242-4	The Shipping News	6
ISBN 0-571-20408-2	The History of the Kelly Gang	6

The five records displayed are those that have been borrowed the most number of times.

How does Access know that it is the Total Loans field whose top values you want to view? Because that is the field on which the results are sorted. If you are sorting on more than one field, the field whose top values you want to view must be the leftmost of those fields.

Note that when you specify a number (instead of a percentage) in the *Top Values* property, the query does not always display exactly that number of records. If the value of the top values field in the last record is shared by other records, those records are also displayed. For example, if more than two records have been borrowed six times, the TopFiveBooks query will display all those records and not just the first two.

Parameter queries

Up until now you have always entered your selection criteria for a query in the design grid. With a parameter query, however, Access instead prompts you for the criteria when you run the query. This means that you can use the same query to retrieve different information.

For example, the BooksInCategory query is designed to list the books in any specified category. When you run the query, Access prompts you for the category you want to view.

Try it and see what happens! Access prompts you to enter a category and then displays all books in that category.

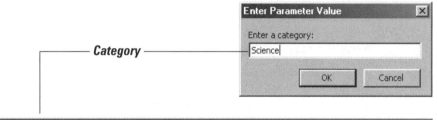

Category

	Category	ISBN	Title	Publisher
	Science	ISBN 1-85702-712-4	Galileo's Daughter	Fourth Estate
	Science	ISBN 0-283-06145-6	New Guide to the Planets	Sidgwick & Jackson
	Science	ISBN 0-297-81410-9	The Man in the Ice	Weidenfeld and Nicholson
	Science	ISBN 0-451-16776-7	Feeling Good: The New Mood	Penguin Books
▶				

You could also use a parameter query in the Village Library database to:

- Display the books by any specified author.

- Display the total cost of books in any specified category.

- Display the total cost of books in any specified category *and* from any specified publisher.

- Display the books still out on loan to any specified member.

- Display the books borrowed in any specified date range.

> ### Parameter query
>
> *A query that prompts for record selection criteria when the query is run.*

Creating a parameter query

To create a parameter query, you enter a parameter in the *Criteria* cell of a field instead of entering specific criteria. The parameter acts as placeholder for the actual criteria entered when the query is run. It consists of the text of the prompt to be displayed enclosed within square brackets.

For example, in the BooksInCategory query, '[Enter a category:]' has been entered as a parameter for the Books.Category field.

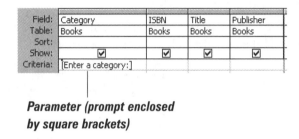

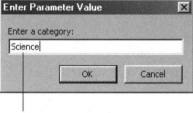

Parameter (prompt enclosed by square brackets)

Criteria entered at run time

When you run the query, Access prompts you for a category and then uses the value you enter as the query criteria. Basically, Access substitutes the parameter in the query with the value that you enter at the prompt.

You can enter a parameter almost anywhere in criteria where you would normally enter a text string, a number, or a date. And you can include more than one parameter in a query. Access displays multiple prompts in the order that they appear in the design grid.

Exercise 10.7: Creating a parameter query

In this exercise you will convert the LoansExtended query to a parameter query. The modified query will prompt for a member's first name and last name and then display the loan records for that member.

1) Open the LoansExtended query in Design View and add the Members table to the query (choose **Query | Show Table** and then select the table in the normal way).

2) Add the Members.MemFirstname and Members.MemLastname fields to the right of the MemID field in the design grid.

3) Enter the following parameters in the *Criteria* rows for the MemFirstname and MemLastname fields respectively:

    [Enter first name:]
    [Enter last name:]

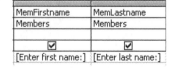

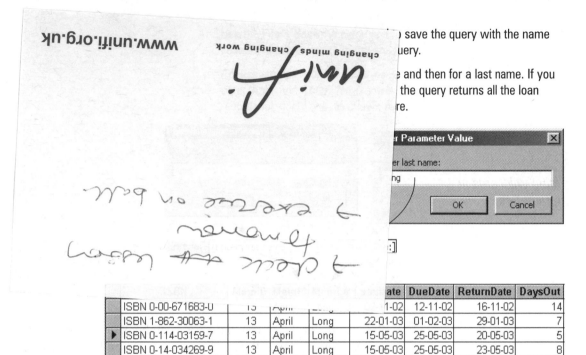

...) save the query with the name
...uery.

...e and then for a last name. If you
... the query returns all the loan
...re.

...r Parameter Value

...er last name:

...ng

| OK | Cancel |

					ate	DueDate	ReturnDate	DaysOut
	ISBN 0-00-671683-U	13	April	Long	1-02	12-11-02	16-11-02	14
	ISBN 1-862-30063-1	13	April	Long	22-01-03	01-02-03	29-01-03	7
▶	ISBN 0-114-03159-7	13	April	Long	15-05-03	25-05-03	20-05-03	5
	ISBN 0-14-034269-9	13	April	Long	15-05-03	25-05-03	23-05-03	8

Prompting for a date range

When you want to use a date range as the selection criteria for a query, you typically use the Between … And … operator. For example:

`Between #01-01-02# And #31-12-02#`

With a parameter query you can prompt for the start and end dates in the range instead of specifying them in the query.

For example, the LoansInPeriod query displays the loan records for books borrowed in any specified date range. Open that query in Design View and you will see that the *Criteria* row for the Loans.LoanDate field contains the following expression:

`Between [Enter start date:] And [Enter end date:]`

The expression includes two parameters instead of the start and end dates of a date range. When you run the query, Access prompts you for the dates that you want to use and then returns all records where the LoanDate value is in that range.

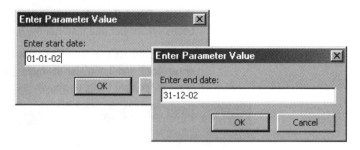

Using wildcards in parameters

Adding parameters to a query creates a more flexible query. Combining wildcards with the parameters creates a yet more flexible query again.

With a standard query you can retrieve all books in a category that begins with 'F' by entering the following criteria expression for the Books.Category field.

```
Like "F*"
```

With a parameter query you can retrieve all books where the category value begins with any character(s) entered by the user. To create this query you would enter the following criteria expression for the Books.Category field:

```
Like [Enter a category:] & "*"
```

Then if the user enters 'C' at the prompt, the query retrieves all books in the Children, Computer, and Cookery categories. And if the user enters 'Co', the query retrieves all books in the Computer and Cookery categories, and so on.

To retrieve records that include the entered characters *anywhere* in their Category value, use the following criteria expression:

```
Like "*" & [Enter a category:] & "*"
```

To retrieve records where the category value *ends with* the characters entered at the prompt, use the following criteria expression:

```
Like "*" & [Enter a category:]
```

Returning all records with a parameter query

When you combine the asterisk (*) wildcard with a parameter, entering nothing at the prompt retrieves all records where the parameter field does not contain Null. This is the same as entering "*" as the field criteria.

If you want to retrieve records that contain Null in the parameter field as well, you must add the following Or expression:

`[parameter] Is Null`

In the case of the BooksInCategory query, for example, entering nothing at the prompt will return all records, including those with Null values, if you enter the criteria shown here.

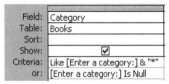

Field:	Category
Table:	Books
Sort:	
Show:	☑
Criteria:	Like [Enter a category:] & "*"
or:	[Enter a category:] Is Null

Chapter 10: summary

Null is a special value that indicates a missing, unknown, or inapplicable value. Access automatically enters a Null value when you leave a field blank. You can use Null values in query criteria and calculated fields but remember that aggregate functions ignore Null values, and expressions that use arithmetic operators always return Null if one of the fields in the expression contains Null.

You can use the Is Null operator in criteria expressions to select only records that contain Null in a particular field, and you can use the Is Not Null operator to select only records that contain non-Null values.

You can use the IsNull() function in calculated fields to test for Null values. Typically you use this function in combination with the IIf() function. You can use the Nz() function to convert Null values to zeros before performing a calculation.

A *duplicate record* is one that contains identical values to another record in all its fields. You can use the *Find Duplicates Query Wizard* to find duplicate records in a table or query and to find records that have the same values in selected fields. You use a query's *Unique Values* property to omit records that have duplicate values in the fields displayed by the query. You use the *Unique Records* property to omit duplicates that represent the same record in the underlying data source.

An *unmatched record* is one that has no matching record in a related table. You can use the *Find Unmatched Query Wizard* to find unmatched records.

In a query that specifies a sort order on a field, you can use the *Top Values* property to return a specified number or percentage of the highest or lowest values in that field.

A *parameter query* is a query that prompts for record selection criteria when you run the query. This allows you to use the same query to retrieve different information.

Chapter 10: quick quiz

Q1	True or false – an arithmetic expression always returns Null if one of the fields in the expression contains a Null value.
A.	True.
B.	False.

Q2	Which of these criteria expressions returns only records that contain Null in the criteria field?
A.	`IsNull()`
B.	`IsNull([ReturnDate])`
C.	`Is Null`

Q3	True or false – you use the *Unique Records* property to omit records that have duplicate values in the fields displayed by a query.
A.	True.
B.	False.

Q4	To display fields from two tables in a query you create with the *Find Unmatched Records Wizard*, you ...
A.	Create a query that contains all the fields you want to display and base the *Find Unmatched Records* query on that query.
B.	Select the two tables and the required fields in the wizard.
C.	Create the query and then modify the query in Design View to include the records from the second table.

Q5	To display the ten earliest publication years for books in the library, you ...
A.	Set the PublicationYear field's *Top Values* property to 10.
B.	Select a descending sort order for the PublicationYear field and set the query's *Top Values* property to 10.
C.	Select an ascending sort order for the PublicationYear field and set the query's *Top Values* property to 10.

Q6	Which of these criteria in the LoanDate field creates a query that allows users to enter a number (*n*) and then lists all books that were borrowed in the previous *n* days?
A.	`Date() – [Enter a number of days:]`
B.	`<=Date() – [Enter a number of days:]`
C.	`>=Date() – [Enter a number of days:]`

Answers

1: A, 2: C, 3: B, 4: A and C, 5: C, 6: C.

11 *Form design: controls*

In this chapter

Forms are the main means of adding and editing data in a database. All information in a form is contained in controls such as labels, text boxes, list boxes and checkboxes. In this chapter you will learn about the most common form controls, when to use them, and how to create them.

New skills

At the end of this chapter you should be able to:

- Create text box, combo box, list box, checkbox and option group controls

- Create bound and unbound controls

- Create a record selector control

- Set the tab order for a form

- Add controls to form headers and footers

New words

In this chapter you will meet the following terms:

- Control
- Bound control

- Unbound control
- Tab order

Exercise file

In this chapter you will work with the following Access file:

- Chp11_VillageLibrary_Database

Syllabus reference

In this chapter you will cover the following items of the ECDL Advanced Database Syllabus:

- **AM5.3.1.1**: Create bound and unbound controls.

- **AM5.3.1.2**: Create, edit a combo box, list box, checkbox, option group.

- **AM5.3.1.4**: Set sequential order of controls on a form.

- **AM5.3.1.5**: Insert data field to appear within form header, footers on the first page or all pages.

About controls

A control is a graphical object that you place on a form to display data, to accept data input, to perform an action, or simply for decorative purposes.

Control types

The following list describes the controls that you need to know about for ECDL. You can see examples of these controls in the BookLoans form in the Chp11_VillageLibrary_Database database. If you open that form now you can try out each control as you read through the descriptions.

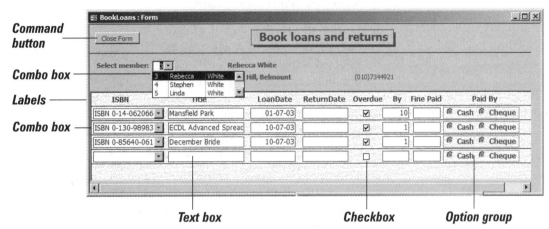

Command button

Combo box

Labels

Combo box

Text box   *Checkbox*   *Option group*

- **Label**. Displays descriptive text such as titles, headings, and instructions. By default, all controls that you add to a form have an attached label control.

Label   *Text box*

- **Text box**. Displays data from a table or query field and accepts input to that field. Text boxes can also display the results of calculations. In the BookLoans form, the member name, book title and loan date fields all use text box controls.

- **List box**. Displays a list from which users select a value. The list is always open, so this type of control is normally used only for short lists. Combo boxes are a more compact and flexible alternative.

- **Combo box**. Combines a text box, where users can type a value, and a drop-down list box, where users can select a value instead. The list opens only when you click the down arrow in the control. In the BookLoans form, Select Member and ISBN are examples of combo box controls.

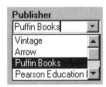

- **Checkbox**. A box that represents a Yes/No choice. Typically, checkboxes are used as stand-alone controls, with each checkbox representing a Yes/No choice that is independent of any other Yes/No choices. In the BookLoans form, Overdue is an example of a checkbox control.

- **Option button**. A small circle that represents a Yes/No choice. A blank circle represents a 'No' value; a small dot in the circle represents a 'Yes' value. Option buttons typically form part of an option group.

- **Option group**. A group of related options, only one of which can be selected at any time. Typically each option is represented by an option button control. Use option groups to present a few options only. If there are a large number of options, use a list box or combo box instead. In the BookLoans form, Paid By is an example of an option group.

- **Command button**. A button control that starts an action or set of actions. In the BookLoans form, the Close Form button is an example of a command button. Clicking it closes the form. See Chapter 15 for further details.

Form control

A graphical object that you place on a form to display data, to accept data input, to perform an action, or simply for decorative purposes.

Bound and unbound controls

The tables and/or queries that provide the data for a form are referred to as the form's *record source*. The form is said to be *bound* to that record source. The form's controls can be either *bound* or *unbound*:

- A *bound control* is linked to a field in the form's record source. You use bound controls to display, enter, and update values in table or query fields.

  For example, in the BookLoans form, the ISBN, Title and Return Date controls are bound to fields in the LoansExtended query and can be used to add and edit values in those fields.

- An *unbound control* is not linked to a field in the form's record source. You use unbound controls, for example, to display descriptive text and to perform calculations and display their results. You cannot use an unbound control to update field values.

  In the BookLoans form, the form title and field labels are unbound. Overdue and By are also unbound, their data sources being calculated expressions.

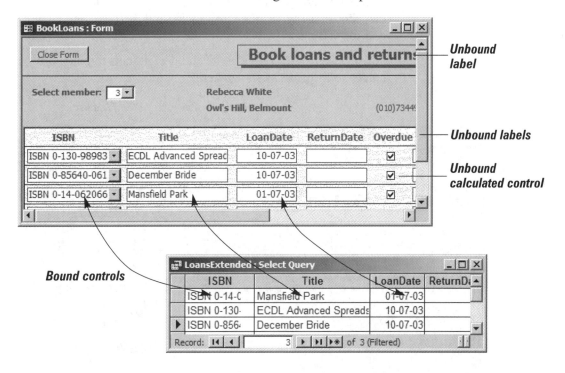

While most control types can be bound or unbound, only labels, text boxes and combo boxes are really useful for unbound data.

Record source

The table or query from which a form gets its data and whose fields it updates.

Bound control

A control that gets its values from a field in the form's record source and that you can use to update values in that field.

> **Unbound control**
>
> *A control that is not linked to a table/query field. You can use unbound controls to display informational text, graphics and the results of calculations.*

Form design tools

When you use a wizard to create a form, Access automatically creates controls for all the form fields. When you create a form in Design View you must create the controls manually, but you can choose the types of control to use and their content, layout and formatting.

Form Design View provides several design tools to help you create your forms, as shown here:

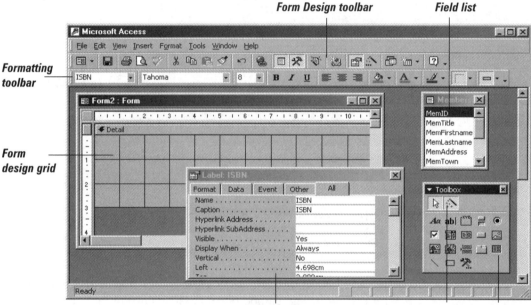

Before you create a form, let's take a look at how you use each of these tools. If you open the DesignToolsPractise form, you can experiment with each design tool as you read the descriptions.

Design grid

This is where you place a form's controls and arrange their layout. The grid lines provide a useful guide for aligning controls. The content and layout of the design grid correspond to the content and layout of the form you are creating.

- To change the height or width of a form, drag the bottom or right border of the design grid until it is the size you want.

This lists all fields in the form's record source and you use it to add bound fields to a form. You can show or hide the list by clicking the **Field List** button on the *Form Design* toolbar.

- To add a bound field to a form, simply drag the field from the field list to the required position in the design grid.

  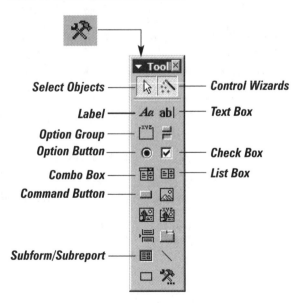

  Access creates an appropriate control for the field, based on the field's data type. In most cases it creates a text box control. However, for a Yes/No or Lookup field it creates the control type specified by the field's *Display Control* property (see 'Lookup fields' in Chapter 4).

  By default, a label control is created for each field you add to the design grid.

- To add a block of fields to the design grid, click the first field in the block, hold down the **Shift** key, click the last field in the block, and then drag the fields to the design grid.

- To add several nonadjacent fields, hold down the **Ctrl** key, click each field to be added, and then drag to the design grid.

Toolbox

This provides tools for creating all types of form controls. You can show or hide the toolbox by clicking the **Toolbox** button on the *Form Design* toolbar. The following are the tools that you need to know about for ECDL.

- To create a bound control of a particular type, select the required tool in the toolbox and then drag the field from the field list to the design grid.

- To create an unbound control, click the required tool in the toolbox. Then either click in the design grid or click in the design grid and drag until the control is the size you want. To specify the content for the control, you can use a Control Wizard or the control's property sheet (see below).

Control wizards

Access provides wizards for creating some control types. These guide you through the process of creating the control and defining its data source.

Control Wizards tool

If the **Control Wizards** tool in the toolbox is currently selected (pressed in), the appropriate wizard starts automatically when you add a combo box, list box or option group to the design grid. This is the simplest means of creating these control types.

Property sheets

Forms, form sections and form controls all have properties that define their appearance, behaviour, content and data sources. Access sets these properties automatically when you create a form, section or control.

You can view and edit properties in the *Property Sheet* window. For help with any property, click that property in the property sheet and press **F1**.

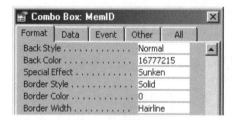
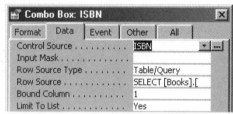

Properties button

To open the *Property Sheet* window, click the **Properties** button on the *Form Design* toolbar. Once the window is open, you can view the property sheet for any form element as follows:

- **Form**. Click the form selector.

- **Section**. Click the section selector.

- **Control**. Click the control.

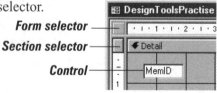

- **Any element**. Select the element in the *Object* list on the *Formatting* toolbar.

Here is a list of the most frequently used *form* properties.

- **Default View** (Format tab). Specifies the opening view for a form (see 'Default View' in Chapter 12).

- **Record Source** (Data tab). Specifies the source for data in the form. If you select a record source when creating the form, it is automatically entered in this property. To change the record source for a form:

  - Click the arrow at the right of the property box and select a table or query from the list displayed.

Build button

  - Click the **Build** button at the right of the property box. This opens the *Query Builder*. You can then modify the current query or create a new query for the form.

Here is a list of the most frequently used *control* properties.

- **Name** (Other tab). Every control has a name that identifies it uniquely, and which you can use to refer to the control's value in expressions.

  - The default name for a bound control is the name of the underlying field.

  - The default name for an unbound control is the control type followed by a unique number (for example, Label1, Combo6 or Text11). If you intend to refer to the control in expressions in other controls, it is a good idea to change the name to something more meaningful.

- **Caption** (Format tab). Specifies the text that appears in label controls.

  - When you create a control, the caption of the attached label is automatically set to the name of the control.

  - When you create a stand-alone label, its caption is whatever you type in the label.

To change a label's caption, type the new caption in the label itself or in its *Caption* property.

- **Control Source** (Data tab). A form's *Record Source* property specifies the table or query to which the form is bound and from which it gets its data. The *Control Source* property for a control specifies the source of the data displayed by that control.

— For a bound control, the source is a field in the form's record source. When you drag a field from the field list to the design grid, this property is set automatically. To change the source field for a control, click the arrow at the right of the property box and select a field from the list displayed.

 — For an unbound control, the source is typically an expression that you enter in the *Control Source* property.

 ▪ **Format and Decimal Places** (Format tab). These have the same function as the *Format* and *Decimal Places* properties for a query or table field. You use them to change the display format of date, number, and currency values.

Formatting toolbar

The *Format* properties for most controls include colour, font, border and other standard formatting options. The *Formatting* toolbar presents the same options and is easier and quicker to use than a property sheet.

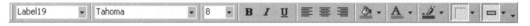

Form Design toolbar

The *Form Design* toolbar includes buttons for showing/hiding the field list and toolbox and the *Property Sheet* window.

Toolbox

Field List   Properties

Creating forms in Design View

In the exercises in this chapter you will create a form for maintaining library membership records, as shown here.

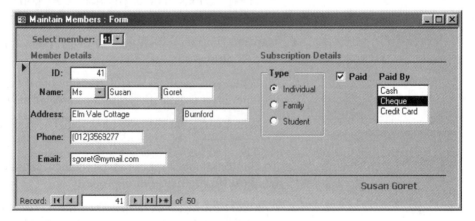

The form's record source is the Members table – that is, the form displays records from that table, and when you add, edit or delete records in the form, the table is updated accordingly.

In order to illustrate the use of combo box, list box, option group and checkbox controls, the following fields have been added to the table:

- **MemTitle**. The member's title.

- **MemType**. The member's membership type.

- **SubPaid**. A Yes/No field that indicates whether or not a member has paid their membership subscription.

- **PaidBy**. This indicates the payment method.

Exercise 11.1: Creating the Maintain Members form

In this exercise you will create a blank form that is bound to the Members table. In subsequent exercises you will add controls to the form.

1) Click *Forms* in the *Objects* list in the Database window and click the **New** button on the window's toolbar.

2) In the *New Form* dialog box, select the *Design View* option, select the Members table as the record source, and then click **OK**.

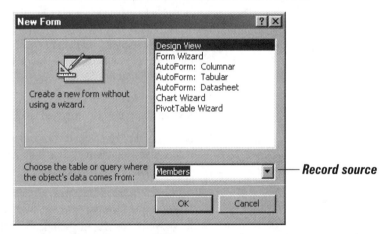

3) Access opens the *Form Design* window with a blank design grid. If you display the property sheet for the form, you will see that the *Record Source* property (Data tab) has been set to the Members table.

4) By default, any new form you create has only a Detail section. The Maintain Members form uses both Form Header and Form Footer sections, so add these by choosing **View | Form Header/Footer**.

5) To fit all the form controls, you need to increase the width of the design grid to about 15.5 cm, and change the height of the Form Header, Detail and Form Footer sections to about 1 cm, 4 cm and

0.75 cm respectively. You can do this by dragging the section borders. Use the horizontal and vertical rulers as guides.

Horizontal ruler —
Vertical ruler —
Height of section —

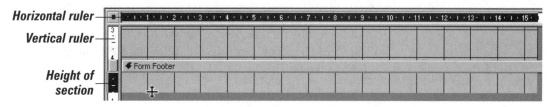

5) Choose **File | Save** to save the form. Name it Maintain Members.

Creating bound controls

In Exercises 11.2 to 11.6 you will add label, text box, combo box, list box, option group and checkbox controls to the Maintain Members form. All the controls, except the labels, will be bound to fields in the Members table.

Creating bound text boxes

A bound text box displays values from a field in the form's record source and you can use it to update the field.

Exercise 11.2: Creating bound text boxes

In this exercise you will create text box controls for the MemID, MemFirstname, MemLastname, MemAddress, MemTown, MemPhone and MemEmail fields.

Text Box tool

1) Select the **Text Box** tool in the toolbox.

2) Select the required fields in the field list. Remember that to select multiple, non-contiguous fields, you press and hold down the **Ctrl** key while selecting the fields.

3) Drag the fields to the centre of the Detail section in the design grid. A text box control, with attached label, is created for each field.

4) Now you need to position, size and format the controls as shown below (see steps 5 to 7). Use the rulers and grid lines to help you with the sizing and positioning.

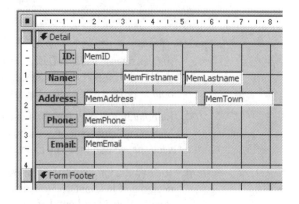

5) First delete the labels for the MemLastname and MemTown fields (click each label and press the **Delete** key), and then change the captions of the other labels as shown.

6) Now select all the label controls so that you can format them together. If the labels are in a single vertical column, you can do this by clicking on the horizontal ruler directly above them.

   – To change the label text to bold type, click the **Bold** button in the *Formatting* toolbar.

   – To right-align the label controls, choose **Format | Align | Right**.

   – To right-align the label text within the controls, click the **Align Right** button on the *Formatting* toolbar.

   – To resize the label controls to the size of the label text, choose **Format | Size | To Fit**.

7) Finally, reposition and resize the controls as shown above. Leave sufficient space between the Name label and the MemFirstname text box to insert a combo box control for the MemTitle field.

8) Save the form and switch to Form View to see how it looks.

If you need help with moving, sizing and aligning controls, the following Microsoft Help topic provides all the information you need: 'Move, size, align, and format text boxes or controls in a form or report'.

Creating bound combo boxes

A bound combo box control displays a list of values from which the user selects one to store in the field to which the control is bound. The control can look up its values either in a table or query, or in a fixed value list that you create manually.

Note that if you create a lookup field in a table and select a combo box as its default display control (see 'Lookup fields' in Chapter 4), Access automatically creates a combo box control for the field when you drag it from the field list to the design grid.

Control Wizards tool

Combo Box tool

Exercise 11.3: Creating a bound combo box control
In this exercise you will create a combo box control for the MemTitle field. This control will allow users to select a title from a predefined list. You will use a wizard to create the control.

1) Make sure that the **Control Wizards** tool is selected (presssed in) and then select the **Combo Box** tool.

2) Drag the MemTitle field from the field list to a blank area of the design grid. This starts the *Combo Box Wizard*.

3) First the wizard prompts you to select the type of combo box you want to create. Only the first two options are relevant for bound combo boxes.

The first option creates a combo box that looks up its values in a table or query. The second option creates a combo box that looks up its values in a fixed value list. You met similar options when you created a lookup field in Chapter 4. Select the second option and click **Next**.

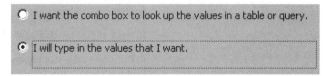

4) The wizard now prompts you for the list of values. Enter the values shown here and then click **Next**.

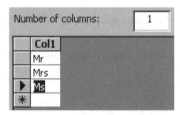

5) The wizard asks you what you want to do with a value selected in the list. Access can either save the value for later use (in a calculation, for example), or it can store the value in a table field. Because you based the combo box on the MemTitle field, the second option and the MemTitle field are selected by default. This is the option you want, so click **Next** to continue.

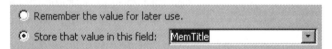

6) The last page of the wizard prompts you for a label for the combo box. The default is the field name. Leave this as it is and click **Finish**.

7) You are now returned to the design grid where the new combo box and attached label have been created for you. Delete the label, resize the combo box to the width of its longest entry, and move the control to the start of the Name row.

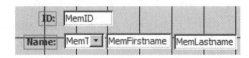

8) Save the form and switch to Form View to try out the new control.

What if you want to change the list displayed in the combo box? You could rerun the wizard and create the control again from scratch. However, the list values are stored in the control's *Row Source* property and can be edited there.

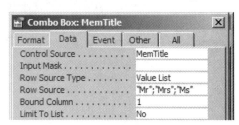

Each entry in the list is enclosed in double quotes and separated from the next entry by a semicolon. To add 'Dr' to the list, for example, you would edit the list as follows:

```
"Mr";"Mrs";"Ms";"Dr"
```

Creating bound option groups

A bound option group presents a set of options from which the user selects one to store in the field to which the group is bound. Each option in the group has a label and a value. The label describes the option; the value is stored in the bound field when you select the option.

Exercise 11.4: Creating a bound option group

In this exercise you will create an option group control for the MemType field. You will use a wizard to create the control.

Option Group tool

1) Make sure that the **Control Wizards** tool is selected and then select the **Option Group** tool.

2) Drag the MemType field from the field list to a blank area of the design grid. This starts the *Option Group Wizard*.

3) First the wizard prompts you for the label for each option in the option group. Enter the values shown here and click **Next**.

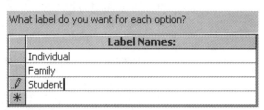

4) Next the wizard asks whether you want to specify a default option. It suggests that you use the first option: 'Individual'. As most library members are individual members, leave this as it is and click **Next**.

5) The wizard now asks you what value you want to assign to each option in the group. Only number values are valid.

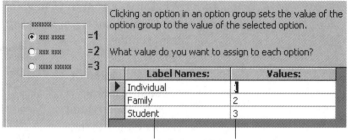

Clicking an option in an option group sets the value of the option group to the value of the selected option.

What value do you want to assign to each option?

Label Names:	Values:
▶ Individual	1
Family	2
Student	3

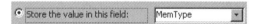

Option labels   Values stored

By default, the wizard assigns sequential numbers to the options. This makes sense, so accept these defaults by clicking **Next**. Now when a user selects the *Individual* option, Access stores 1 in the MemType field, when a user selects the *Family* option, Access stores 2 in the field, and so on.

6) The wizard now asks you what you want Access to do with the value of a selected option. Because you based the option group on the MemType field, the second option and the MemType field are selected by default. This is the option you want, so click **Next** to continue.

⊙ Store the value in this field: MemType ▾

7) The wizard prompts you for the type of controls you want to use in the option group and the style to apply to the group and its controls. In the left part of the dialog box, your option group is displayed using the currently selected control type and style.

For this exercise, accept the default options (*Option Buttons* and *Etched*) and click **Next**.

8) The last page of the wizard prompts you for a label for the option group. Enter 'Type' and click **Finish**.

9) You are now returned to the design grid where the new option group has been created for you. Make the option group label bold and resize it accordingly. Then select the option group by clicking its border, and move it to the position shown here.

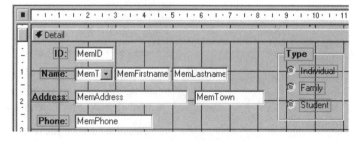

10) Save the form and switch to Form View to try out the new control.

What if you want to update the option group after you've created it?

- To change the label of an option button control within the group, type directly in the label control.

- To delete an option button control from the group, select it and press the **Delete** key.

- To add a new option button to the group, select the **Option Button** tool in the toolbox and click within the option group's borders. Then type the new option button's description in its label control.

A value is assigned to the new option automatically. For example, if you add a fourth option to an option group, it is given the value 4, if you add a fifth option, it is given the value 5, and so on.

Creating bound checkboxes

A bound checkbox displays values from a Yes/No field and you can use it to update the field. By default, Access automatically creates a checkbox control when you drag a Yes/No field from the field list to the design grid. If it does not, you can use the **Check Box** tool to create the control.

Exercise 11.5: Creating a bound checkbox
In this exercise you will create a checkbox control for the SubPaid field. There is no control wizard for creating checkboxes, but the procedure is simple.

Check Box tool

1) Select the **Check Box** tool in the toolbox.

2) Drag the SubPaid field from the field list to a blank area of the design grid. This creates a checkbox control that is bound to the SubPaid field. The attached label displays the field name.

3) Change the label to 'Paid', make it bold, and size it to the width of the text. Then position the check box and its label as shown here.

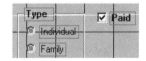

4) Save the form and switch to Form View to try out the control.

Creating bound list boxes

A bound list box control displays a list of values from which the user selects one to store in the field to which the control is bound. You create the control in the same way that you create a bound combo box control. The *List Box Wizard* presents the same options as the *Combo Box Wizard*; the only difference is the type of control created.

Exercise 11.6: Creating a bound list box

In this exercise you will create a list box control for the PaidBy field. This control will allow users to select a payment type from a predefined list. You will use a wizard to create the control.

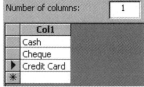

List Box tool

1) Make sure that the **Control Wizards** tool is selected, and then select the **List Box** tool.

2) Drag the PaidBy field from the field list to a blank area of the design grid. This starts the *List Box Wizard*.

3) First the wizard prompts you to select the type of list box you want to create. Select the second option and click **Next**.

4) The wizard prompts you for the list of values to be displayed by the control. Enter the values shown here and click **Next**.

5) The wizard asks you what you want Access to do with a value selected in the list. Because you based the list box on the PaidBy field, the second option and the PaidBy field are selected by default. This is the option you want, so simply click **Next** to continue.

6) The last page of the wizard prompts you for a label for the list box. Enter 'Paid By' and click **Finish**.

7) You are now returned to the design grid where the new list box and attached label have been created for you. Note that the label may be positioned some distance from the list box, possibly overlying some other control in the design grid.

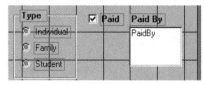

Position and resize the list box and label as shown here and make the label bold.

8) Save the form and switch to Form View to try out the list box.

If you want to change the values in the list you can edit the control's *Row Source* property, as described under 'Creating bound combo boxes' above.

In Form View and in Design View, your form should now resemble that shown here.

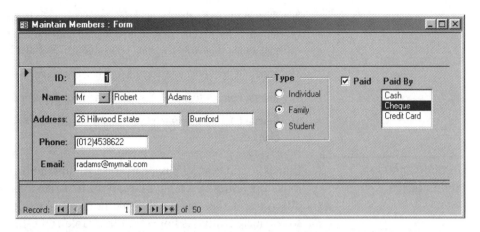

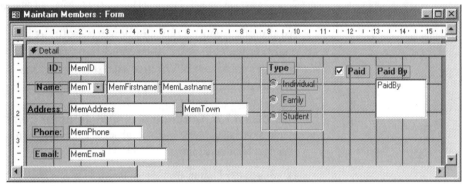

Creating unbound controls

In Exercises 11.7 to 11.9 you will add unbound label, combo box and text box controls to the Maintain Members form.

Creating unattached labels

Access automatically creates a label for each control you add to the design grid. These are attached labels that move with the control and describe its content. You use unattached (or stand-alone) labels for form titles, headings, instructions, and so on.

Exercise 11.7: Creating unattached label controls

In this exercise you will create label controls for the form headings, as shown here.

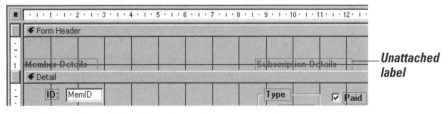

Unattached label

Aa

Label tool

1) Display the Maintain Members form in Design View and select the **Label** tool in the toolbox.

2) Click in the Form Header section where you want the upper left corner of the first heading to be and drag until the control is the size you want. Then type the label text – that is, 'Member Details'.

3) Make the text bold and apply a font colour of blue.

4) Repeat steps 1 to 3 for the second heading: Subscription Details.

5) Save the form and switch to Form View to see the result of your changes.

Creating unbound combo boxes

Like a bound combo box or list box, an unbound combo box looks up values in a table or query or in a fixed value list. The difference is that you do not bind the control to a table field and so a selected value is not stored in a table field. Instead Access stores the value internally for use by another control.

An unbound combo box can be very useful as a record selector, enabling users to select the record they want to view from the control's lookup list. When a user selects a value in the list, Access displays the corresponding record in the form.

Exercise 11.8: Creating a record selector combo box

In this exercise you will create a record selector combo box for the Maintain Members form.

1) Select the **Combo Box** tool in the toolbox and click in the Form Header section. This starts the *Combo Box Wizard*.

2) First the wizard prompts you to select the type of combo box you want to create. Select the *Find a record on my form* . . . option and click **Next**.

> ⊙ Find a record on my form based on the value I selected in my combo box.

3) The wizard prompts you for the fields you want to display in the combo box list. Select MemID, MemFirstname and MemLastname and click **Next**.

4) You can now adjust the layout of the columns. Access suggests that you hide the MemID column. However, users need to be able to differentiate between members with the same first and last names, so deselect the *Hide key column* option. Then size the columns as shown here and click **Next**.

☐ Hide key column (recommended)		
Men	MemFirst	MemLast
▶ 1	Robert	Adams
2	Sylvia	Turner
3	Rebecca	White

5) The wizard prompts you to select the field whose value Access will use to find a record. Select MemID and click **Next**.

6) The wizard asks you what you want Access to do with a value selected in the list. Make sure the *Remember the value for later use* option is selected and click **Next**.

7) The last page of the wizard prompts you for a label for the combo box. Enter 'Select member:' and click **Finish**.

8) You are now returned to the design grid where the new combo box and attached label have been created for you. Make the label text bold and apply a font colour of blue. Then position and size the controls as shown here.

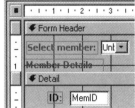

9) Save the form and switch to Form View to try out the new control. Select a member in the combo box and you will see that Access immediately displays the record for that member.

What if you want to add or remove columns from the combo box list or adjust the column widths? These attributes are all properties of the control and you can edit them in the control's property sheet.

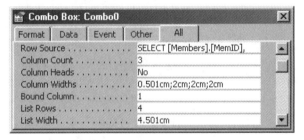

Many of the properties are the same as those for a lookup field in a table. For an explanation of these properties, see 'Creating and modifying lookup fields manually' in Chapter 4.

Creating unbound text boxes

You use unbound text box controls to display the results of expressions. An expression can consist of a calculation or a reference to a value in another control.

In the following exercise, you will create a text box control that references a value in another control. You will learn about calculated controls in Chapter 12.

Exercise 11.9: Creating an unbound text box

In this exercise you will create an unbound text box in the Footer section of the Maintain Members form. The text box will display the name of the member whose record is currently displayed in the form.

1) Select the **Text Box** tool in the toolbox and click in the Form Footer section. This creates an unbound text box and attached label. Delete the label.

2) Type the following expression in the text box:

```
=[MemFirstname] & [MemLastname]
```

Control
name   *Concatenation*   *Control*
                operator   *name*

The & (concatenation) operator is a very useful operator that merges the values from two fields or controls and displays them as a single string. So the above expression combines the values in the MemFirstname and MemLastname controls.

3) As the control cannot be used to update a member's name, it is a good idea to use different formatting than you use for interactive text boxes.

Use the **Fill/Back Colour** and **Line/Border** buttons on the *Formatting* toolbar to change the control's background colour and border colour to *Transparent*. Increase the font size to 10 point, change its colour to blue, and then position the control at the far right side of the Footer section.

4) Save the form and switch to Form View. Notice that the first and last names are merged without any space in between. To insert a space, you need to change the control's expression as follows:

```
=[MemFirstname] & " " & [MemLastname]
```

This combines a member's first name, a space character, and the member's last name. Update the expression now and then save the form again.

In Form View and in Design View, your form should now resemble that shown here.

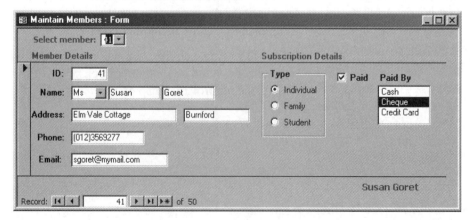

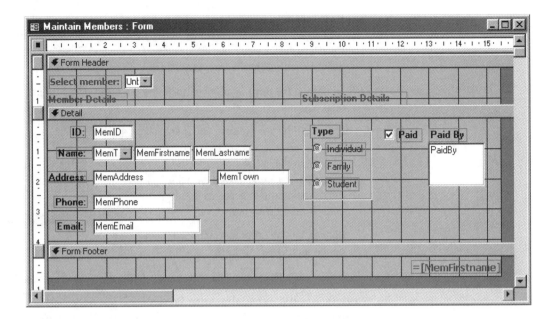

Setting the tab order for a form

In Form View users can press the **Tab** key to move from control to control. The order in which the focus moves through the controls is referred to as the *tab order*.

By default, the tab order corresponds to the order in which the controls were created. However, this may not be the most logical order for the form. In the Maintain Members form, for example, the MemTitle control comes after the MemEmail control in the tab order.

Exercise 11.10: Setting the tab order for a form

In this exercise you will set the tab order for the Maintain Members form.

1) Open the Maintain Members form in Design View and choose **View | Tab Order**. This displays the *Tab Order* dialog box.

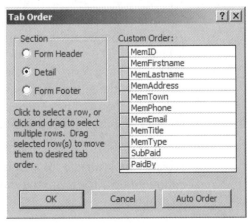

2) Each section in a form has a separate tab order. You select the section with which you want to work by selecting a *Section* option in the dialog box. Select the *Detail* option. The *Custom Order* box now lists the controls in the Detail section in their current tab order.

3) To change the position of a control in the tab order, drag it to its new position.

First click the control selector. Then click it again and drag the control to its new position in the list. As you drag the control, a black line moves with the mouse pointer to indicate where the control will be inserted.

Change the tab order to that shown here on the right. Then click **OK**.

Custom Order:

MemID
MemTitle
MemFirstname
MemLastname
MemAddress
MemTown
MemPhone
MemEmail
MemType
SubPaid
PaidBy

Control selectors **Insertion point**

4) Save the form.

Note that you can use the **Auto Order** button in the *Tab Order* dialog box to apply a left-to-right, top-to-bottom tab order automatically.

Tab order

The order in which the focus moves from control to control when a user tabs through a form.

Chapter 11: summary

All information in a form is contained in *controls* such as text boxes, list boxes, combo boxes and checkboxes. These controls can be either bound or unbound. A *bound control* is linked to a field in the form's record source and can be used to update that field. An *unbound control* (other than a label) is typically used as a record selector or to display the result of a calculation.

Access provides several tools for creating a form in Design View. The *field list* lists all fields in the form's record source. To create a bound field, drag the field from the field list to the design grid. The *toolbox* provides tools for all the controls you can include in a form. To create a bound control of a particular type, select the relevant tool in the toolbox before dragging the field from the field list. To create an unbound control, select the relevant tool in the toolbox and then click in the design grid where you want to position the control.

Wizards are available for creating combo boxes, list boxes and option groups. These are the simplest means of creating these control types.

Forms, form sections and form controls all have properties that define their appearance, behaviour, content and data sources. You can view and edit these properties in the *Property Sheet* window.

The *tab order* of a form is the order in which the focus moves from control to control when a user tabs through the form. The default tab order is the order in which the controls were created.

Chapter 11: quick quiz

Q1	True or false – a bound control displays data from a table or query field and can be used to update that field.
A.	True.
B.	False.

Q2	True or false – an unbound control can display data from a table or query field but cannot be used to update that field.
A.	True.
B.	False.

Q3	Which of these tools do you use to create a text box?
A.	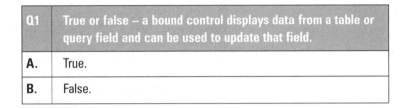
B.	
C.	

Q4	Which of these can you use as the source for a bound combo box or list box control?
A.	A field in the form's record source.
B.	A fixed value list.
C.	A field in any table or query in the database.

Q5	Which of these can you use as the source for a record selector combo box?
A.	A field in the form's record source.
B.	A fixed value list.
C.	A field in any table or query in the database.

Q6	Which of these expressions concatenates a member's title, firstname and lastname?
A.	=[MemTitle] & [MemFirstname] & [MemLastname]
B.	=[MemTitle] # [MemFirstname] # [MemLastname]
C.	=[MemTitle] & " " & [MemFirstname] & " " & [MemLastname]

Q7	Which of these properties defines the field that a bound control updates?
A.	Record Source.
B.	Control Source.
C.	Row Source.

Q8	Which of these properties defines the table/query from which a form gets its data?
A.	Record Source.
B.	Control Source.
C.	Row Source.

Answers

1: A, **2**: A, **3**: B, **4**: All, **5**: A, **6**: A and C (this latter expression inserts spaces between the concatenated fields), **7**: B, **8**: A.

12

Form design: calculated controls

You use calculated controls to display the results of calculations. The controls are unbound, so the calculation results are not stored in a database table. Instead Access reruns the calculation each time you open the form and whenever a value in the calculation expression changes.

In this chapter you will learn how to create calculated controls for single records and for summarizing and totalling values across records.

New skills

At the end of this chapter you should be able to:

- Create calculated controls

- Use aggregate functions in calculated controls

- Use the IIf(), Nz() and IsNull() functions in calculated controls.

New words

There are no new words in this chapter.

Exercise file

In this chapter you will work with the following Access file:

- Chp12_VillageLibrary_Database

Syllabus reference

In this chapter you will cover the following items of the ECDL Advanced Database Syllabus:

- **AM5.3.1.3**: Create arithmetic, logical expression controls on a form.

Calculated controls versus calculated fields

Calculated fields are query fields that display the results of calculations on other query fields (see Chapter 9). *Calculated controls* are controls that display the results of calculations on other controls in a form or report. You can use the same operators and functions in both cases.

**When to use
calculated fields**

When you base a form on a query that includes calculated fields, those fields are available to the form in the same way as any other field. If you intend using the same calculations in multiple forms or reports, then put them in a query and base the forms/reports on that query. Otherwise you will find yourself creating the same calculated controls again and again.

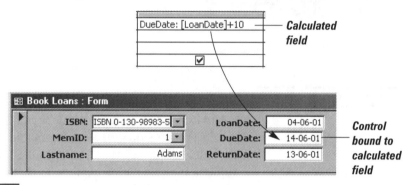

DueDate: [LoanDate]+10 —— *Calculated field*

Control bound to calculated field

**When to use
calculated controls**

Tables cannot include calculated fields. So when you base a form/report on a table, you must use calculated controls for any calculations you want to perform.

You also use calculated controls for summarizing values across multiple records. For example, this form here is based on a parameter query that allows users to retrieve the records for books in any specified category. The calculated control in the form's footer calculates the total cost of books in the category specified at the parameter prompt.

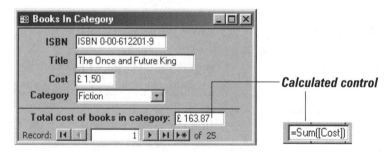

Calculated control

=Sum([Cost])

If you want to take a look at this form, it is included in Chp12_VillageLibrary_Database under the name BooksInCategory.

Exploring the Loans and Returns form

In the exercises in this chapter you will create the Loans and Returns form, which library staff use for processing book loans and returns.

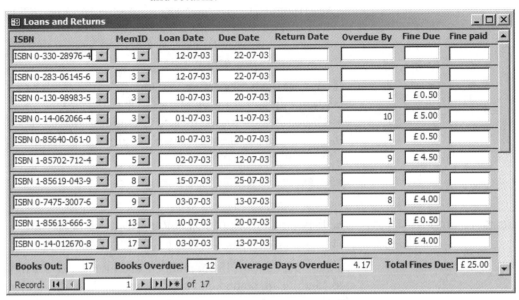

A finished copy of this form is available in Chp12_VillageLibrary_Database under the name LoansAndReturnsFinishedVersion. Open the latter form now and let's take a look at its contents, data sources, properties and behaviour.

Record source

When checking books out and in, library staff are not interested in records for books that have already been returned. To filter out these records, the form is bound to a query instead of to the Loans table.

Record Source . . . . BookReturns

The query (BookReturns) returns all fields in the Loans table but only for records that have no return date. You can view this query by opening it in Query Design View.

Default view

Forms can be presented to users in one of three different views. You set the view in which a form opens by using the form's *Default View property*. The available views are:

- **Single Form**. One record is displayed at a time. This is the view used for the Maintain Members form in Chapter 11.

- **Continuous Forms**. Multiple records are displayed at a time, each in its own copy of the form's Detail section.

Typically you use this view for records that have no more than two or three rows of controls.

- **Datasheet**. Multiple records are displayed at a time in rows and columns, in the same way as records are displayed in table and query datasheets. This view cannot display option groups, list boxes, graphics, headers and footers, or more than a single row of controls.

When checking books out and in, library staff want to be able to view multiple records at a time, so the *Default View* property for the LoansAndReturnsFinishedVersion form has been set to *Continuous Forms*. If set to *Datasheet* instead, the headers and footers would not display.

Bound controls

The ISBN, MemID, LoanDate, ReturnDate and FinePaid controls are all bound to fields in the BookReturns query.

To facilitate entry of ISBN numbers and member IDs, ISBN and MemID are combo box controls that look up their values in the Books and Members tables respectively. The other bound fields all use text box controls.

Calculated controls

Two types of calculated controls are included in the form:

- **Single-record calculated controls**. These perform calculations on values in a single record, in order to provide additional information about that record – that is, information that can be calculated from existing values in the record and does not need to be stored in a database table. You create this type of calculated control in the Detail section of a form.

DueDate, OverdueBy and FineDue are all single-record calculated controls. They perform calculations on values in a single Loans record in order to provide information on the overdue status of a book loan. Any or all of these calculations could be performed by calculated fields in the BookReturns query instead of by calculated controls in the form.

Overdue By	Fine Due
8	£ 4.00
8	£ 4.00

Note that DueDate, OverdueBy and FineDue are the control names (as defined in their *Name* properties) and not their labels. When the controls were first created, they were automatically given names like Text8, Text9, and so on. It is difficult to keep track of controls with names like these, particularly when you want to refer to them in calculations. So the names of the controls have been changed to something more meaningful.

- **Multi-record calculated controls.** These perform calculations that summarize values in a group of records by using Access's aggregate functions. You create this type of control in the Header or Footer sections of a form. The calculations are always performed on all records retrieved by the form.

   BooksOut, BooksOverdue, AverageDaysOverdue and TotalFinesDue are calculated controls that summarize information about all books that are currently out on loan. Again the control names have been changed from their default values to make them more meaningful.

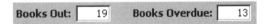

The calculations in a calculated control are rerun each time the form is opened and whenever a value in the calculation expression changes.

Exercise 12.1: Using the LoansAndReturnsFinishedVersion form

In this exercise you will update and add records in the form in order to see the calculated controls in action.

1) Open the LoansAndReturnsFinishedVersion form in Form View.

2) Go to any record with a loan date of 10-07-03 and take a look at the values in the DueDate, OverdueBy and FineDue controls.

   (Note that the calculations in the form use 21-07-03 as today's date, so a book with a loan date of 10-07-03 is overdue by one day.)

3) Change the loan date to 08-07-03. When you now move to another control, all the calculated controls for the record are automatically updated. When you move to another record, all the calculated controls in the form footer are also updated.

4) Now add a new record. Select a book in the ISBN control, a member in the MemID control, and enter 21-07-03 as the loan date. As soon as you leave the LoanDate control, the DueDate control will calculate and display the due date.

5) Enter a return date for any of the records. Then press **Shift+F9**. This command reruns the query on which the form is based and redisplays the records in the form. Notice that the record for which you entered

the return date is no longer displayed. This is because it no longer meets the criteria for the BookReturns query, which returns only records for which there is no return date.

6) Close the form.

Creating calculated controls

Typically you use text box controls for calculations. You can enter the calculation expression directly in the text box or in its *Control Source* property.

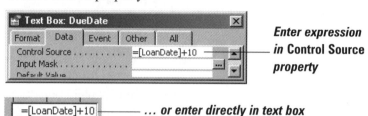

Enter expression *in* **Control Source** *property*

=[LoanDate]+10 ———— *... or enter directly in text box*

An expression in a calculated control must be preceded by the equal to (=) symbol. Otherwise the rules for control expressions are similar to those for calculated field expressions. And most expressions that you can enter in a calculated field you can also enter in a calculated control.

For example, all the calculation examples in 'About custom calculations' in Chapter 9 could also be used in calculated controls. Similarly, information in that chapter about the IIf() function applies equally to calculated controls, as does information in Chapter 10 about Null values, and the IsNull() and Nz() functions.

Appendix A summarizes all that you need to know about the operators, values, functions and field and control references that you can include in an expression.

Creating single-record calculated controls

In the exercises in this section you will create the DueDate, OverdueBy, and FineDue controls for the Loans and Returns form.

The form has already been started for you. All the bound controls have been created, and unbound text boxes have been created for the calculated controls. The controls are laid out in a single row in the Detail section. The labels have been moved to the Header section so that they are not repeated for each record in the form.

Exercise 12.2: Creating single-record calculated controls

1) Open the Loans and Returns form in Design View.

2) Click the DueDate text box control and type the following expression:

```
=[LoanDate]+10
```

In Form View this control will now display the due date for a book — that is, the loan date plus ten.

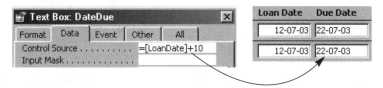

3) Display the property sheet for the OverdueBy text box control and click the **Data** tab to display its *Control Source* property. At the moment this is blank, but you will now enter an expression that calculates the number of days (if any) that a book is overdue, as follows:

```
=IIf(Date()-[DueDate]>0,Date()-[DueDate],Null)
```

As the expression is quite long, you will find it easier to enter and edit it in the *Zoom* dialog box. To open this, click in the *Control Source* property box and press **Shift+F2**. When you have finished, click **OK** and the expression is automatically entered in the *Control Source* property.

4) Switch to Form View to see the calculation results. The OverdueBy control now displays the number of days by which each book is overdue.

5) Note that the most recent loan dates in the database are in July 2003, so the number of days that books are overdue may be quite high by now. The data in the illustrations in this and subsequent chapters are based on a current date of 21-07-03. You can simulate this in your form by changing the OverdueBy expression as follows:

```
=IIf(#21-07-03#-[DueDate]>0,#21-07-03#-
[DueDate],Null)
```

Switch back to Design View and do this now. Then take a look at the new calculation results.

6) In Design View, display the property sheet for the FineDue control and click the **Data** tab to display the control's *Control Source* property. Then enter this expression:

```
=[OverdueBy]*0.5
```

7) Click the **Format** tab, and change the control's *Format* property to *Currency*.

8) Switch to Form View to see the results of this calculation. Then save the form.

In the exercises in this section you will create the BooksOut, BooksOverdue, AverageDaysOverdue and TotalFinesDue controls for the Loans and Returns form. The calculations for these controls use the Count(), Avg() and Sum() functions. The controls are all located in the Form Footer section, as you want them to calculate totals for all records retrieved by the form and not just for a single record.

There is one important limitation when using aggregate functions in forms and reports. The functions *cannot* refer to the name of a *control*.

This isn't a problem when performing calculations on bound values. The calculation can refer to the bound *field* instead of to the *control*. So Count([ISBN]) will work.

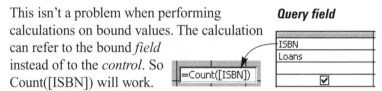

Query field

However, calculated controls do not store their values in table or query fields. So an aggregate function that summarizes the values in a calculated control can take its values from neither the calculated control nor an underlying field. In the case of the BooksOverdue control, for example, you can't use the expression Count([OverdueBy]).

The best solution is usually to create your single-record calculations as calculated query fields, as shown here on the right. Aggregate functions can then take their values from those fields.

Query field

Another solution is to repeat the expression from the single-record calculated control in the aggregate function, as shown here.

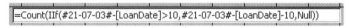

This is the method you will use in the following exercise.

Exercise 12.3: Creating multi-record calculated controls
1) Open the Loans and Returns form in Design View.

2) Enter the following expression in the BooksOut text box control:

    =Count([ISBN])

This calculates the number of books that are currently out on loan. Remember that the Count() function ignores Null values. So, to count all the records in the form, you must specify a field that always contains a value. As a primary key field, ISBN is never Null and so is suitable for the calculation.

3) Enter the following expression in the BooksOverdue text box control:

   =Count(IIf(#21-07-03#-[LoanDate]>10,#21-07-03#-[LoanDate]-10,Null))

   This calculates the number of books that are overdue, by counting only records for books that have been out on loan for longer than ten days.

   Note that in a real-life scenario you would enter Date() instead of #21-07-03#. However, use #21-07-03# to maintain consistency between your calculation results and those shown in illustrations in this chapter.

4) Enter the following expression in the AverageDaysOverdue text box control:

   =Avg(IIf(#21-07-03#-[LoanDate]>10,#21-07-03#-[LoanDate]-10,Null))

   This calculates the average number of days that books are overdue. Average() ignores Null values and so averages only books that have been out on loan for more than ten days.

5) Change the control's *Format* property to *Standard* and its *Decimal Places* property to *2*.

6) Enter the following expression in the TotalFinesDue text box control:

   =Sum(IIf(#21-07-03#-[LoanDate]>10,#21-07-03#-[LoanDate]-10,Null))*0.5

   This calculates the total fines due on overdue books. The IIf() function returns the number of days that each overdue book is overdue and the Sum() function then adds these values.

7) Change the control's *Format* property to *Currency*.

8) Save the form and then switch to Form View to see the results of your changes.

In Form View and Design View, your form should now resemble that shown here.

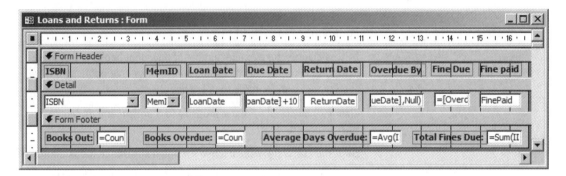

Chapter 12: summary

Calculated controls display the results of calculations. The controls are unbound, so the calculation results are not stored in the database. Instead Access reruns the calculation each time you open the form and whenever a value in the calculation expression changes.

If you intend to use the same calculations in multiple forms/reports, create them as calculated fields in a query and then base your forms/reports on that query.

Single-record calculated controls perform calculations on values in a single record, in order to provide additional information about that record. You create these controls in the Detail section of a form.

Multi-record calculated controls perform calculations that summarize values across multiple records by using Access's aggregate functions. You create these controls in the Header or Footer sections of a form.

When using aggregate functions in a calculated control, you cannot refer to the name of another control. For bound controls, you refer to the underlying field instead. For unbound controls, you can either add a calculated field to the record source and refer to that field in the aggregate function, or you can repeat the expression from the unbound control in the aggregate function.

Typically you use text boxes for calculated controls. You can enter the calculation expression directly in the text box or in its *Control Source* property. The expression must always be preceded by an equal to (=) symbol.

Chapter 12: quick quiz

Q1	True or false – form headers and footers do not display in Continuous Forms view.
A.	True.
B.	False.

Q2	True or false – a single-record calculated control performs calculations on the values in individual records.
A.	True.
B.	False.

Q3	True or false – a multi-record calculated control performs calculations across records retrieved by a form.
A.	True.
B.	False.

Q4	True or false – an equal to (=) symbol is optional at the start of a calculated control's expression.
A.	True.
B.	False.

Q5	Which of these control expressions calculates the average fine due for overdue books?
A.	=Avg[OverdueBy]*0.5
B.	=Avg([OverdueBy])*0.5
C.	=Avg((IIf(Date()-[LoanDate]>10,Date()-[LoanDate]-10,Null))*0.5

Q6	Which of these control expressions calculates the maximum number of overdue days for books in the library?
A.	=Max([OverdueBy])
B.	=Max(Date()-[LoanDate]-10)
C.	=Max(IIf(Date()-[LoanDate]>10,Date()-[LoanDate]-10,Null))
D.	=TopValue([OverdueBy])

Answers

1: B, **2**: A, **3**: A, **4**: B, **5**: C, **6**: B and C.

13

Form design: subforms

In this chapter

In previous chapters you created forms that display records from a single table or query. A form can also display a record from one table and all related records from another table. The records in the related table are displayed in a subform.

In this chapter you will learn about subforms and the various methods you can use to create them.

New skills

At the end of this chapter you should be able to:

- Understand subforms and their uses
- Create a subform with the *Form Wizard*
- Create a subform with the *Subform Wizard*
- Use an existing form as a subform
- Modify a subform to display different records

New words

In this chapter you will meet the following terms:

- Main form
- Subform

Exercise file

In this chapter you will work with the following Access file:

- Chp13_VillageLibrary_Database

Syllabus reference

In this chapter you will cover the following items of the ECDL Advanced Database Syllabus:

- **AM5.3.2.1**: Create a subform and link to parent.
- **AM5.3.2.2**: Modify the subform to change records displayed.

About subforms

A subform is a form that is contained within another form. The container or parent form is referred to as the main form.

In itself, a subform is not a special type of form. You can create and use it independently of the main form. It is a subform only when included in another form.

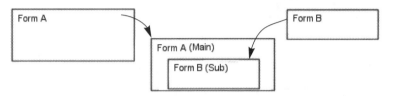

Subforms are especially useful for displaying records from tables with a one-to-many relationship, such as Books and Loans. For example, it would be very useful to be able to browse through the Books table and, as you move to each book, to see all the loans for that book. The BookLoans form shown here enables you to do just that.

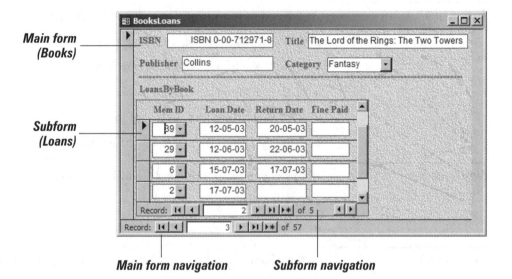

Main form
(Books)

Subform
(Loans)

Main form navigation   Subform navigation

The main form displays a single record from the Books table – that is, from the 'one' side of the relationship. The subform displays multiple records from the Loans table – that is, from the 'many' side of the relationship. The two forms are linked in such a way that the subform displays only records related to the current record in the main form.

Exercise 13.1: Using forms with subforms

In this exercise you will explore the BookLoans form and its subform.

1) Open the BookLoans form in Form View.

2) Use the main form's navigation buttons to browse through the book records.

3) Use the subform's navigation buttons or its scroll bar to browse through the loan records for the current book.

***New Record
button***

4) Use the subform's **New Record** button to enter a new loan record for the current book. The MemID field in the Loans table is a lookup field, so you can select a member from its lookup list. The ISBN number from the record in the main form is automatically saved as the ISBN number for the loan record.

5) Close the BookLoans form.

6) The subform exists as a form in its own right. It is named LoansByBook. Open that form now in Form View.

   Notice that when not acting as a subform, the form displays all records in the Loans table. Close the form.

Subform
A form that is contained within another form.

Main form
A form that contains a subform.

Creating subforms

You can use any of the following methods to create a form that contains a subform:

- Use the *Form Wizard* to create both forms.

- Use the *Subform Wizard* to create a subform in an existing form.

- Use an existing form as a subform.

Which method you use depends, for example, on whether you have existing forms that would be suitable as a main form or subform, whether you want to include headers and footers in the forms, and whether you want to include multiple subforms in the main form.

Note that you must use *Single Form* view for a main form. You can use any view for the subform, but *Continuous Form* view is generally the most useful.

In the following exercises you will create forms and subforms for processing book loans and returns. In each case, the main form will display details of an individual library member and the subform will list that member's loan records.

The main form will be based on the Members table (the 'one' side of the Members/Loans relationship). The subform will be based on the Loans table (the 'many' side of the relationship).

Using the Form Wizard

You use the *Form Wizard* to create a main form and subform at the same time.

Exercise 13.2: Using the *Form Wizard* to create a form and subform

1) Start the *Form Wizard*. To do this, click *Forms* in the *Objects* list in the Database window and then double-click the *Create form by using wizard* option in the forms list.

2) In the first page of the wizard, select the Members table in the *Tables/Queries* list and add all its fields to the *Selected fields* list. These are the fields that will be included in the main form.

   Then select the Loans table and add its ISBN, LoanDate, ReturnDate, and FinePaid fields to the list. These are the fields that will be included in the subform. You can omit Loans.MemID from the subform as it displays the same value as the MemID field in the main form.

   Select the Books table and add its Title field immediately below the ISBN field in the list. To do this, select the ISBN field in the right list before adding the Title field. Click **Next**.

   Note that you can select the tables and fields in any order. You don't have to select the table and fields for the main form first.

3) The wizard now asks you how you want to view your data. This is where you indicate the table/query to which you want to bind the main form. You must select a table on the 'one' side of a relationship. If you select a table on the 'many' side (in this case, Loans), the wizard creates a single form in which each record displays all the selected fields.

   Make sure that the *by Members* option is selected. This will create a main form that displays member records and a subform that displays loan records.

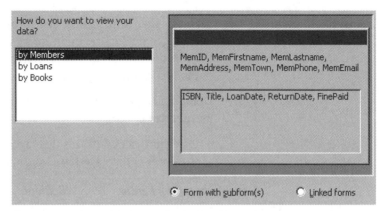

How do you want to view your data?

by Members
by Loans
by Books

MemID, MemFirstname, MemLastname, MemAddress, MemTown, MemPhone, MemEmail

ISBN, Title, LoanDate, ReturnDate, FinePaid

○ Form with subform(s)   ○ Linked forms

4) You now have the option of creating either a form with a subform or two linked forms. Make sure that the *Form with subform(s)* option is selected and click **Next**.

5) When prompted for a layout for the subform, select *Tabular* and click **Next**. This sets *Continuous Forms* as the default view for the subform.

6) When prompted for a form style, select *Expedition* and click **Next**.

7) When prompted for names for the two forms, enter FormWizard for the main form and FormWizardSubform for the subform. Click **Finish**.

Access now creates the main form and subform and displays the main form in Form View, as shown below.

Main form (Members) —

Subform (Loans) —

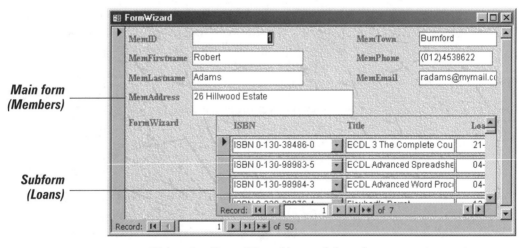

Using the *Form Wizard* is a quick and easy way to create a form and subform. However, the layout and formatting need some editing.

For example, the subform records don't display in full, the size of most fields needs to be adjusted, and the labels in the main form would be better without the 'Mem' prefix. You can make all these changes in Form Design View.

Like all other information in a form, a subform is displayed within a control in the main form. The control used is a Subform/Subreport control (referred to as the Subform control in the rest of this chapter).

Open the *FormWizard* form in Design View and take a look at its subform control:

■ The subform control is displayed as a rectangular box. The subform is displayed in Design View within the box.

Subform control border   **Subform**

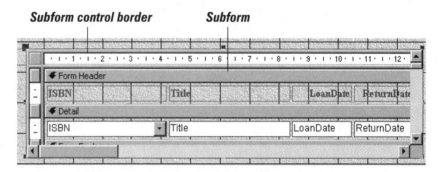

If the control is blank, it means that the subform is already open in a separate window; if this happens, close the main form and subform, and then reopen the main form.

■ To select the subform control, click on its border. Alternatively, select the subform control in the *Object* list on the *Formatting* toolbar (it has the same name as the subform it contains).

■ Once the control is selected, you can view its properties in its property sheet. The *Name* property specifies the name of the control; the *Source Object* property specifies the form that the control contains; and the *Link Child Fields* and *Link Master Fields* properties specify the fields that link the main form and the subform.

Object list

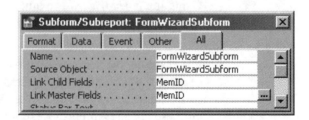

- Once the control is selected, you can also select any element of the subform in the normal way. For example, click the form selector to select the form, click a section selector to select a section, and click a control to select a control.

- When you select an element of the subform, you can edit it in the normal way.

While you can edit a subform from within a main form, it is usually easier to work with a subform in its own Design View window. To do this, close the main form, and then open the subform in Design View from the Database window.

Using the Subform Wizard You use the *Subform Wizard* to create a subform within an existing form.

Exercise 13.3: Using the *Subform Wizard* to create a form and subform

For this exercise, a form based on the Members table has been prepared for you. You will create the subform that displays the loan records.

1) Open the Process Loans form in Form View.

   Notice that the form displays member records in *Single Form* view. A record selector combo box allows you to select the record you want to view from a lookup list. The MemFirstname and MemLastname values have been merged into a single string, as have the MemAddress and MemTown fields.

2) Switch to Form Design View and make sure that the **Control Wizards** tool is selected (pressed in) in the toolbox.

Subform tool

3) Click the **Subform** tool in the toolbox and click near the left edge of the Detail section, a little below the existing controls. This starts the *Subform Wizard*.

4) The wizard first asks you whether you want to use an existing form as the subform or whether you want to create a new subform. Make sure the *Use existing Tables and Queries* options is selected and click **Next**.

   ⦿ Use existing Tables and Queries

5) When prompted for the fields to include in the subform, select the following fields, in the order listed, and click **Next**:
   - Loans.ISBN
   - Books.Title
   - Loans.LoanDate
   - Loans.ReturnDate
   - Loans.FinePaid

6) The wizard next prompts you to specify the fields that link the subform and main form. The default options are *Choose from a list* and *Show Loans for each record in Members using MemID*. Leave these as they are and click **Next**.

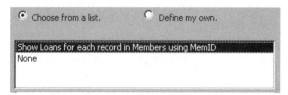

7) When prompted for a name for the subform, enter LoansSubform and click **Finish**. Access now creates the LoansSubform form and adds it to the subform control in the Process Loans form.

8) Switch to Form View to see what the subform looks like and how it works. When you select a member in the main form, the loan records for that member are displayed in the subform. This is what you want. However, the layout and formatting of the subform still need some work.

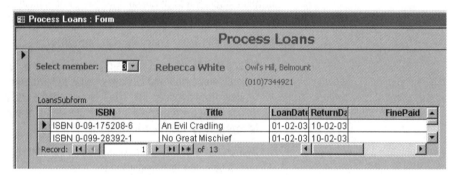

The height of the subform needs to be increased in order to display more records at a time; the field sizes need to be adjusted, and some of the labels could be more user friendly.

9) In the next exercise you will use the same main form and insert an existing form as the subform. So, switch back to Design View now and delete the subform control you have just created.

To do this, select the control and press **Delete**. Then save and close the main form.

Using an existing form

Why go to the effort of creating a new subform when you already have a suitable form that you can use instead? The Loans and Returns form you created in Chapter 12 is well laid out and formatted, it displays only the records for current loans, and its calculated controls provide useful additional information.

Loans and Returns is an ideal candidate for the subform required by the Process Loans form. Just a few modifications are necessary, and these have already been made in the version of the form included in the Chp13_VillageLibrary_Database database.

Open the Loans and Returns form in Form View to see the changes:

- The Loans.MemID field has been removed from the form as it would have the same value as the ID in the main form. And the Books.Title field has been added to make the loan records more meaningful. The Books.Title field was first added to the BookReturns query on which the form is based.

- A new text box control has been added to the footer. This calculates the total amount of fines paid.

- The form's navigation buttons have been removed to avoid confusion with those on the main form. To do this the form's *Navigation Buttons* property was set to 'No'. You can still browse through the loan records by using the scroll bar.

Exercise 13.4: Using an existing form as a subform

In this exercise you will add the Loans and Returns form as a subform in the Process Loans form.

1) Make sure that the Loans and Returns form is closed. Then open the Process Loans form in Design View.

2) Rearrange the Database window and the form window so that you can see them both on your screen.

3) Click on the Loans and Returns form in the Database window and drag it into the form window, dropping it at the position shown here.

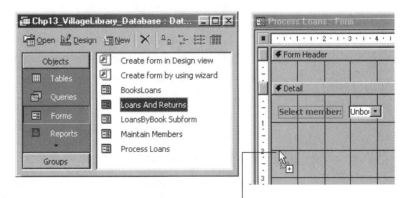

Drop here

Access creates a subform control and displays the Loans And Returns form in Design View within it, as shown here.

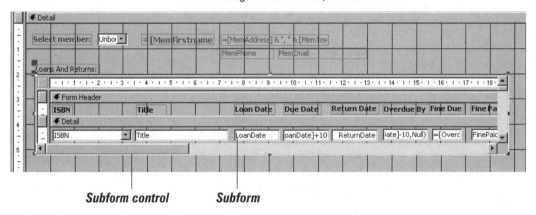

Subform control   **Subform**

4) Save the Process Loans form and switch to Form View. Access has automatically linked the main form and subform so that the subform always displays the loans for the current member.

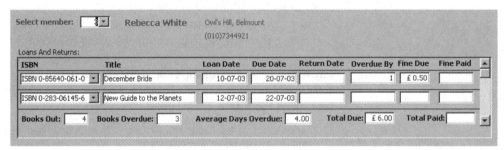

The form is now almost ready for use. Just two small changes: the subform's label should be the same colour as the other labels in the form; and the size of the subform control needs to be adjusted to display more than two records. Switch back to Design View to make these changes.

5) Change the subform control's label to 'Loans'. Make the text bold and the same colour as the other labels in the main form.

6) Members of the Village Library can have up to five books out on loan at the same time. To accommodate five records, the height of the subform control needs to be increased. Select the subform control to display its sizing handles. Then drag the lower edge of the control down to the end of the main form's Detail section and the beginning of the main form's Form Footer section. The control should have a height of about 5.5 cm.

7) Save the form and switch to Form View to see the result of your changes. Your form should now resemble that shown here.

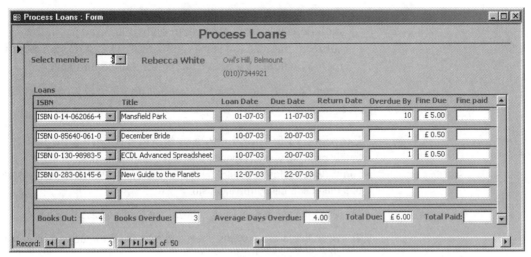

In this exercise, you added the Loans and Returns form to the Process Loans form by dragging it from the Database window. Here are two other methods you can use:

- Use the *Subform Wizard* and, in the first page of the wizard, select the Loans and Returns form as the subform.

- Create a blank subform control and then set its *Source Object* property to the Loans and Returns form.

Modifying the record source for a subform

Which records a subform displays is determined both by the current selection in the main form and by the subform's record source. The record source can be a table, a query or an SQL statement.

- Take a look at the *Record Source* property for the LoansByBook subform and you will see that its record source is the Loans table. The subform displays all records in the Loans table that relate to the book selected in the main form.

- Take a look at the *Record Source* property for the Loans and Returns subform and you will see that its record source is the BookReturns query, which retrieves only current loans – that is, loans where the ReturnDate value is Null.

- Take a look at the *Record Source* property for the FormWizardSubform and you will see that its record source is an SQL statement that retrieves all records from the Loans table and also the Title field from the Books table.

The record source is always an SQL statement when you include fields from more than one table or query in the subform and use a wizard to create it. The SQL statement is the equivalent of a query but is not named and saved.

You can change the record source for any form by changing its *Record Source* property.

Exercise 13.5: Modifying a subform's record source

In this exercise you will modify the record source for the FormWizardSubform subform so that it displays only current loans instead of a member's full borrowing history.

1) Open the subform in Design View from the Database window.

2) Open the form's property sheet and click the **Data** tab to display the *Record Source* property.

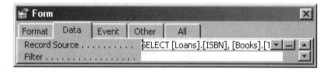

The property box displays both an arrow button and a **Build** button.

3) Click the arrow button. This displays a list of the tables and queries in the database and allows you to select one as the record source for your form instead of the SQL statement. Close the list without selecting an option. To do this, press the **Esc** button.

4) Click the **Build** button. This opens the *Query Builder*, which displays the SQL statement in Query Design View. You can now add and remove fields and specify criteria in the normal way.

5) Enter the following criteria for the ReturnDate field:

    Is Null

6) Close the *Query Builder* window. When prompted to confirm your changes, click **Yes**. This updates the SQL statement in the *Record Source* property.

7) Close the form, saving it as you do.

8) Open the FormWizard form in Form View. When you select a member in the main form, the subform now displays only current loans.

You can modify the record source for the Loans and Returns subform in exactly the same way. Because the record source is a query, any changes you make are saved to that query. Alternatively, you can open the query in Design View from the Database window and make your changes there. The result is the same.

Chapter 13: summary

A *subform* is a form that is contained within another form. The container form is referred to as the *main form*.

Typically you use a main form and subform to display data from tables or queries with a one-to-many relationship. The main table displays records from the 'one' side of the relationship; the subform displays records from the 'many' side. The two forms are linked in such as a way that the subform displays only records that are related to the current record in the main form.

You use the *Form Wizard* to create a main form and subform at the same time. You use the *Subform Wizard* to create a subform in an existing main form. To use an existing form as a subform, open the main form in Design View and then drag the subform from the Database window to the Detail section of the main form.

You can change which records a subform displays by changing its *Record Source* property.

Chapter 13: quick quiz

Q1	True or false – you use a main form to display records from the 'many' side of a relationship.
A.	True.
B.	False.

Q2	To use an existing form as a subform ...
A.	Open the main form in Design View and drag the subform from the Database window into the main form.
B.	Create a blank subform control in the main form and set its *Source Object* property to the name of the subform.
C.	Open the main form in Design View and use the *Subform Wizard* to select the subform.

Q3	Which of these views can you use for a main form?
A.	Single Form.
B.	Datasheet.
C.	Continuous Forms.

Q4	True or false – you can modify a subform from within a main form.
A.	True.
B.	False.

Q5	True or false – you cannot view and use a subform independently of a main form.
A.	True.
B.	False.

Q6	True or false – a subform displays only records related to the current record in the main form.
A.	True.
B.	False.

Answers

1: B, **2**: All, **3**: A, **4**: A, **5**: B, **6**: A.

14

Report design

In this chapter

Reports are the main means of organizing, grouping and summarizing database information in a format suitable for printing and for online review. You can group records on significant fields, summarize and subtotal data within and across groups, create running sums, and perform complex calculations.

In this chapter, you will learn how to use these and other report features.

New skills

At the end of this chapter you should be able to:

- Create calculated controls in a report
- Use aggregate functions in a report
- Calculate percentages in a report
- Create running sums in a report
- Number items in a report
- Display data in headers and footers
- Display report sections on separate pages

New words

In this chapter you will meet the following term:

- Running sum

Exercise file

In this chapter you will work with the following Access file:

- Chp14_VillageLibrary_Database

Syllabus reference

In this chapter you will cover the following items of the ECDL Advanced Database Syllabus:

- **AM5.4.1.1**: Create arithmetic, logical calculation controls in a report.
- **AM5.4.1.2**: Calculate percentage calculation control in a report.

- **AM5.4.1.3**: Use formulas, expressions in a report such as sum, count, average, max, min, concatenate.

- **AM5.4.1.4**: Create running summaries in a report.

- **AM5.4.2.1**: Insert a data field to appear within report header, footers on the first page or all pages.

- **AM5.4.2.2**: Force page breaks for groups on reports.

Report controls

As with forms, all information in a report is contained in controls. The same controls are available for reports as for forms, and you create and modify them in the same way and with the same tools.

Most information in reports is presented in text box controls and labels. Reports are not interactive, so controls such as combo boxes, list boxes, option groups and command buttons are not appropriate.

Calculated controls

Calculated report controls are controls that display the results of calculations on other controls or fields in a report. You create them in the same way that you create calculated controls in a form and the same rules and guidelines generally apply.

- You can use calculated controls to perform calculations on values in single records, in order to provide additional information about those records. If you intend using the same calculations in multiple forms or reports, it is often easier to put the calculations in a query and base your report on that query.

- As with forms, you can use calculated controls to summarize values across all records. But, with reports, you can also group records and summarize values within each group.

- Remember that aggregate functions *cannot* refer to the name of a *control*. So an aggregate function cannot summarize values in a calculated control by referring to the control name.

  Instead you can either put the calculation in a query field and refer to that field in the aggregate function, or you can repeat the calculation expression in the aggregate function. For an example, see 'Creating multi-record calculated controls' in Chapter 12.

Exploring the Books By Category report

In the exercises in this chapter you will create the Books By Category report, which lists the full library catalogue, grouped by category, and summarizes the number and cost of books in each category and in the full catalogue.

A finished copy of this report is available in the Chp14_VillageLibrary_Database database under the name BooksByCategoryFinishedVersion. Open the report now in Print Preview View and take a look at its content and design.

Report header

The first page you see is the report header. A *report header* is displayed once at the start of a report. You use it to display items such as the report title and date.

In this report, the report header displays the report title, the report date, and a picture. It is displayed on a page by itself.

Category groups

Use the report's navigation buttons to browse through the next few pages of the report. You can see that the main body of the report consists of a list of books and their cost. The books are grouped by category, with each category displayed on a separate page.

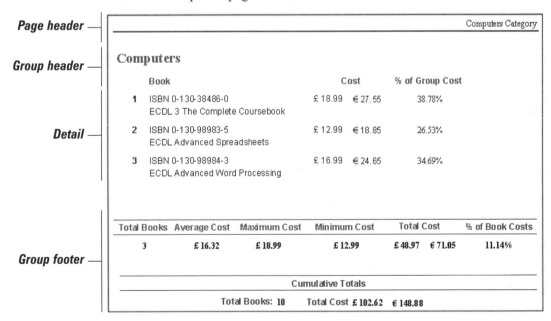

Page header —

Computers Category

Group header —

Computers

	Book	Cost	% of Group Cost
1	ISBN 0-130-38486-0 ECDL 3 The Complete Coursebook	£ 18.99 € 27.55	38.78%
2	ISBN 0-130-98983-5 ECDL Advanced Spreadsheets	£ 12.99 € 18.85	26.53%
3	ISBN 0-130-98984-3 ECDL Advanced Word Processing	£ 16.99 € 24.65	34.69%

Detail —

Total Books	Average Cost	Maximum Cost	Minimum Cost	Total Cost	% of Book Costs
3	£ 16.32	£ 18.99	£ 12.99	£ 48.97 € 71.05	11.14%

Group footer —

Cumulative Totals

Total Books: 10   Total Cost £ 102.62   € 148.88

For each group there is a group header section, a detail section and a group footer section.

- The *group header* is displayed at the start of each group and you use it to display information that applies to the entire group. In this report, the group header displays the Category value and the column headings. Putting the column headings here means that they are displayed only once at the top of each group. If you include them in the detail section, they are repeated for each record in the group.

- The *detail* section displays the main report data. In this report, it lists the books in the current category and numbers the books sequentially within the group. For each book, the value of the BooksConfidential.Cost field is displayed and the euro equivalent is calculated. The percentage value displays the book cost as a percentage of the total cost of books in the category.

  Some books were donated to the library. In these cases, the word 'Donated' is displayed instead of costs. For examples of this, go to the Science and Reference categories.

- The *group footer* is displayed at the end of each group. You typically use it to display group totals. In this report, the group footer displays summary information about the number and cost of books in the current category. The percentage value displays the total cost of books in the category, as a percentage of the total cost of books in the library.

  The group footer in this report also displays running sums – that is, totals for all categories up to and including the current category.

Report footer

The *report footer* is displayed once at the end of a report. You use it to display items such as report totals. In this report, the report footer displays summary information about the number and cost of books in the library. It is displayed on a page by itself.

```
                    Totals for All Books
                      10 April 2003


        Total Books:     58
           Total cost:  £ 439.77    € 638.02
        Average cost:   £ 7.85      € 11.39
      Maximum Cost:     £ 24.80     € 35.98
       Minimum cost:    £ 1.50       € 2.18
```

Page headers and footers

Page headers and *page footers* are displayed at the top and bottom of each page. Typically you use the page header to display column headings, and the page footer to display page numbers.

In this report, the page header displays the name of the current category. The page footer displays the date and page number.

Page header ————
```
                                                                   Science Category
```

Page footer ————
```
  10-Apr-03                                                        Page 11 of 12
```

Design View

Now let's take a look at the report in Design View and see how it is defined.

- First display the property sheet for the report and take a look at its *Record Source* property. The report is based on a query named BooksByCategoryReportSource. You can open and view the query by clicking the **Build** button in the *Record Source* property box.

  This query joins the Books and BooksConfidential tables, and retrieves the ISBN, Title, Category and Cost fields from those tables. The tables are joined with a left outer join so that the query returns *all* records from the Books table, including those that have no matching record in the BooksConfidential table.

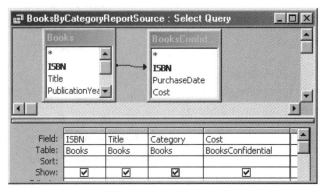

If you have opened the *Query Builder*, close it before continuing.

- If you open the **View** menu, you can see that both the **Page Header/Footer** and **Report Header/Footer** options are selected, so the report includes these sections.

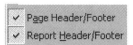

- If you open the *Sorting and Grouping* dialog box (choose **View | Sorting and Grouping**), you can see that a Category group has been created by selecting the Category field in the *Field/Expression* column and setting its *Group Header* and *Group Footer* properties to *Yes*. An ascending sort order has also been selected for the group.

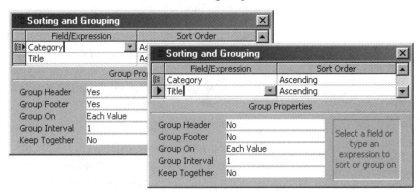

- To sort the books in ascending order of title, the Title field has been selected in the *Field/Expression* column and *Ascending* has been selected in the *Sort Order* column.

You can now close the BooksByCategoryFinishedVersion report. Do not save any changes you may have made.

Creating calculated controls

The BooksByCategoryFinishedVersion report includes calculated controls for a variety of calculation types and for different report sections. In the exercises in this section you will add these calculations to the Books By Category report.

This report has already been started for you. Open it now in Print Preview mode. You can see that it includes all the relevant sections and labels, but no calculations, no page breaks between sections, and no information in the page header and footer.

Switch to Design View and you can see that most of the text box controls for the calculations have been created for you. Your task is to add the calculations themselves.

Note that in the exercises, controls are referred to by the names specified in their *Name* properties. For unbound controls, the names have been changed from the default names (Text1 and Text2, for example) to make them more meaningful.

Report width wider than page width warning

The Books By Category report is designed to be printed on A4 size paper. The report itself is a little less than 16 cm wide; the margins take up the rest of the page width. If the following message appears at any stage when you switch from Design View to Print Preview, it means that the report width has been increased beyond what will fit on one page.

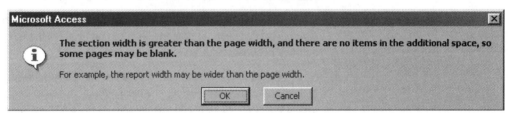

This can happen when you create a new control near the right edge of the report. If the control extends beyond the edge of the report, Access automatically increases the report width to accommodate it. If this happens, first move the control back from the edge of the report; then drag the report edge back to its original position (16 cm or less).

Creating calculated controls in the detail section

In the detail section of a report you create calculated controls that perform calculations on values in individual records.

Exercise 14.1: Creating calculated controls in the detail section

In this exercise you will add a calculation to display the euro cost of each book, and you will create a calculated field that displays the word 'Donated' for books that have no Cost value.

1) Open the Books By Category report in Design View and scroll to the detail section.

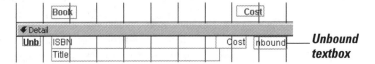

Notice that there are two controls below the Cost heading. The first is a text box control that is bound to the Cost field. The second is an unbound text box control (named EuroCost) that currently has no source.

2) Enter the following expression in the EuroCost text box control (you can type the expression directly in the control or in its *Control Source* property):

`=[Cost]*1.4508`

This calculates the euro equivalent of the values in the Cost field.

3) Display the property sheet for the EuroCost control and select the *Euro* option in its *Format* property. This format displays the € symbol and two decimal places only.

4) Now create a new unbound text box control by clicking the **Text Box** tool in the toolbox and clicking in a blank area of the detail section. Delete the attached label and change the control's *Name* property to 'DonatedBook'.

5) Enter the following expression in the control:

`=IIf(IsNull([Cost]),"Donated",Null)`

This checks if the Cost field is empty. If it is, the control displays the word 'Donated'. If it isn't, the control displays nothing.

6) You want the word 'Donated' to be displayed below the Cost heading, in place of the cost values. So change the width of the control to just fit the word 'Donated'; then position it on top of, and centred on, the Cost and EuroCost controls.

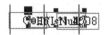

This may look confusing in Design View, but in Print Preview the DonatedBook control will always be empty if the other two controls contain values and vice versa.

7) Save the report and switch to Print Preview to see the result of your changes. To see the DonatedBook control in action, go to the Science or Reference category.

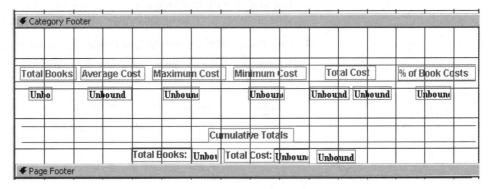

Print Preview button

Creating calculated controls in a group footer

In a group footer section of a report you typically create calculated controls that display group totals.

Exercise 14.2: Creating calculated controls in the group footer

In this exercise you will add calculations that display summary information about the number and cost of books in each category.

1) Open the Books By Category report in Design View and scroll to the group footer section (named Category Footer in this report).

An unbound text box control has been created under each of the headings in the upper part of the section. These are where you will enter the group calculations.

2) In the TotalBooks text box control, enter the following expression:

`=Count(*)`

This counts all books in a group.

3) In the AverageCost text box control, enter the following expression:

`=Avg([Cost])`

This calculates the average cost of books in a group.

4) In the MaximumCost text box control, enter the following expression:

`=Max([Cost])`

This returns the maximum book cost in a group.

5) In the MinimumCost text box control, enter the following expression:

`=Min([Cost])`

This returns the minimum book cost in a group.

6) In the GroupTotalCostGBP text box control, enter the following expression:

`=Sum([Cost])`

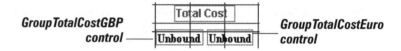

GroupTotalCostGBP control — Total Cost / Unbound Unbound — *GroupTotalCostEuro control*

This totals the cost of books in a group.

7) In the GroupTotalCostEuro text box control, enter the following expression:

`=Sum([Cost]*1.4508)`

This totals the costs of books in a group, in euros. To include the euro symbol, select the *Euro* option in the control's *Format* property.

8) Save the report and switch to Print Preview to see the result of your changes. For example, the group footer for the Children category should now look as shown here.

Total Books	Average Cost	Maximum Cost	Minimum Cost	Total Cost	
6	£ 6.82	£ 18.99	£ 2.99	£ 40.90	€59.34

In the report footer section of a report you typically create
calculated controls that display report totals.

Exercise 14.3: Creating calculated controls in the report footer

In this exercise you will add calculations that display summary information
about the number and cost of books in the library as a whole.

1) Open the Books By Category report in Design View and scroll to the
report footer section.

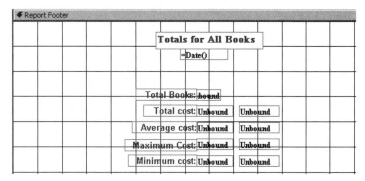

There are unbound text box controls beside each label in the section.
These are where you will enter the overall report calculations.

2) In the ReportTotalBooks text box control, enter the following expression:

   `=Count(*)`

   This counts all books in the report.

3) In the ReportTotalCostGBP text box control, enter the following
expression:

   `=Sum([Cost])`

   This calculates the total cost of books in the report.

4) In the ReportTotalCostEuro text box control, enter the following
expression:

   `=Sum([Cost]*1.4508)`

   This calculates the total cost of books in euros.

5) In the ReportAverageCostGBP text box control, enter the following
expression:

   `=Avg([Cost])`

   This calculates the average cost of books in the report.

6) In the ReportAverageCostEuro text box control, enter the following expression:

```
=Avg([Cost]*1.4508)
```

This calculates the average cost of books in euros.

7) In the ReportMaxCostGBP text box control, enter the following expression:

```
=Max([Cost])
```

This returns the maximum book cost in the report.

8) In the ReportMaxCostEuro text box control, enter the following expression:

```
=Max([Cost]*1.4508)
```

This returns the maximum book cost in euros.

9) In the ReportMinCostGBP text box control, enter the following expression:

```
=Min([Cost])
```

This returns the minimum book cost in the report.

10) In the ReportMinCostEuro text box control, enter the following expression:

```
=Min([Cost]*1.4508)
```

This returns the minimum book cost in euros.

11) Save the report and switch to Print Preview to see the result of your changes. The report footer should now look as shown here.

Totals for All Books

10 April 2003

Total Books:	58	
Total cost:	£ 439.77	€ 638.02
Average cost:	£ 7.85	€ 11.39
Maximum Cost:	£ 24.80	€ 35.98
Minimum cost:	£ 1.50	€ 2.18

Creating calculated controls in the report header

In the report header section of a report you typically create calculated controls for the date and perhaps for some summary data.

Exercise 14.4: Creating a calculated control in the report header

In this exercise you will add the current date to the report header.

1) Open the Books By Category report in Design View. There is an unbound text box control immediately below the report title. This is where you will enter the date expression.

Note that the report header includes a decorative line and an image. For your information, these were created with the **Line** and **Unbound Object Frame** tools respectively. In the latter case, the image was selected from Microsoft's Clip Gallery.

2) In the HeaderDate text box control, enter the following expression:

```
=Date()
```

This returns the current date.

3) Save the report and switch to Print Preview to see the result of your change.

Creating calculated controls in the page header

You typically use the page header section to display column headings, but you can also use it to repeat the report date, the report title or a group heading, for example.

Exercise 14.5: Creating a calculated control in the page header

In this exercise you will add a calculated control to the page header to display the category heading for the first group on each page.

1) Open the Books By Category report in Design View.

2) Create a new text box control at the right side of the page header section. Delete the attached label, and make the text box about 3 cm wide.

3) Enter the following expression In the control:

```
=[Category] & " Category"
```

This expression references the Category control in the group header. On each page, it will display the value of that control for the first group on the page. The concatenation expression appends the word 'Category' after the category value.

4) Save the report and switch to Print Preview to see the result of your change.

Computers Category

Computers

Book	Cost	% of Group Cost
ISBN 0-130-38486-0 ECDL 3 The Complete Coursebook	£ 18.99 € 27.55	38.78%

Creating calculated controls in the page footer

You typically use the page footer section of a report to display the date and page numbers.

Exercise 14.6: Creating calculated controls in the page footer

In this exercise you will add the date and page number to the page footer. You could create the controls and expressions for these items manually, but it is quicker and easier to use the **Insert** menu options.

1) Open the Books By Category report in Design View.

2) Choose **Insert | Page Numbers**. This displays the *Page Numbers* dialog box, which presents various options for displaying page numbers. Select the following options:

- *Format – Page N of M*

- *Position – Bottom of page (Footer)*

- *Alignment – Right*

Deselect the *Show Number on First Page* option. Then click **OK**.

3) Scroll to the page footer section and you can see that a text box control and appropriate expression have automatically been created for the page numbering.

4) Choose **Insert | Date and Time**. This displays the *Date and Time* dialog box.

5) Make sure the *Include Date* option is selected and then select the Medium Date format (for example, 10-Apr-03).

6) Deselect the *Include Time* option and click **OK**.

7) Scroll to the report header section and you can see that a text box control and appropriate expression have automatically been created for today's date.

Select the control and drag it to the left side of the page footer section, as shown here.

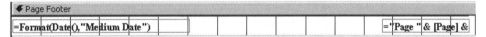

8) Save the report and switch to Print Preview to see the result of your changes.

Calculating percentages in a report

In a report you often need to calculate what percentage one value is of another. For example, what percentage a field value is of a group total and what percentage a group total is of a report total.

To do this you simply create an unbound text box control and enter an expression that divides the smaller value by the larger value. You then set the control's *Format* property to *Percent*.

Exercise 14.7: Calculating percentages

In this exercise you will add percentage calculations to the detail and group footer sections of the report.

1) Open the Books By Category report in Design View and scroll to the detail section.

2) There is an empty text box control (named PercentOfGroup) below the % of Group Costs heading. Enter the following expression in this control:

=[Cost]/[GroupTotalCostGBP]

This divides the cost of each book by the total cost of books in the group (as calculated in the GroupTotalCostGBP control), indicating what percentage the book cost is of the total group cost.

Select *Percent* in the *Format* property for the PercentOfGroup control.

3) There is another empty text box control (named PercentOfReport) in the Category Footer section, below the % of Book Costs heading. Enter the following expression in this control:

```
=[GroupTotalCostGBP]/[ReportTotalCostGBP]
```

This divides the total cost of books in a category by the total cost of books in the report (as calculated by the ReportTotalCostGBP control in the report footer), indicating what proportion the total category cost is of the total report cost.

Select *Percent* in the *Format* property for the PercentOfReport control.

4) Save the report and switch to Print Preview to see the result of your changes. For example, the information for the Reference category should now look as shown.

Reference

Book	Cost	% of Group Cost
ISBN 0-00-447823-1 Atlas of the World	Donated	
ISBN 0-7548-0731-2 The New Guide to Cat Care	£ 14.95 € 21.69	100.00%

Total Books	Average Cost	Maximum Cost	Minimum Cost	Total Cost	% of Book Costs
2	£ 14.95	£ 14.95	£ 14.95	£ 14.95 € 21.69	3.40%

Creating running sums

A running sum is a cumulative total of values in a report. You use a running sum to calculate record-by-record or group-by-group subtotals.

On the right is an example of a running sum that you could include in the Books By Category report. It displays a cumulative total for the Cost values in the detail section.

Cost	Running Sum
£ 18.99	£ 18.99
£ 2.99	£ 21.98
£ 3.99	£ 25.97
£ 3.99	£ 29.96
£ 5.99	£ 35.95
£ 4.95	£ 40.90

For each record, the running sum calculation adds the value of the Cost field to the previous value of the running sum, so accumulating the total Cost values record-by-record.

To create this running sum, you would create a text box control that is bound to the BooksConfidential.Cost field and then set the control's *Running Sum* property to either *Over Group* or *Over All*.

To create a running sum that increases for each record, you put it in the detail section. To create a running sum that increases for each group, you put it in the group header or group footer section.

You can choose to reset the running sum at the start of each group or to accumulate the totals through the entire report.

Running sum
A cumulative total of values in a report.

Exercise 14.8: Creating running sums

In this exercise you will add three running sums to the group footer.

1) Open the Books By Category report in Design View and scroll to the Category Footer section.

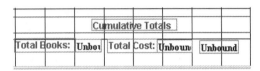

There are three unbound text box controls below the Cumulative Totals heading. These are where you will create the running sums.

2) You are going to use the TotalCostCumulativeGBP control (the second in the row) to calculate a running sum for the total cost of books in each group.

   – To calculate the total cost of books in a group, enter the following expression in the TotalCostCumulativeGBP control:

   =Sum([Cost])

   – To create a running sum that accumulates until the end of the report, select the *Over All* option in the control's *Running Sum* property (**Data** tab).

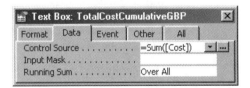

3) You are going to use the TotalCostCumulativeEuro control (the last in the row) to create an equivalent running sum in euros.

   – To calculate the total cost of books in a group in euros, enter the following expression in the TotalCostCumulativeEuro control:

   =Sum([Cost]*1.4508)

- To create a running sum that accumulates until the end of the report, select the *Over All* option in the control's *Running Sum* property.

4) You are going to use the TotalBooksCumulative control to calculate a running sum for the total number of books in each group.

   - To calculate the total number of books in a group, enter the following expression in the TotalBooksCumulative control:

   ```
   =Count(*)
   ```

   - To create a running sum that accumulates until the end of the report, select the *Over All* option in the control's *Running Sum* property.

5) Save the report and switch to Print Preview to see your running sums in action. Browse through the report from group to group and you will see that the running sum values accumulate through the report.

   Note that the running sum values for the last group represent the grand totals for the entire report, as shown here.

Cumulative Totals		
Total Books: 58	Total Cost £439.77	€ 638.02

Exercise 14.9: Repeating the grand total in the report footer

When a running sum is set to accumulate through the entire report, its final value represents the grand total for the report. In this exercise you will use this value to repeat the grand total in the report footer.

1) Open the Books By Category report in Design View and scroll to the report footer section.

2) The ReportTotalBooks text box control currently uses the Count() function to calculate the total number of books in the report. However, by the end of the report, the running sum in the TotalBooksCumulative control contains the same value.

3) To demonstrate this, change the expression in the ReportTotalBooks control to the following:

```
=[TotalBooksCumulative]
```

This simply references the value in the TotalBooksCumulative control.

4) Save the report and switch to Print Preview. Go to the report footer and you will see that the Total Books value is the same as before.

Numbering report items

In a report, it is often useful to number records and groups for easy reference. The running sum feature provides a very handy way to do this.

In the example here, a running sum is used to sequentially number book records in the detail section of a report.

1	ISBN 0-14-023171-4	A Good Man In Africa
2	ISBN 0-552-99702-1	A Walk in the Woods
3	ISBN 0-14-012670-8	Animal Farm
4	ISBN 0-14-014658-X	Brazzaville Beach
5	ISBN 0-552-99893-1	Chocolat

How do you create the running sum? Simply create an unbound text box control, set its *Control Source* property to '=1' and set its *Running Sum* property to either *Over Group* or *Over All*.

How does this work? The source value for the running sum is 1 and this is the running sum value for the first record. For each subsequent record, the running sum calculation adds its source value (that is, 1) to the current running sum value. This effectively increments the value of the control by 1 for each record.

Exercise 14.10: Number records in a report

In this exercise you will use a running sum to number the records in the Books By Category report.

1) Open the report in Design View and scroll to the detail section. There is a small, unbound text box control (named BookNumbers) at the start of this section. You will use this for the record numbers.

BookNumbers control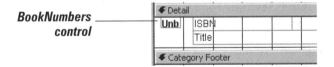

2) Enter the following expression in the BookNumbers control:

=1

3) To create a running sum that is reset to its source value at the start of each group, select the *Over Group* option in the control's *Running Sum* property.

4) Save the report and switch to Print Preview to see the record numbering. For example, the Science category in the report should now look as shown below.

Science

	Book	Cost		% of Group Cost
1	ISBN 0-451-16776-7 Feeling Good: The New Mood Therapy	£ 4.99	€7.24	12.83%
2	ISBN 1-85702-712-4 Galileo's Daughter	£ 10.40	€15.09	26.75%
3	ISBN 0-283-06145-6 New Guide to the Planets	£ 10.99	€15.94	28.27%
4	ISBN 0-00-219169-5 The Living Planet	Donated		
5	ISBN 0-297-81410-9 The Man in the Ice	£ 12.50	€18.14	32.15%

Working with page breaks

By default, report sections have no page breaks between them. Each section and group is displayed on the same page as the previous section or group, provided there is sufficient space.

The report header and footer, group header and footer, and detail sections all have a *Force New Page* property that you can use to create page breaks before and/or after the sections. The options available are:

- **None**. The section is displayed on the same page as the previous section.

- **Before Section**. The section is displayed at the top of a new page.

- **After Section**. The next section is displayed at the top of a new page.

- **Before & After**. The section is displayed at the top of a new page, and the next section is also displayed at the top of a new page.

Exercise 14.11: Creating page breaks between sections

In this exercise you will modify the Books By Category report so that individual groups and the report header and footer are all displayed on separate pages.

1) Open the Books By Category report in Design View.

2) Display the property sheet for the Report Header section and select the *AfterSection* option in the *Force New Page* property. This inserts a page break after the report header, so that it appears on a page by itself.

3) Display the property sheet for the Category Header section and select the *BeforeSection* option in its *Force New Page* property. This inserts a page break before each group header, so that each group is displayed on a separate page.

4) Select *Yes* in the section's *Repeat Section* property. If a group spans more than one page, this causes the group header to be repeated on those pages.

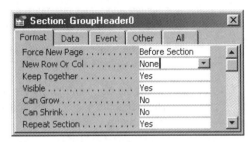

5) Display the property sheet for the report footer section and select the *BeforeSection* option in its *Force New Page* property.

This inserts a page break before the report footer, so that it is displayed on a page of its own.

6) Save the report and switch to Print Preview to see the result of your changes.

Omitting page headers and footers

If you include page header and footer sections in a report, they are displayed on all pages by default. However, when you are using the report header as a title page, for example, you may want to omit the page header and footer from that page. Similarly, you may want to omit the page header and footer from the page that displays the report footer.

You use the report's *Page Header* and *Page Footer* properties to do this. The options are:

- **All Pages**. Displays the page header or footer on all pages.

- **Not with Rpt Hdr**. Omits the page header or footer from the report header page.

- **Not with Rpt Ftr**. Omits the page header or footer from the report footer page.

- **Not with Rpt Hdr/Ftr**. Omits the page header or footer from both the report header and report footer pages.

Exercise 14.12: Omitting page headers/footers from the report header/footer pages

In this exercise you will modify the Books By Category report so that the page header and footer are omitted from the report header page and the page header is omitted from the report footer page.

1) Open the Books By Category report in Design View and display the report's property sheet.

2) Select the *Not with Rpt Hdr/Ftr* option in the *Page Header* property. This omits the page header from both the report header and report footer pages.

3) Select the *Not with Rpt Hdr* option in the *Page Footer* property. This omits the page footer from the report header page but not from the report footer page.

4) Save the report and switch to Print Preview to see the result of your changes.

Chapter 14: summary

Reports are the main means of organizing, grouping and summarizing database information in a format suitable for printing and for online review. As with forms, all information in a report is contained in *controls*. The same controls are available for reports as for forms, and you create and modify them in the same way and with the same tools.

Calculated report controls are controls that display the results of calculations on other controls or fields in a report. You create them in the same way that you create calculated controls in a form, and the same rules and guidelines generally apply.

To perform calculations on single records in a report, put the calculated controls in the detail section. To summarize values in a group with Access's aggregate functions, put the calculated controls in the group header or footer. To summarize values across the entire report, put the calculated controls in the report footer. To include a data value on all pages, put the calculated control in the page header or footer.

A *running sum* is a cumulative total of values in a report. To create a running sum that increases for each record, put it in the detail section. To create a running sum that increases for each group, put it in the group header or footer section. In both cases you use the calculated control's *Running Sum* property to create the running sum.

You can also use a running sum to number records in a group and to number groups in a report.

The report header and footer, group header and footer, and detail sections all have a *Force New Page* property that you can use to create page breaks before and/or after the sections. The report itself has *Page Header* and *Page Footer* properties that you can use to omit the page header and footer from the pages that display the report header and/or report footer.

Chapter 14: quick quiz

Q1	True or false – aggregate functions cannot reference calculated controls.
A.	True.
B.	False.

Q2	Where do you create calculations that summarize group values?
A.	Detail section.
B.	Group header section.
C.	Group footer section.
D.	Report footer section.

Q3	Where do you create calculations that summarize values for an entire report?
A.	Detail section.
B.	Group header section.
C.	Report header section.
D.	Report footer section.

Q4	You can use a running sum to …
A.	Number records sequentially within a group.
B.	Display a cumulative, record-by-record total for a value in a report.
C.	Number groups sequentially through an entire report.
D.	Display a cumulative, group-by-group total for a value in a report.

Q5	To display each group on a separate page, you …
A.	Set the group header's *Force New Page* property to *Before Section*.
B.	Set the group footer's *Force New Page* property to *After Section*.
C.	Set the page header's *Force New Page* property to *Before & After*.
D.	Set the report header's *Force New Page* property to *Before & After*.

Q6	True or false – expressions in calculated report controls must start with an equal to (=) symbol.
A.	True.
B.	False.

Answers

1: A, **2**: B and C, **3**: C and D, **4**: All, **5**: A and B, **6**: A.

15

Macros

In this chapter

Macros provide a simple means of automating common database tasks. You can use them to automatically perform tasks that you repeat frequently and to make your database objects work together.

In this chapter, you will learn how to create macros and how to attach them to forms, reports and controls.

New skills

At the end of this chapter you should be able to:

- Create a macro
- Run a macro
- Attach macros to controls, forms and reports

New words

In this chapter you will meet the following terms:

- Macro
- Event

Exercise file

In this chapter you will work with the following Access file:

- Chp15_VillageLibrary_Database

Syllabus reference

In this chapter you will cover the following items of the ECDL Advanced Database Syllabus:

- **AM5.5.1.1**: Record a simple macro (e.g. close a form).
- **AM5.5.1.2**: Run a macro.
- **AM5.5.1.3**: Assign/attach a macro to a form, report, control.

About macros

A macro consists of a sequence of one or more database actions that can be triggered automatically or executed with a single command. A typical macro is one that opens a form or prints a report. But why create a macro to perform such a simple action?

The power of macros lies is their ability to run automatically in response to events that occur on forms, reports and controls. For example, a macro that simply opens the Maintain Members form is not very useful by itself. But, if it runs automatically when you click a command button in the Process Loans form, it becomes a useful tool for integrating the two forms.

In the exercises in this chapter you will add macros to the Process Loans form that you created in Chapter 13. A finished copy of this form is available in the Chp15_VillageLibrary_Database database under the name ProcessLoansFinishedVersion. Open that form now in Form View.

You can see that the main form has four command buttons, each of which triggers a macro. Click each command button in turn to see what happens.

- The **View Member** button displays the Maintain Members form for the currently selected member. If you change and save the member's details in the Maintain Members form, the changes are automatically reflected in the Process Loans form.

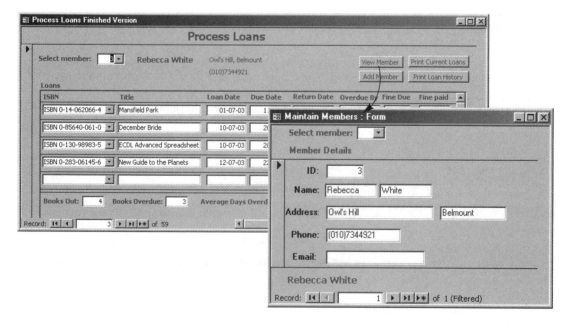

- The **Add Member** button opens the Maintain Members form at a new record, ready for you to enter details of a new member.

- The **Print Current Loans** button runs a report that lists the selected member's current loans. You can then print the report.

- The **Print Loan History** button runs a report that lists the selected member's past loans. You can then print the report.

With each of these examples, clicking a command button is the event that triggers execution of the macro. But there are many other events that can trigger macros, including opening and closing a form or report, moving from one record to another in a form, updating data in a form, deleting data in a form, and moving the focus to a particular form control.

> ### Macro
> *A sequence of one or more database actions that can be triggered automatically or executed with a single command.*

> ### Event
> *An action that occurs on a form, report or control and that can trigger execution of a macro.*

Creating a macro

Unlike Microsoft Office applications such as Word and Excel, Access does not have a facility for recording macros. Instead, you create macros manually in the Macro window, as shown here.

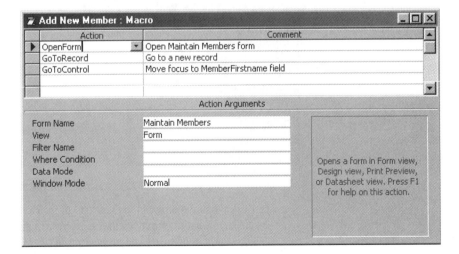

- In the *Action* column, you specify the actions you want the macro to perform, in the order you want them performed. The down arrow in an *Action* cell displays a list of actions and you select the action you want from this list.

- In the *Action Arguments* section of the window you specify the arguments for each action – that is, any additional information required to carry out the action. For example, an *OpenForm* action needs to know the name of the form to open and a *GoToRecord* action needs to know which record to go to.

- In the *Comment* column, you enter a description of each action. This is optional, but helps you to understand exactly what a macro does without having to browse through all its actions and arguments.

- A help message to the right of the action arguments provides help for the currently selected action or argument. For further help on the action or argument, press **F1**.

Exercise 15.1: Creating a macro that opens a form

In this exercise you will create a simple macro that opens the Maintain Members form.

1) Open the Chp15_VillageLibrary_Database database.

2) Click *Macros* in the *Objects* list in the Database window and click the **New** button on the window's toolbar. This opens the Macro window.

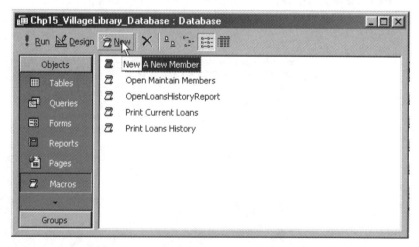

3) Click the down arrow in the first row of the *Action* column. This displays a list of all actions that a macro can perform. Select the *OpenForm* action. The arguments for the *OpenForm* action are now displayed in the *Action Arguments* section of the window.

4) Click the down arrow in the *Form Name* argument. This displays a list of all forms in the current database. Select *Maintain Members*, as this is the form that you want the macro to open.

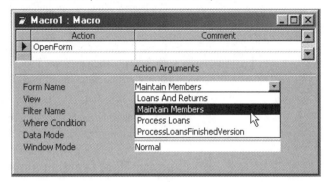

5) You can leave the other arguments as they are. The *View* argument specifies the View in which to open the form; the default is Form View. The *Where* argument allows you to specify which records the form displays. You will learn how to use this argument in a later exercise.

6) Close the Macro window, and when prompted to save the macro, click **Yes**. When prompted for a name for the macro, enter OpenMaintainMembersForm and click **OK**.

7) The new macro is now listed in the Database window. To run the macro, simply double-click it. The Maintain Members form automatically opens.

Exercise 15.2: Creating a macro that runs a report

The Current Loans By Member report lists all current loans, grouped by member. In this exercise you will create a simple macro that runs this report.

1) Click *Macros* in the *Objects* list in the Database window and click the **New** button on the window's toolbar. This opens the Macro window.

2) Click the down arrow in the first row of the *Action* column and select the *OpenReport* action. The arguments for this action are now displayed in the *Action Arguments* section of the window.

3) Click the down arrow in the *Report Name* argument. This displays a list of all reports in the current database. Select *Current Loans By Member*.

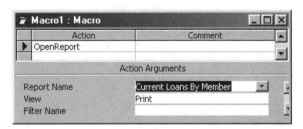

4) Click the down arrow in the *View* argument. This lists the views in which you can open the report. The *Print* option sends the report directly to the printer; the *Print Preview* option opens the report in Print Preview; and the *Design* option opens the report in Design View. Select the *Print Preview* option.

5) Close the Macro window, and when prompted to save the macro, click **Yes**. When prompted for a name for the macro, enter OpenCurrentLoansReport and click **OK**.

6) The new macro is now listed in the Database window. To run the macro, simply double-click it. The Open Current Loans By Member report automatically opens in Print Preview.

Exercise 15.3: Creating a macro that opens a blank record in a form

In this exercise you will create a macro that displays a blank record in the Maintain Members form, ready for you to enter a new record. The macro consists of several actions.

1) Open the Macro window for a new macro.

2) In the first row of the *Action* column, select the *OpenForm* action.

3) In the *Form Name* argument for this action, select *Maintain Members*.

4) In the second row of the *Action* column, select the *GoToRecord* action. With this action you can specify which record you want the macro to display in the form.

5) The arguments for the *GoToRecord* action include the type of object that contains the record you want to go to and the name of the object. In this case, there is no need to fill these two arguments; the previous action opens the Maintain Members form and this is taken as the default object.

6) The *Record* argument provides a list of options for specifying the record you want to go to in the form. Select the *New* option. This displays a blank record, the same as when you select the **New Record** button in the form itself.

7) In the third row of the *Action* column, select the *GoToControl* action. With this action you can specify which control you want the macro to put the focus on in the form.

8) There is only one argument for the *GoToControl* action – the control name. In the Maintain Members form, the first field that must be filled manually is the MemFirstname field (the MemID is generated automatically by Access). So enter MemFirstname in the *Control Name* argument.

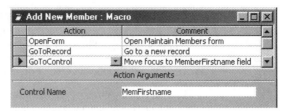

9) Close the Macro window and save the macro with the name AddNewMember.

10) Run the macro. The Maintain Members form opens automatically at a new record, with the focus on the MemFirstname field ready for you to enter details of a new member.

Attaching macros to control events

The power of macros lies in their ability to run in response to form, report, and control events. Every form control has a variety of associated events. These events are listed on the **Event** tab of the control's property sheet. Report controls do not have associated events.

Open the Process Loans form now in Design View and display the property sheet for the Print Loan History command button control. Then click the **Event** tab to see the list of control events. These include mouse events, keyboard key events and focus events.

For example, the *On Click* event occurs when you click the control, the *On Dbl Click* event occurs when you double-click the control, and the *On Got Focus* event occurs when the focus moves to the control.

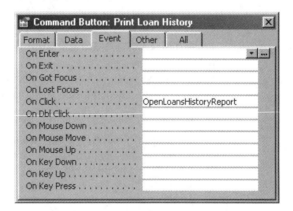

To attach a macro to a control, you simply click the event that you want to trigger the macro and then select the macro from the event's drop-down list.

In the case of the Print Loan History command button, the OpenLoansHistoryReport macro has been attached to the *On Click* event. This means that the macro runs automatically when you click the command button.

Exercise 15.4: Attaching macros to command buttons

In this exercise you will attach macros to the View Member and Add Member command buttons in the Process Loans form.

1) Open the Process Loans form in Design View.

2) Display the property sheet for the View Member command button control and click the **Event** tab to display the control's event properties.

3) In Exercise 15.1 you created the OpenMaintainMembersForm macro. To run this macro when a user clicks the View Member command button control, you attach the macro to the control's *On Click* event. To do this, click the *On Click* event and select *OpenMaintainMembersForm* from its drop-down list.

4) Now display the property sheet for the Add Member command button control and click the **Event** tab to display the control's event properties.

5) In Exercise 15.3 you created the AddNewMember macro. To run this macro when a user clicks the Add Member command button control, you attach the macro to the control's *On Click* event. To do this, click the *On Click* event and select *AddNewMember* from its drop-down list.

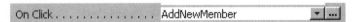

6) Save the form and switch to Form View to try out the command buttons. Note that clicking the **View Member** button opens the Maintain Members form. It does not, however, automatically display the record for the member currently selected in the Process Loans form. You will learn how to do this in a later exercise.

Exercise 15.5: Creating a command button that runs a macro

In this exercise you will create a new command button that runs the OpenCurrentLoansReport macro you created in Exercise 15.2.

1) Open the Process Loans form in Design View.

2) Make sure that the **Control Wizards** button in the toolbox is *not* selected.

Command Button tool

3) Click the **Command Button** tool in the toolbox and then click in the form where you want the top left corner of the control to be positioned. This creates a new command button control, as shown here. By default, the name of the control is used as the button's caption.

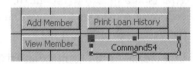

ECDL Advanced Databases

4) Display the property sheet for the new command button and enter Print Current Loans in the *Caption* property. This specifies the text to display on the button.

5) Click the **Event** tab to display the control's event properties.

6) To attach the OpenCurrentLoansReport macro to the control's *On Click* event, click that event and select OpenCurrentLoansReport from its drop-down list.

7) Save the form and switch to Form View to try out the new command button. When you click the button, the Current Loans By Member report is automatically run. It does not, however, automatically display the records for the member currently selected in the Process Loans form. You will learn how to do this in Exercise 15.6.

Synchronizing two forms or a form and a report

The **Print Loan History** button in the Process Loans form runs the Loans History By Member report and displays just the records for the member currently selected in the Process Loans form. To see how this is done, open the form in Design View and display the property sheet for the Print Loan History button.

The OpenLoansHistoryReport macro is attached to the control's *On Click* event. Take a look at that macro now by clicking the **Build** button at the right of the *On Click* property box.

 —— **Build button**

The macro consists of a single *OpenReport* action that opens the Loans History By Member report. The following expression is entered in the *Where Condition* argument for that action (click the argument and press **Shift+F2** to open the expression in the *Zoom* window):

[MemID]=[Forms]![Process Loans]![SelectMember]

This tells the macro to select only records where the MemID value equals the value in the SelectMember control in the Process Loans form.

You can use a similar expression whenever you want to open a form or report and restrict its records to those that match the value of a control on another form. The syntax for the expression is:

[*field*]=Forms![*form*]![*control*]

where *field* is the name of a field in the record source of the form/report you want to open, *form* is the name of another form, and *control* is the name of a control on the other form.

You can close the Macro window now. Do not save any changes you may have made.

Exercise 15.6: Synchronizing forms and reports

In this exercise you will modify the OpenMaintainMembersForm and OpenCurrentLoansReport macros so that they display only records related to the member currently selected in the Process Loans form.

1) Open the Process Loans form in Design View.

2) Display the *On Click* event property for the View Member command button. Click in the property box and then click its **Build** button. This displays the OpenMaintainMembersForm macro in the Macro window.

3) Click the *Where Condition* argument for the *OpenForm* action and press **Shift+F2**. This opens the *Zoom* dialog box. Enter the following expression and then click **OK** to close the *Zoom* dialog box:

   `[MemID]=[Forms]![Process Loans]![SelectMember]`

4) Close the Macro window, saving the macro as you do.

5) Now repeat steps 2 to 4 for the Print Current Loans command button.

6) Save the form and switch to Form View to see the result of your changes.

   For example, display the record for Rebecca White in the Process Loans form and then click the **Print Current Loans** button. This runs the Current Loans By Member report and displays the current loans for Rebecca White only.

Attaching macros to form and report events

Clicking a command button in a form is one of the most common ways of running a macro. However, you can also attach a macro to form/report events such as the opening or closing of a form/report and the insertion or deletion of data in a form.

Exercise 15.7: Attaching a macro to a form event

In this exercise you will create a macro that runs automatically when the Process Loans form opens. The macro will display a message that tells users how to use the form.

1) Open the Macro window for a new macro.

2) In the first row of the *Action* column, select the *MsgBox* action.

3) Click the *Message* argument for this action and type the following text:

   This form displays the current loans for the member you select in the Select Member combo box. You can then add, delete, and edit loan records.

4) Close the Macro window and save the macro with the name ProcessLoansMessage.

5) Open the Process Loans form in Design View and display the property sheet for the form itself (double-click the form selector).

6) Click the **Event** tab to display the form events. Click the *On Open* event and select ProcessLoansMessage from its drop-down list.

7) Close the form, saving it as you do.

8) Now open the form in Form View from the Database window. Access displays your message and then opens the form when you click **OK**.

Exercise 15.8: Attaching a macro to a report event

In this exercise you will create a macro that runs automatically when you open the Current Loans By Member report. The macro will display a message that tells users about the report.

1) Open the Macro window for a new macro.

2) In the first row of the *Action* column, select the *MsgBox* action.

3) Click the *Message* argument for this action and type the following text:

```
This report lists current loans only. To view
non-current loans, run the Loans History By
Member report, or click the Print Loan History
button in the Process Loans form.
```

4) Close the Macro window and save the macro with the name CurrentLoansMessage.

5) Open the Current Loans By Member report in Design View and display the property sheet for the report itself (double-click the report selector).

6) Click the **Event** tab to display the report events. Click the *On Open* event and select CurrentLoansMessage from its drop-down list.

7) Close the report, saving it as you do.

8) Now open the report in Print Preview from the Database window. Access displays your message and then runs the report when you click **OK**.

Chapter 15: summary

A *macro* consists of a sequence of one or more database actions that can be triggered automatically or executed with a single command. The power of macros lies in their ability to run automatically in response to *events* that occur on forms, reports and controls.

In a form, *command button* controls are often used to trigger macros. You can also run a macro when the form opens or closes and when data in the form changes. You cannot attach macros to report controls, but you can run a macro when the report opens or closes, for example.

The **Event** tab on the property sheet for a form, report or control lists all the events to which you can attach a macro. You attach a macro to an event by clicking the event in the property sheet and then selecting the macro from the event's drop-down list.

You create macros in the *Macro* window. In the *Action* column you select the actions you want the macro to perform. In the *Action Arguments* section, you specify any additional information that the macro needs to perform these actions. For actions that open forms and reports, you can use the *Where Condition* argument to restrict the records displayed to those that match the value of a control on another form.

Chapter 15: quick quiz

Q1	Which of these events can trigger a macro?
A.	Opening a form.
B.	Double-clicking a form control.
C.	Opening a query.
D.	Closing a report.

Q2	Which of these macro actions would you use to open a report in Print Preview?
A.	SelectObject.
B.	PrintOut.
C.	OpenReport.
D.	OutputTo.

Q3	To run a macro when a form opens, to which form event would you attach the macro?
A.	On Activate.
B.	On Got Focus.
C.	On Open.
D.	On Current.

Q4	To view the definition of a macro that is attached to a command button . . .
A.	Run the macro from the Database window.
B.	Select the macro in the Database window and click the **Design** button on the window's toolbar.
C.	Open the form that contains the command button, display the button's event properties, click the event with which the macro is associated, and then select the macro from the event's drop-down list.
D.	Open the form that contains the command button, display the button's event properties, click the event with which the macro is associated, and then click the **Build** button for that event.

Q5	To run a macro when a report closes, to which event would you attach the macro?
A.	On Deactivate.
B.	On Unload.
C.	On Lost Focus.
D.	On Close.

Q6	Which of these *Where Condition* expressions restricts the records displayed by a report to those related to the record displayed in the Process Loans form?
A.	[MemID]=[Process Loans]![SelectMember]
B.	[MemID]=[Forms]![Process Loans]![SelectMember]
C.	[MemID]=[Forms]![Process Loans.SelectMember]
D.	[Reports]![MemID]=[Forms]![Process Loans]![SelectMember]

Answers

1: A, B, and D, 2: C, 3: C, 4: B and D, 5: D, 6: B.

16

Importing, linking and exporting data

With Access you aren't limited to working with data in a single Access database. You can import data from other Access databases and from other file formats, you can link to data in external sources, and you can export data in various formats for use in other applications.

In this chapter, you will learn how to import, link to and export data in a variety of file formats.

New skills

At the end of this chapter you should be able to:

- Import dBASE, Paradox, spreadsheet and text files into an Access database
- Import database objects from another Access database
- Link to external data
- Export data to dBASE, Paradox, spreadsheet and text files

New words

In this chapter you will meet the following terms:

- Import
- Link
- Export
- Delimited text file
- Fixed-width text file

Exercise files

In this chapter you will work with the following Access file:

- Chp16_VillageLibrary_Database

You will also work with the following non-Access files:

- MemPx (a Paradox table)
- MemDB (a dBASE table)
- LibraryExcel (an Excel workbook)

- ■ LoansTxt (a delimited text file)

- ■ MemTxt (a fixed-width text file)

All these files are located in the folder to which you copied the contents of the CD that accompanies this book.

Syllabus reference

In this chapter you will cover the following items of the ECDL Advanced Database Syllabus:

- ■ **AM5.6.1.1**: Import text, spreadsheet, csv, dBASE, Paradox files into a database.

- ■ **AM5.6.1.2**: Export data in spreadsheet, txt, dBASE and Paradox formats.

- ■ **AM5.6.1.3**: Link external data to a database.

About importing and linking data

Access provides two methods for working with data from external sources: *importing* and *linking*.

- ■ **Importing**. When you import data, it is copied from the source file and converted from its original format to a set of Access records. There is no ongoing connection between the source data and the data in Access – changes to one do not affect the other.

  You use this method of working with external data when you no longer need to work with the data in its original format.

- ■ **Linking**. When you link to external data, the data is not copied to your Access database. Instead, a connection is created between the external data and a table in Access, allowing you to view and work with the data in the source file from within Access. Changes you make to the data in Access are saved to the source file, and changes to the source file are reflected in your view of the data in Access.

  You use this method of working with external data when you need to share the data with users of a different database or application.

You can import and link to data from many different sources, including other Access databases, Paradox and dBASE database tables, spreadsheet files and text files.

Converts data from its original format and saves it to a new or existing Access table. There is no ongoing connection between the original data and the data in Access.

Creates a link to external data, allowing you to view and work with that data from within Access.

About exporting data

When you want to use data from an Access table or query in another application, you can export the data to a file format appropriate for that application. There is no ongoing connection between the data in Access and the exported data. Changes in one are not reflected in the other.

You can export data to a wide variety of file formats, including dBASE, Paradox, spreadsheet and text files.

Importing dBASE and Paradox tables

Both dBASE and Paradox are relational database applications. Paradox is part of the WordPerfect Office Suite from Corel. dBASE is a product of dBASE Inc.

All dBASE and Paradox tables are stored in separate table files, with the extensions .db (Paradox) and .dbf (dBASE). This means that you can import a single table to Access by importing the table file.

Exercise 16.1: Importing a Paradox table

In this exercise you will import a Paradox table to an Access database.

1) Open the Chp16_VillageLibrary_Database database.

2) Choose **File | Get External Data | Import**. This displays the *Import* dialog box.

3) In the *File of type* box, select the *Paradox* option. Then locate the MemPx file, select it, and click **Import**.

Select the file to import

Select the type of file to import

4) When the file has been successfully imported, a message to this effect is displayed. Click **OK** to close this message. Then click **Close** to close the *Import* dialog box.

5) In the Database window you can see that Access has created a new table named MemPx. If your database already contains a MemPx table, Access appends a number to the name to make it unique.

6) Open the MemPx table now in Datasheet View. You can see that it contains five records with similar fields to your own Members table.

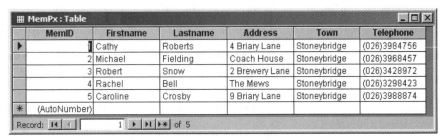

7) When you import data from any source, Access attempts to assign an appropriate data type and field size to the imported fields. However, you should always check these attributes to make sure that they meet your requirements.

Switch to Design View now to see the data types and field sizes that Access has assigned to the fields in the MemPx table. Then close the table.

You use almost exactly the same procedure to import a dBASE table. The only difference is that you select one of the dBASE file types in the *Import* dialog box instead of the Paradox file type. If you wish, you can try this with the MemDB file, which is in dBASE IV format.

Once you have imported a table, you can use an append query to add the new records to an existing table if you want (see Chapter 7). For example, to append the records in the MemPx table to the Members table, you would use the append query shown here.

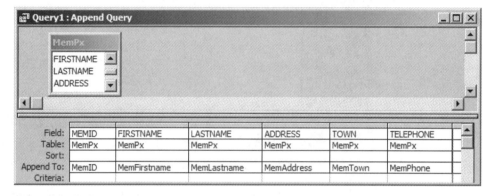

Importing spreadsheet data

You can import spreadsheet data from both Microsoft Excel and Lotus 1-2-3. The procedure is the same in both cases.

You can create a new table with the imported data or you can append the data to an existing table. However, in the latter case, the column headings must exactly match the field names in the Access table.

Preparing spreadsheet data

Before importing spreadsheet data, make sure that it is in a format suitable for conversion to an Access table:

- The data must be in tabular format, with each record on a separate row, and each field in a separate column. All data in a column must have the same data type. You can include column headings – Access converts these to field names.

- If a spreadsheet includes additional information such as totals and titles, you must either delete these from the spreadsheet or create a named range that includes only the data to be imported. A *named range* is a set of worksheet cells to which a name has been assigned.

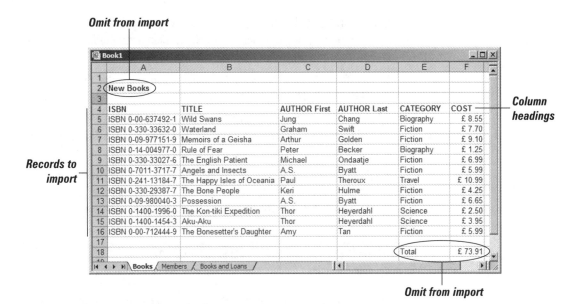

Omit from import

Column headings

Records to import

Omit from import

- When importing from Excel (version 5.0 or later), you can import data from any worksheet within a workbook. When importing data from other multiple-spreadsheet sources, you must save each spreadsheet as a separate file before importing data from them.

Importing an Excel worksheet

The `LibraryExcel` file is an Excel workbook that contains book, member and loan records suitable for importing into the Village Library database. Open that workbook now and take a look at the contents of the Books worksheet.

The records include information relevant to three different tables in the Village Library database: Books, BooksConfidential and Authors. This means that you cannot import the records directly into an existing table. Instead, you must import the records to a new table and then use one or more append queries to add selected fields to the other tables.

Exercise 16.2: Importing an Excel worksheet

In this exercise you will import the Books worksheet from the LibraryExcel workbook to the Chp16_VillageLibrary_Database database.

1) Switch to the Database window and choose **File | Get External Data | Import**.

2) In the *Import* dialog box, select *Microsoft Excel* as the file type, locate and select the LibraryExcel file, and click **Import**. This starts the *Import Spreadsheet Wizard*.

3) In the first page of the wizard you choose the worksheet or named range that you want to import. For this exercise, make sure that the *Show Worksheets* option and the *Books* worksheet are selected. Then click **Next**.

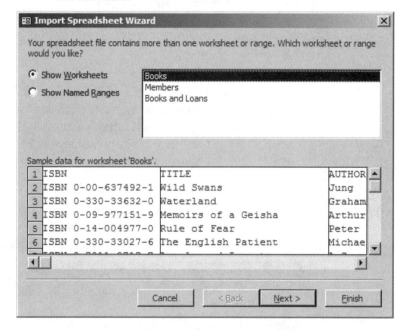

4) In the next page of the wizard, you specify whether or not the first row in the spreadsheet contains column headings. Select the *First Row Contains Column Headings* option and click **Next**.

5) When asked where you want to store the imported records, select the *In a New Table* option and click **Next**.

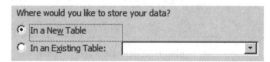

6) In the next page of the wizard you can specify various settings for the fields you are importing. The *Field Options* section of the dialog box displays the settings for the currently selected column.

Click in a
column to
select it

For this exercise, you do not need to make any changes to these options. Just click **Next**.

If you want to change the field settings, you can use the *Field Options* as follows:

- Use the *Field Name* option to change the name of the field to which the selected column will be imported.

- Use the *Data Type* option (when available) to change the data type for the field.

- Use the *Indexed* option to specify index settings for the field.

- Use the *Do not import field (Skip)* option to prevent a particular column being imported. This is particularly useful for omitting blank columns that may be included in a spreadsheet to separate other columns.

7) In the next page of the wizard you can specify a primary key for the new table. The records you are importing relate to three tables in your database and need to be appended to those tables at a later stage. So the table created to store the data is for temporary use only and does not need a primary key. Select the *No primary key* option and click **Next**.

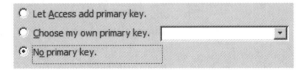

If you select the *Let Access add primary key* option instead, Access generates an AutoNumber primary key field for the table. If you select the *Choose my own primary key* option, you can select a primary key from the associated drop-down list.

8) The last page of the wizard prompts you for a name for the new table. The default is the name of the worksheet or named range being imported. Change this to BooksExcel and click **Finish**.

Import to Table:
BooksExcel

9) When the worksheet has been successfully imported, a message to this effect is displayed. Click **OK** to close this message.

10) In the Database window you can see that Access has created a new table named BooksExcel. Open that table now in Datasheet View. It contains all the records from the Books worksheet.

11) Switch to Design View and you can see that Access has assigned a Text data type to the first five fields, and has set their field size to 255 characters. It has also correctly assigned a Currency data type to the Cost field. When you have finished, close the table.

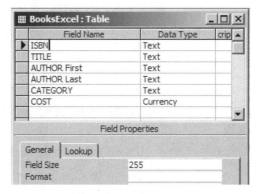

Importing text files

You can import data from text files provided that the data is organized and formatted appropriately:

- Each record must be on a separate line and the line must end with a paragraph break.

- All records must include the same fields and each field must contain the same type of data in all records.

- The file must be saved as a text file. The text file types to which you can save a file depend on the application you are using. The following are all appropriate for files you want to import to Access: Plain Text, Text Only, Text Document.

In order to convert data in a text file to a database table, Access needs to know where each field begins and ends. So the text file must be in one of the following formats:

- **Delimited text file**. Fields are separated by a special delimiter character such as a comma, tab or semicolon. Delimited files are often referred to as comma-delimited files or CSV (comma-separated values) files.

```
"ISBN 0-09-980040-3",2,01-07-03,
"ISBN 0-00-712444-9",6,03-06-31,
"ISBN 0-1400-1996-0",1,07-07-03,
```

- **Fixed-width text file**. Fields are aligned in columns. Spaces are inserted to fill out the fields so that they are the same width in all rows.

```
1··Cathy·····Roberts···4·Briary·Lane··Stoney·Bridge··(026)3679288¶
2··Michael···Fielding··Coach·House····Stoney·Bridge··(026)3388676¶
3··Robert····Snow······2·Brewery·Lane·Stoney·Bridge··(026)3847100¶
```

Preparing delimited text files

Before importing data from a delimited text file, make sure that the data is organized and formatted appropriately:

- Use the same delimiter character throughout the file – typically a comma.

- Enclose text values within double quotes.

- If you are including field names, enter them on the first row.

The LoansTxt file is a delimited text file that contains loan records suitable for appending to the Loans table in your database. Open the file now and take a look at its contents. You can open it in Notepad, WordPad, Microsoft Word, or some other word processing application.

Field names

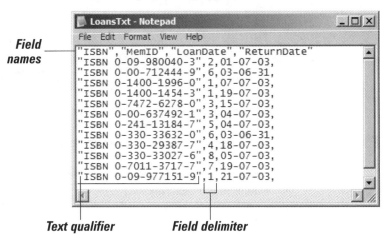

Text qualifier   *Field delimiter*

Note that each record is on a line of its own, with a paragraph break at the end of the line. The delimiter character is a comma (,). Text values, including the field headings, are enclosed within double quotes. Note also that the ReturnDate field is blank in all records.

Importing delimited text files

Exercise 16.3: Importing a delimited text file

In this exercise you will import the LoansTxt file and append its records to the Loans table.

1) Switch to the Database window and choose **File | Get External Data | Import**.

2) In the *Import* dialog box, select *Text Files* as the file type, locate and select the LoansTxt file, and click **Import**. This starts the *Import Text Wizard*.

3) The wizard first prompts you for the file type – that is, *Delimited* or *Fixed Width*. Make sure that the *Delimited* option is selected and click **Next**.

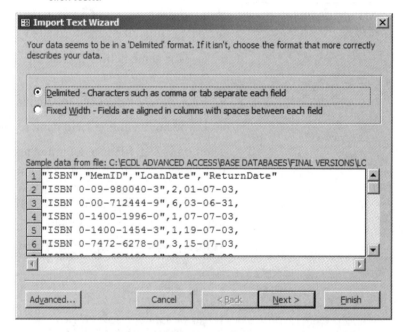

4) Next the wizard prompts you for information about the file format. Typically the wizard automatically selects the appropriate options, based on the contents of the text file. Make sure that *Comma* is selected as the field delimiter and that double quotes (") are selected as the text qualifier. Then select the *First Row Contains Field Names* option and click **Next**.

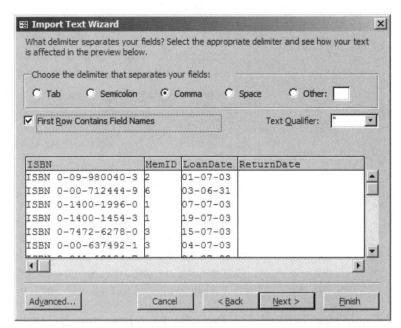

5) Next the wizard asks where you want to store the imported data. Select the *In an Existing Table* option and select the Loans table from the drop-down list. Then click **Next**.

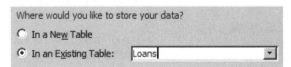

6) The last page of the wizard displays the name of the table to which the data will be imported. Make sure that this is the Loans table and then click **Finish**.

7) When the records have been successfully imported, a message to this effect is displayed. Click **OK** to close this message.

8) Now open the Loans table in Datasheet View and check that the records have been imported correctly. When you have finished, close the table.

Preparing fixed-width text files

Before importing data from a fixed-width text file, make sure that the data is organized and formatted appropriately:

- Access cannot import field names from a fixed-width text file. So, if the first row contains field names, delete that row.

- Make sure that each field is the same width in all rows. You need to apply a monospaced font (such as Courier New) to see this. If necessary, add or delete spaces in order to make fields the same width.

The MemTxt file is a fixed-width text file that contains several member records. Open the file now and take a look at its contents. You can open it in Notepad, WordPad, Microsoft Word, or some other word processing application.

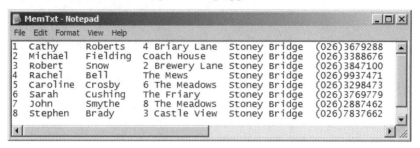

Note that each record is on a line of its own, with a paragraph break at the end of the line, and each field starts at the same position in every row. Spaces are used to fill out the fields so that they are the same width in each row.

Importing fixed-width text files

Exercise 16.4: Importing a fixed-width text file

In this exercise you will import the MemTxt file to a new table in your Access database.

1) Switch to the Database window and choose **File | Get External Data | Import**.

2) In the *Import* dialog box, select *Text Files* as the file type, locate and select the MemTxt file, and click **Import**. This starts the *Import Text Wizard*.

3) The wizard first prompts you for the file type. Make sure that the *Fixed-Width* option is selected and then click **Next**.

4) On the next page of the wizard, the records being imported are displayed with arrowed lines indicating the field breaks. The wizard makes a best guess at where field breaks occur, based on the contents of the source file.

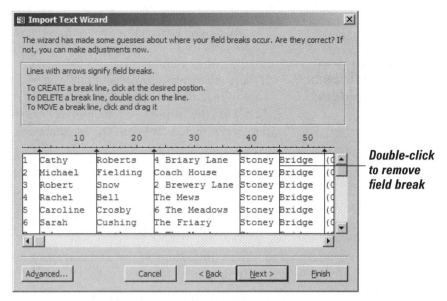

Import Text Wizard

The wizard has made some guesses about where your field breaks occur. Are they correct? If not, you can make adjustments now.

Lines with arrows signify field breaks.

To CREATE a break line, click at the desired postion.
To DELETE a break line, double click on the line.
To MOVE a break line, click and drag it

	10	20	30	40	50

1	Cathy	Roberts	4 Briary Lane	Stoney	Bridge	(C
2	Michael	Fielding	Coach House	Stoney	Bridge	(C
3	Robert	Snow	2 Brewery Lane	Stoney	Bridge	(C
4	Rachel	Bell	The Mews	Stoney	Bridge	(C
5	Caroline	Crosby	6 The Meadows	Stoney	Bridge	(C
6	Sarah	Cushing	The Friary	Stoney	Bridge	(C

[Advanced...]   [Cancel]   [< Back]   [Next >]   [Finish]

Double-click to remove field break

As you can see, the town name has been split into two fields. To remove the field break between the two parts of the name, double-click on the arrowed line. Then click **Next**.

5) Next the wizard asks you where you want to store the imported data. Select the *In a New Table* option and click **Next**.

6) In the next page of the wizard you can specify various settings for the fields you are importing. For this exercise, change the field names as follows:

Default name	New name
Field1	MemID
Field2	MemFirstname
Field3	MemLastname
Field4	MemAddress
Field5	MemTown
Field6	MemPhone

To change a field name, click the field in the lower part of the page and then type the new name in the *Field Name* box. When finished entering the new names, click **Next**.

7) In the next page of the wizard you can specify a primary key for the new table. Select the *No primary key* option and then click **Next**.

8) The last page of the wizard displays the name of the table to which the data will be imported. The default name is the name of the text file. Click **Finish** to create a new table with this name.

9) When the data has been successfully imported, a message to this effect is displayed. Click **OK** to close this message.

10) Now open the `MemTxt` table in Datasheet View and check that the records have been imported correctly. When you have finished, close the table.

Importing Access database objects

If there are database objects in one Access database that you want to include in another Access database, you can import them with the **Import** command. Here are some tips for importing objects from an Access database:

- When importing a table that contains lookup fields, also import the tables to which those fields refer (unless the tables already exist in your current database).

- When importing a form or report that is based on a query, import the query also.

- When importing a form that contains a subform, import the subform also.

- When importing a form that references other queries, forms, reports or macros, import those objects also.

Exercise 16.5: Importing a form from another Access database

In this exercise you will import the ProcessLoansFinishedVersion form from the `Chp15_VillageLibrary_Database` file.

1) With the `Chp16_VillageLibrary_Database` open in Access, switch to the Database window and choose **File | Get External Data | Import**.

2) In the *Import* dialog box, select *Microsoft Access* as the file type, locate and select the `Chp15_VillageLibrary_Database` file, and click **Import**. This displays the *Import Objects* dialog box.

3) Switch to the **Forms** tab and click the ProcessLoansFinishedVersion form to select it.

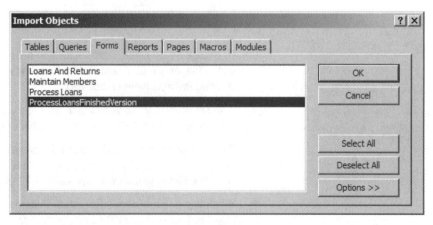

This form has a number of associated forms, queries, reports and macros, as follows:

- *Forms*: Loans and Returns; Maintain Members.

- *Query*: BookReturns.

- *Reports*: Current Loans by Member; Loans History by Member.

- *Macros*: Add a New Member; Open Maintain Members; Print Current Loans; Print Loans History; CurrentLoansMessage.

You need to import these objects also if you want to be able to use the ProcessLoansFinishedVersion form properly. So, switch to the relevant tabs and click each object to select it. When you have finished, click **OK**. Access now imports all the selected objects.

4) Open the ProcessLoansFinishedVersion form and check that it is working correctly. If any of its associated objects are missing, you can simply repeat the import operation for those objects. When you have finished, close the form.

Linking to an Excel worksheet

You can link to data in other Access databases, in Paradox and dBASE tables, in spreadsheet files, and in text files. The procedures are similar to those for importing data from those file types.

However, when you link to external data, you cannot change the table structure from within your database. And, depending on the source application, there may be some limitations to the operations you can perform on the data.

Exercise 16.6: Linking to an Excel worksheet

In this exercise you will create a link to the Books worksheet in the LibraryExcel workbook.

1) Switch to the Database window and choose **File | Get External Data | Link Files**.

2) In the *Link* dialog box, select *Microsoft Excel* as the file type, locate and select the `LibraryExcel` file, and click **Link**. This starts the *Link Spreadsheet Wizard*.

3) In the first page of the wizard, make sure that the *Show Worksheets* option and the *Books* worksheet are selected. Then click **Next**.

4) In the next page of the wizard select the *First Row Contains Column Headings* option and click **Next**.

5) The last page of the wizard displays the name that will be given to the linked table in Access. The default is the name of the worksheet. Change this to BooksExcelLinked and then click **Finish**.

6) When Access has successfully created the linked table, a message to this effect is displayed. Click **OK** to close this message.

7) BooksExcelLinked is now listed as a table in the Database window. As you can see, the table has a special icon consisting of the Excel logo preceded by an arrow. All linked tables in Access have this type of icon – an image that represents the source application preceded by an arrow, as shown below:

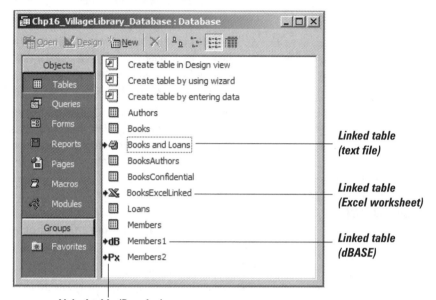

Linked table
(text file)

Linked table
(Excel worksheet)

Linked table
(dBASE)

Linked table (Paradox)

Open the BooksExcelLinked table in Datasheet View. As you can see, it looks the same as any other table in Access and you can base queries, forms, and reports on it in the normal way. However, the records are stored in the source file and not in your Access database. Also, you cannot make any changes to the table in Design View.

8) To see how linked tables work, open the BooksExcelLinked table in Datasheet View and make some changes to the data – for example, add a new record and change some values in existing records. Notice that you cannot delete a record here. When you have finished, close the table.

9) Now open the LibraryExcel workbook in Excel. Notice that the changes you made in Access have been saved to the workbook file and are included in the Books worksheet.

In the same way, any changes (including record deletions) that you make in Excel are included in the BooksExcelLinked table in Access the next time you open it. When you have finished viewing or updating the records in Excel, close the application.

Exporting data

You can export Access tables and queries to Paradox, dBASE, spreadsheet and text files. You use the same procedure for exporting to Paradox, dBASE and spreadsheet files. For text files, you use the *Export Text Wizard*, which enables you to choose a delimited or fixed-length format, and to specify various settings for the selected format.

Exercise 16.7: Exporting to an Excel spreadsheet

In this exercise you will export data from an Access query to an Excel worksheet.

1) Click *Queries* in the *Objects* list in the Database window and select the ExportQuery query. This query is a version of the LoansExtended query that you have worked with in previous chapters.

2) Choose **File | Export**. This displays the *Export Query* dialog box.

3) Select one of the *Excel* options in the *File of type* box, enter BookLoans as the destination file name, navigate to the folder where you want to save the file, and then click **Save**. The query data is now saved to an Excel workbook named BookLoans.

4) Open the BookLoans workbook in Excel. You can see that the query data has been copied to a worksheet with the same name as the query.

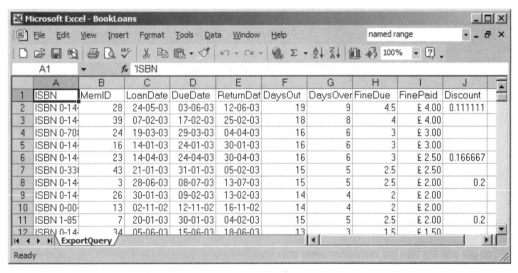

You can now work with the data in Excel. There is no connection between the data in Excel and the data in Access, so any changes you make affect only the Excel worksheet.

You use almost exactly the same procedure to export data to a dBASE or Paradox table. The only difference is that you select a dBASE or Paradox file type in the *Export* dialog box.

Exercise 16.8: Exporting to a text file

In this exercise you will export data from the Members table to a delimited text file.

1) In the Database window, click the Members table and then choose **File | Export**. This displays the *Export Table* dialog box.

2) Select *Text Files* in the *File of Type* box, enter MembersDelimited as the name of the destination file, navigate to the folder where you want to save the file, and then click **Save**. This starts the *Export Text Wizard*.

3) In the first page of the wizard you specify whether you want to export to a delimited text tile or to a fixed-width text file. Select each option in turn and see how this affects the format of the records displayed in the lower part of the window.

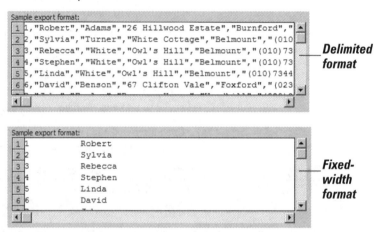

Delimited format

Fixed-width format

4) You are going to export the table to a delimited text file, so select this option and click **Next**.

5) In the next page of the wizard, you can change the field delimiter and text qualifier. You can also choose whether or not to export the field names with the records. Select the *Include Field Names on First Row* option and click **Finish**.

6) The wizard now creates a delimited text file named MembersDelimited and displays a confirmation message. Click **OK** to close this message.

7) Now open the MembersDelimited file to see the result of the export operation. You can open the file in Notepad, WordPad or Microsoft Word, for example.

ECDL Advanced Databases

Chapter 16:
summary

Access provides two methods for working with data from external sources: *importing* and *linking*.

When you *import* data, it is copied from the source file and converted from its original format to a set of Access records. There is no ongoing connection between the source data and the data in Access – changes to one do not affect the other. You use this method of working with external data when you no longer need to work with the data in its original format.

When you *link* to external data, a connection is created between the external data and a table in Access, allowing you to view and work with the data in the source file from within Access. Changes you make to the data in Access are saved to the source file, and changes to the source file are reflected in your view of the data in Access. You use this method of working with external data when you need to share the data with users of a different database or application.

You can import and link to data from many different sources, including other Access databases, Paradox and dBASE database tables, spreadsheet files and text files. You use the **File | Get External Data | Import** option to import data and the **File | Get External Data | Link Files** option to link to data. Where necessary a wizard guides you through the procedure. Before importing a spreadsheet or text file, you usually need to prepare the file so that it is in a format suitable for conversion to an Access table.

When you want to use data from an Access database in another application, you can export the data to a file type appropriate for that application. There is no ongoing connection between the data in Access and the exported data. Changes in one are not reflected in the other. You can export Access tables and queries to a wide variety of file formats, including dBASE, Paradox, spreadsheet and text files.

Chapter 16: quick quiz

Q1	True or false – a linked table allows you to view and work with the same data in Access and in another application.
A.	True.
B.	False.

Q2	True or false – imported data is copied from the source file without retaining a link to that file.
A.	True.
B.	False.

Q3	When importing from a spreadsheet, the source data must not include . . .
A.	Column headings.
B.	Column totals and subtotals.
C.	Blank columns.

Q4	When importing from a text file, which of these requirements must the source data meet?
A.	Each field must contain the same type of data on all rows.
B.	Each record must be on a separate row.
C.	Each row must end with a paragraph break.
D.	All records must include the same fields.

Q5	True or false – when you import an object from another Access database, all associated objects are automatically imported as well.
A.	True.
B.	False.

Q6	True or false – when you export data from Access, a link is created between the source table or query and the exported data.
A.	True.
B.	False.

Answers

1: A, **2**: A, **3**: B, **4**: All, **5**: B, **6**: B.

17 *In conclusion*

In this chapter

Now that you have completed the topics and tasks in the previous chapters, you have covered the syllabus requirements for ECDL Advanced Databases.

This chapter summarizes what you have learnt. It also presents a final version of the Village Library database, with a more complete set of queries, forms, and reports than previous versions. An integrated Help file explains how and why the various elements of this database were created.

Exercise file

In this chapter you will work with the following Access file:

`Village Library Database`

Table design: summary

At the core of any database are the tables and fields that store the database data and the relationships that link the tables. These are determined by the purpose of the database, its subjects, and the tasks it is required to handle.

In Chapters 2 to 6 of this book you learnt how to:

- Design a set of tables that support the purpose of a database and the tasks it is intended to perform.

- Create relationships between the database tables.

- Enforce referential integrity to ensure consistency between related tables.

- Use the *Cascade Update* and *Cascade Delete* options to override referential integrity restrictions in a controlled manner.

- Specify a default join type for each relationship.

- Assign an appropriate data type and field size to each field.

- Create lookup fields, input masks, and default values to facilitate data entry.

- Create validation rules and specify required fields to ensure valid data entry.

- Select appropriate field formats to control how data is displayed.

You can view the resulting structure of the Village Library database by opening the `Village Library Database` and then opening the Relationships window (**Tools | Relationships**).

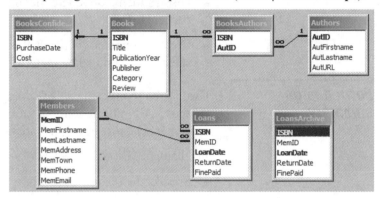

This provides an overview of the database structure, including the relationships between tables, the default join types, and the referential integrity options applied.

Query design: summary

You use select queries to retrieve data from your database, specifying the source tables and fields for the data and the criteria you want the retrieved data to meet. You can then use these queries as the record sources for forms and reports.

You use action queries to retrieve data from your database and then copy, delete, or modify the records retrieved.

In Chapters 7 to 10 of this book, you learnt how to:

- Create update, make-table, append and delete queries that enable you to act on multiple records at a time.

- Group records in a query.

- Create total queries that summarize (for example, count, sum, or average) field values in all records or in groups of records returned by the query.

- Create crosstab queries that calculate totals for records that are grouped on more than one field and display the results in a compact, spreadsheet-like format.

- Create calculated fields that return the result of calculations on other fields.

- Use calculations as criteria for determining which records are returned by a query.

- Include or exclude duplicate records and records that share the same value(s) in one or more fields.

- Find records that have no matching values in related tables.

- Display the records with the highest or lowest values in a particular field.

- Create parameter queries that prompt users for record selection criteria when they run the queries.

Form design: summary

Forms are the main means of adding and editing data in a database. All information in a form is contained in controls such as labels, text boxes, list boxes, and so on.

In Chapters 11 to 13 of this book, you learnt how to:

- Specify the record source for a form.

- Create controls that are linked to fields in the form's record source (bound controls).

- Create record selector controls.

- Create calculated controls that perform calculations on values in individual records.

- Create calculated controls that summarize values in a group of records.

- Specify the tab order for a form.

- Create a main form and subform that display records from one table/query and all related records from another table/query.

Report design: summary

Reports are the main means of organizing, grouping, and summarizing database information for printing or online review. All information in a report is contained in controls such as text boxes and labels.

In Chapter 14 you learnt how to:

- Create calculated controls that perform calculations on values in individual records in a report.

- Create calculated controls that display group totals.

- Create calculated controls that display report totals.

- Create calculated controls that display concatenated values, dates, and other expressions.

- Calculate percentages in a report.

- Create running sums and use running sums to number report items.

- Insert page breaks.

- Display/hide page headers and footers.

Macros: summary

Macros provide a simple means of automating common database tasks. You can use them to automatically perform tasks that you repeat frequently and to make your database objects work together.

In Chapter 15 you learnt how to:

- Create a macro.

- Create command buttons that trigger macros.

- Attach macros to form control events.

- Attach macros to form and report events.

- Use a macro to synchronize two forms or a form and a report.

Importing, exporting, and linking: summary

With Access you aren't limited to working with data in a single Access database. You can import data from other Access databases and from other file formats, you can link to data in external sources, and you can export data in various formats for use in other applications.

In Chapter 16 you learnt how to:

- Import dBASE and Paradox tables.

- Import spreadsheet data and text files.

- Import Access database objects.

- Link to data in an Excel worksheet.

- Export tables and queries to dBASE, Paradox, spreadsheet, and text files.

Village Library Database: final version

The case study in this book has been designed to illustrate the features required to cover the ECDL Advanced Database syllabus. Each chapter has its own version of the Village Library database, designed to support the skill sets dealt with in that chapter. This chapter presents a final version of the database (`Village Library Database.mdb`), which incorporates a more complete set of features than previous versions.

Remember that the database does not represent a complete functioning database for a real library. Such a database would require a more complex structure – one that is capable of storing and manipulating information about, for example, multiple copies and editions of books, media other than books, subscription rates, cancelled memberships, interlibrary loans, and so on. It might also exploit some of Access's more advanced features, such as SQL and the Visual Basic for Applications programming language.

Village Library Database: application

A database application consists of a set of database objects that are organized and linked together so that users can easily perform their tasks without having to work their way through long lists of queries, forms, reports, and so on.

Visual Basic for Applications (VBA) code is the most powerful tool that Access provides for developing database applications. However, you can create simple applications without any programming, using just the Access features you learnt about in this book or variations thereon.

The Village Library Database application accompanying this chapter uses only two features that you have not already met: the **Startup** feature and the **Help** feature. It consists of a set of tables, queries, forms, reports, and macros similar to those you created in earlier chapters. The features that turn it into a user-friendly application include:

- Startup settings
- Unbound forms
- Macros

Let's look at each of these now in turn.

Open the Village Library Database. You are immediately presented with a Welcome screen from which you can access all the application functionality.

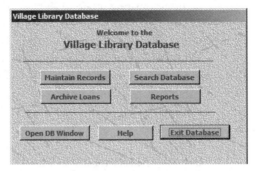

Notice that Access's Database Window is not displayed. Typically when you create an application, you automate access to all user functionality and you hide the underlying database objects so that users cannot interfere with them. So when you open the Village Library Database, Access's Database Window is hidden.

How do you get Access to display the Welcome screen and hide the Database Window? By using Access's **Startup** feature. Let's see how this works.

Having opened the database, choose the **Tools | Startup** command. This displays the *Startup* dialog box, as shown here.

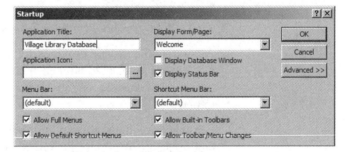

This controls how your application looks and behaves when it starts. The options relevant to the Village Library Database application are as follows:

- *Application Title*: This specifies the text displayed in Access's title bar, allowing you to use the name of your application in the title bar instead of 'Microsoft Access'.

- *Display Form/Page*: This enables you to specify a form to be displayed automatically when the database opens. In this case it is the Welcome form.

- *Display Database Window*: When this option is not selected, the Database Window is automatically hidden when the database is opened.

The other options relate to the use of built-in and custom menus and toolbars, which are not covered in this book. However, it is useful to know that you can customize Access's built-in menus and toolbars and that you can also create you own custom menus and toolbars. This gives you full control over the functionality available to users of your database, preventing access to all functionality except the user interface you have created.

Unbound forms

In this book you learnt how to create forms that display data from one or more tables and/or queries – that is, forms that are bound to some record source. It is also possible to create unbound forms – that is, forms with no record source. These are very useful for creating a user interface to your database objects.

The Welcome form is one such unbound form. Instead of displaying database records, it contains a set of command buttons that provide access to the main tasks that users will want to perform – that is:

- Maintaining records in the various database tables.

- Searching the database for particular records.

- Viewing reports.

- Archiving records from the Loans table.

A command button is provided for each of these tasks. The *On Click* event associated with each command button triggers a macro that takes the user to the next step in the task they want to perform.

For example, the **Maintain Database** button triggers a macro that opens the *Maintain Records* form. This is another unbound form, used only for navigating to the forms used for maintaining different tables.

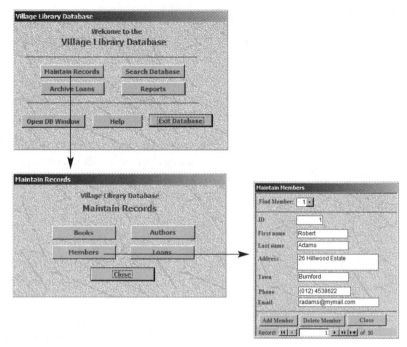

Additional command buttons on the Welcome form are shortcuts for displaying the Database Window, closing the Village Library Database, and accessing the Village Library Database's Help file.

Take some time now to browse through the user interface. You will see that it consists of a hierarchy of forms that allows users to quickly and easily access the functionality they want to use – all created with features you have already met in earlier chapters.

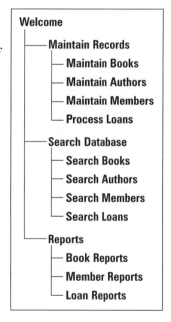

Macros

Macros form an important part of the user interface. They tie together the various forms and reports, and automate access to them.

- On all the unbound forms, macros are attached to each of the command buttons. These macros specify the action to be taken when a command button is clicked.

- On bound forms, such as the Maintain Members form, command buttons with attached macros are used to perform the various tasks associated with the form and to access related functionality.

- Macros have also been attached to some form and report events in order to refine the form/report functionality.

The following diagram illustrates the functionality of the Maintain Members form and the macros used to complete the table maintenance tasks.

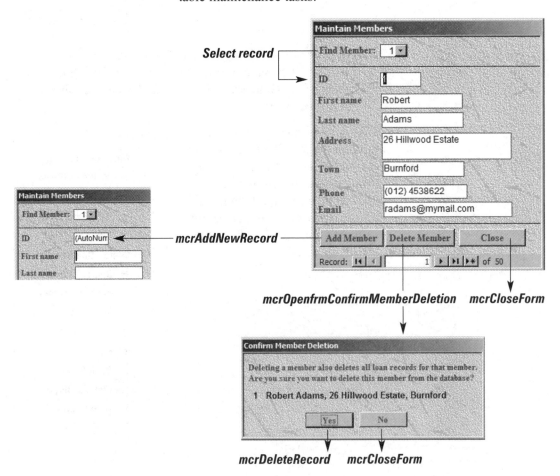

Village Library Database Help

A Help file is provided for the Village Library Database application and is integrated with it. This provides information on why and how the various elements of the database were created.

To display the Village Library Database Help, you can either:

- Click the **Help** button on the Welcome form. This opens a Help window with **Contents**, **Index**, and **Search** tabs.

  The **Contents** tab provides a table of contents for the entire Help file. The **Index** and **Search** tabs allow you to enter keywords to find particular help topics you want to view.

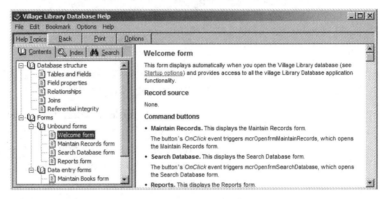

- Press **F1** (forms only). This displays help information specific to the active form.

As well as using the Village Library Help to get information about how the database was built, it will also be useful to open the database objects in Design View and take a look at their record sources, components, and properties.

Naming conventions

To make it easier to identify database objects when selecting them from lists and when referring to them in expressions, it is a good idea to use a consistent naming convention throughout the database.

Prefixes

One useful convention prefixes object names with a three/four letter tag that identifies the object type, as follows:

Object	Prefix	Example
Table	tbl	tblBooks
Query	qry	qryAllBooks
Form	frm	frmMaintainRecords
Subform	fsub	fsubLoansAndReturns
Report	rpt	rptLoansHistory
Macro	mcr	mcrCloseForm

This convention is used in the Village Library Database accompanying this chapter.

There is also a clear benefit to prefixing control names with the control type. This makes it easy to differentiate between controls and their underlying fields in expressions. The Village Library Database uses the following standard naming convention for controls:

Control	Prefix
Check box	chk
Combo box	cbo
Command button	cmd
Label	lbl
Line	lin
Listbox	lst
Option button	opt
Option group	grp
Subform/report	sub
Text box	txt

Spaces

Access supports spaces in object, field, and control names. However, there are disadvantages to including spaces in names.

In particular, Access does not recognize such names in expressions, unless you enclose them in square brackets – for example, [Purchase Date]. If you omit the spaces, Access will recognize the string as a name and automatically insert the square brackets for you.

In the Village Library Database accompanying this chapter, all object, field, and control names consist of a single string, with the first letter of each word (except the prefix) capitalized. This is a standard naming convention.

The default text displayed in the title bar of forms and reports, and in column headings in tables and queries, is the object or field name. To make these more user friendly, you can specify different text by using the object or field's *Caption* property.

And that's it!

The Village Library Database gives you a good idea of what you can achieve with the Access skills you have acquired while following this book. Good luck in your ECDL Advanced Databases examination!

Expressions

In this appendix

Expressions are a fundamental part of many Access operations. You use them, for example, when defining validation rules, default values, query criteria, and calculated fields.

This appendix presents all you need to know about the operators, values, functions, and field and control references that you can include in an expression.

What is an expression?

An expression consists of any combination of operators, identifiers, literal values, and functions that returns a result when applied to data in your database.

- **Literal value**. A value, such as a number, text string, or date, that Access uses exactly as written. You can use wildcard characters in literal values. See 'Literal values' and 'Wildcard characters' below.

- **Identifier**. Specifies the name of a field or control whose value you want to include in the expression. See 'Identifiers' below.

- **Operator**. Specifies the type of operation to be performed. In general, if you do not include an operator in an expression, Access assumes an equal to (=) operator. See 'Operators' below.

- **Function**. Returns a value based on a calculation or other operation. See 'Functions' below.

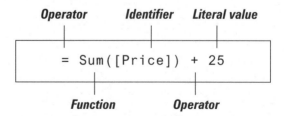

In form and report controls, all expressions must be preceded by the equal to (=) symbol.

Literal values

When including literal values in an expression:

- Enclose dates within hash (#) symbols – for example, #01-02-03#.

- Enclose strings within double quotes (") – for example, "Excellent".

Identifiers

When including field and control identifiers in an expression:

- Enclose the field or control name within square brackets ([ ]) – for example, [Cost].

- When a macro in one form refers to a control in another form, the reference must be in the following format:

  `Forms![Formname]![Controlname]`

Operators

Access provides several types of operators, including comparison, arithmetic, logical, and concatenation operators.

Operator	Meaning
Comparison	
=	Equal to.
<>	Not equal to.
<	Less than.
<=	Less than or equal to.
>	Greater than.
>=	Greater than or equal to.
In	Specifies a list of values. For example, the following validation rule specifies that only values from the list are valid in the field: `In ("Ireland", "England", "Scotland", "Wales")`
Between ... And ...	Specifies a range of values. For example, the following validation rule specifies that values entered must be between 1 and 100: `Between 1 And 100`

Operator	Meaning
Comparison	
Like	Searches for strings that match a specified pattern. (Typically used with wildcard characters.)
	For example, when used as selection criteria in a query field, the following expression specifies all values that begin with the word 'The':
	`Like "The*"`
Is Null	Is equal to Null.
Is Not Null	Is not equal to Null.
Arithmetic	
+	Add.
-	Subtract.
*	Multiply.
/	Divide.
Logical	
And	Use to combine expressions. All the expressions must evaluate to True.
	For example, the following validation rule specifies that values entered in the field must be *both* greater than 1 *and* less than 100:
	`>1 And <100`
Or	Use to combine expressions. Only one of the expressions need evaluate to True.
	For example, the following validation rule specifies that values entered in the field must begin *either* with 'A' *or* with 'B':
	`Like("A*") Or Like("B*")`
Not	Negates the result of an expression. For example, the following validation rule specifies that values in the field cannot begin with 'A':
	`Not Like ("A*")`
Concatenation	
&	Combines text strings from different fields or controls. If using to combine number values, Access automatically converts the numbers to text strings.

Functions

Access provides many different functions for use in expressions. Here is a list of the functions you are most likely to use.

Function	Meaning
Aggregate functions	
Sum()	Calculates the sum of a set of values.
Avg()	Calculates the average of a set of values (excluding Null values).
Min()	Returns the lowest value of a set of values (excluding Null values.)
Max()	Returns the highest value of a set of values (excluding Null values).
Count()	Returns a count of the values in a set of values (excluding Null values).
Count(*)	Returns a count of the values in a set of values (including Null values).
Date and time functions	
Date()	Returns the current date.
Time()	Returns the current time.
Now()	Returns the current date and time.
Year()	Returns the year of a specified date. For example, Year(01-01-03) returns 2003 and Year(Date()) returns the year part of the current date.
Logical functions	
IIf()	Returns one of two values, depending on the evaluation of an expression. The syntax is as follows: `IIf(expression, value_if_true, value_if_false)`
IsNull()	Tests whether or not a value is Null. Returns True if the value is Null. Otherwise returns False.
Conversion function	
Nz()	Converts Null values to zeros. The syntax is: `Nz(expression,0)`

Wildcard characters

A wildcard character is a special character that represents one or more other characters in a literal value.

Character	Meaning
?	Represents any single character in the same position. For example, the following represents 1002, 1112, 1562, 1762, 1222, 1AB2, 1FG2, and so on: 1??2
*	Represents zero or more characters in the same position. For example, the following represents 'Bn', 'Brian', 'Brendan', 'Bern', 'Bergen', and so on: B*n
#	Represents any single number in the same position. For example, the following represents any three-digit number beginning with 1: 1##
[ ]	Represents any single character within the brackets. You can specify either a list of characters or a range of characters. For example, the following represents 'fan', 'fin' and 'fun', but not 'fen' or 'faun': f[aiu]n And the following represents 'ban', 'can', and 'dan', but not 'fan': [b-d]an You can also specify multiple ranges. For example, the following represents 'ban', 'Ban' 'can', 'Can', and so on: [B-D,b-d]an
!	Represents any character except those listed within the brackets. For example, the following represents 'fen' but not 'fan', 'fin' or 'fun': f[!aiu]n

Glossary

In this appendix

This appendix presents a glossary of terms that you can use to quickly find definitions for most database terms used in this book.

Glossary terms and definitions

Action query
A query that copies or changes groups of records from one or more *tables*.

Aggregate function
An Access *function* that summarizes *field* values. Examples are Sum(), Avg() and Count().

Append query
A type of *query* that copies *records* from one or more *tables* and appends them to the end of another table.

Argument
A value or expression that provides information required by a *function* or *macro* action to perform its task.

AutoNumber data type
Access automatically generates unique sequential numbers in the *field*. This *data type* is typically used for *primary key* fields.

Bound control
A *control* that gets its values from a *field* in the *record source* of a *form* or *report*, and that you can use to update values in that field (forms only).

Calculated control
In a *form* or *report*, a *control* that displays the result of calculations.

Calculated field
A *query field* that contains a calculation *expression* and displays the result of that expression. Calculated fields are not stored in a database *table*. Instead Access reruns the calculations each time you run the query.

Checkbox control

A *control* that represents a Yes/No choice. Typically, checkboxes are used as stand-alone controls, with each checkbox representing a Yes/No choice that is independent of any other Yes/No choices.

Combo box control

A *control* that combines a *text box*, where users can type a value, and a drop-down *list box*, where users can select a value instead. A down-arrow appears when you click in the control; the drop-down list opens when you click this arrow.

Command button control

A *control* that starts an action.

Concatenation

The creation of a single string from a combination of *field* values and literal values.

Control

A graphical object that you place on a *form* or *report* to display data, to accept data input, to perform an action, or simply for decorative purposes.

Control name

The name that uniquely identifies a *control* within a *form* or *report*. The default name for a *bound control* is the name of the underlying *field*. The default name for an *unbound control* is the name of the control type followed by a unique number.

Control source

The source of the data displayed by a *control*. For a *bound control*, the control source is a *field* in the *form/report record source*. For an *unbound control*, the source is typically a calculation *expression*.

Criteria

See *Query criteria*.

Crosstab query

A *query* that calculates totals for *records* that are grouped on more than one *field* and displays the results in a spreadsheet-like format.

Currency data type

Stores numeric data with one to four decimal places. The data can be used in calculations and sorted in numeric order. By default, values are displayed with the currency symbol specified in your Windows Regional Settings.

Data and information
Data is the values that you store in the database. Information is data that you retrieve from the database in some meaningful way.

Datasheet View
Displays database information arranged in columns (one for each *field*) and rows (one for each *record*). Datasheet View is available for *tables*, *queries* and *forms*.

Data type
This determines the kind of data that can be stored in a *field* and the operations that can be carried out on that data.

Date/Time data type
Stores dates and times. The *Format* property allows you to specify the format in which dates and times are displayed.

Default value
A value that is automatically entered in a *field* when you create a new *record*.

Delete query
A type of *query* that deletes *records* from one or more *tables*.

Delimited text file
A text file in which fields are separated by a special delimiter character such as a comma, tab or semicolon. Delimited files are often referred to as comma-delimited files or CSV (comma-separated values) files.

Design View
The view in which you design *tables*, *queries*, *forms* and *reports*.

Duplicate records
Records that contain identical values in all their *fields*.

Event
An action that occurs on a *form*, *report* or *control* and that can trigger execution of a *macro* or an *event procedure*.

Event procedure
A procedure, written in Microsoft Visual Basic, that is executed in response to an *event*. *Macros* provide similar, though less powerful, functionality. For ECDL, you do not need to know how to create or use event procedures.

Expression
A combination of *operators*, *identifiers*, *literal values* and *functions* that returns a result when applied to data in your database.

Field

A single piece of information about the subject of a *table*.

Field size property

Determines the maximum size for data in a *field*.

Field validation rule

A rule that sets limits or conditions on the values that you can enter in a *field*.

Fixed-width text file

A text file in which fields are aligned in columns. Spaces are inserted to fill out the fields so that they are the same width in all rows.

Fixed value list

See *Value list*.

Flat database

A flat database consists of a single *table*.

Foreign key

One or more *fields* in a *table* that refer to the *primary key* field(s) of a related table.

Form

A database object used mainly for data input or onscreen display. Typically a form displays a single *record*, laid out and formatted in a user-friendly manner. A variety of *control* types are used to facilitate quick data entry and easy access to related data.

Form View

This is the view in which *forms* are presented to users. Single Form View displays a single *record* at a time. Continuous Form View displays multiple records at a time.

Format property

Determines how values in a *table field*, *query field*, *form control* or *report* control are displayed and printed. The format does not affect how the data is stored.

Function

A predefined formula that performs an operation (for example, a calculation or logical evaluation) and returns a value. The values on which the operation is performed are referred to as the function's *arguments*.

Grouped report
A *report* in which information is grouped by the values in one or more *fields*. Calculations may be performed on the data within each group.

Hyperlink data type
Stores hyperlinks to websites, folders and files. Users can click a hyperlink to start the source application and display the destination website, folder or file.

Identifier
The name of a *field* or *control* whose value you want to include in an *expression*.

Importing
Converts data from its original format and saves it to a new or existing Access *table*. There is no ongoing connection between the original data and the data in Access.

Index
A database feature that speeds up searching and sorting operations and that can force a *field* to have unique values. The *primary key* of a *table* is automatically indexed. You do not need to know about indexes for ECDL.

Inner join
When two *tables* are joined by an inner *join*, a *query* returns only records that have matching values in their related *fields*. Unmatched values in both tables are omitted.

Input mask
A template that assists data entry and controls the type, number and pattern of characters that can be entered in a *field*.

Join
The process of combining *records* from two *tables*.

Label control
A *form* or *report control* that displays descriptive text such as field captions, titles, headings and instructions.

Left outer join
When *two tables* are joined by a left outer *join*, a *query* returns all *records* from the *primary table* but only matching records from the related table.

Linked table
A *table* that is linked to external data, allowing you to view and work with that data from within Access. Changes you make to data in the linked table are saved to the external data source and not to your database.

Linking
Creates a link to external data, allowing you to view and work with that data from within Access.

List box control
A *form control* that displays a list from which users select a value. The list is always open and so is typically used to display a small number of options only.

Literal value
A value, such as a number, text string or date, that Access uses exactly as entered.

Lookup field
A *field* that displays a list from which you select the value to store in the field. The list can look up values either from a *table* or *query* or from a *fixed value list*.

Macro
A sequence of one or more database actions that can be executed with a single command or triggered automatically in response to a *form*, *report* or *control event*.

Main form
A *form* that contains a *subform*.

Make-table query
A type of *query* that creates a new *table* from data in one or more existing tables.

Many-to-many relationship
A *relationship* in which each *record* in the first *table* can have many matching records in the second table, and each record in the second table can have many matching records in the first table.

Memo data type
Stores alphanumeric data that is more than 255 characters long. The data can contain tabs and paragraphs but no formatting.

Multipart field
A *field* that includes more than one data item.

Multivalue field
A *field* that contains multiple values for the same data item.

Null
A special value (displayed as a blank *field)* that indicates missing or unknown data, or a field to which data is not applicable.

Number data type
Stores numeric data that can be used in calculations and sorted in numeric order.

One-to-one relationship
A *relationship* in which each *record* in *one* table can have no more than one matching record in the other table.

One-to-many relationship
A *relationship* in which each *record* in the first *table* can have many matching records in the second table. But each record in the second table can have only one matching record in the first table.

Operator
Specifies the type of calculation to be performed on data in an *expression*. Access supports the following types of operators: arithmetic, comparison, logical and concatenation.

Option button control
A *control* consisting of a small circle that represents a Yes/No choice. A blank circle represents a 'No' value; a small dot in the circle represents a 'Yes' value. Option buttons typically form part of an option group.

Option group control
A *control* consisting of a group of related options, only one of which can be selected at any time. Typically each option is represented by an *option button control*.

Parameter query
A *query* that prompts for *record* selection *criteria* when the query is run.

Primary key
A *field* (or combination of fields) in a database *record* that identifies that record uniquely.

Primary table
When two *tables* are related, the primary table is the one whose *primary key* is used as the linking *field*. So, in a *one-to-many relationship*, the table on the 'one' side of the relationship is always the primary table. In a *one-to-one relationship*, either table can be the primary table. You make the choice when you create the *relationship*.

Print Preview View
A view of database data as it will look when printed. This view is available for *forms*, *reports* and *datasheets*.

Query

A request to the database for *records* that match specified *criteria*. Queries are named and saved in the database and allow you to repeatedly retrieve up-to-date records that meet the query definition.

Query criteria

Expressions that restrict the *records* returned by a *query* to those that match specified conditions.

Record

One complete set of *fields* relating to the same item in a table.

Record source

The *table* or *query* from which a *form* or *report* gets its data and whose *fields* it updates (forms only).

Redundancy

Redundancy refers to the unnecessary duplication of data in a database.

Referential integrity

A set of rules that ensures that the *relationships* between *records* in related *tables* are valid, and that you do not accidentally delete or change related data.

Relational database

A collection of data organized into *tables*.

Relationship

A relationship is a connection between two *tables* that allows them to share data. It is based on the tables having at least one *field* in common.

Report

A database object used to organize, group and summarize database information in a format suitable for printing and for online review.

Required field

A *field* in which it is mandatory to enter a value.

Right outer join

When two *tables* are joined by a right outer *join*, a *query* returns all *records* from the related table but only matching records from the *primary table*.

Running sum

An accumulating total of values in a *report*.

Select query

A type of *query* that retrieves *records* for viewing and updating.

Self join

Joins a *table* to itself. A self *join* is based on a *one-to-one relationship* between two instances of the same table.

SQL

SQL (Structured Query Language) is the standard language used to create and query *relational databases*. For your convenience, Access provides graphical building tools for *tables*, *queries*, *forms*, and so on. Internally, however, it generates SQL statements to define these database objects. You do not need to know how to use SQL for ECDL.

Subform

A *form* that is contained within another form.

Subform control

A *form control*, represented by a rectangular box, that contains a *subform*.

Table

A collection of *records* with the same *fields* and relating to the subject.

Table subject

The people, things or events about which a *table* stores data.

Tab order

The order in which the focus moves from *control* to control when a user tabs through a *form*.

Text box control

Bound text boxes display data from a *table* or *query field* and accept input to that field. Unbound text boxes display the results of calculations.

Text data type

Stores alphanumeric data that does not exceed 255 characters in size.

Total query

A *query* that calculates summary values for all *records* or for groups of records in *tables/queries*.

Unbound control

A *control* that is not linked to a *table/query field*. You can use unbound controls to display informational text, graphics, and the results of calculations. You cannot use an unbound control to update field values.

Unique record

A *record* that contains a unique value in at least one of its *fields*.

Updateable query

A *query* that allows you to edit the *records* it returns. The changes are applied to the underlying *table(s)*.

Update query

A type of *query* that makes changes to values in multiple *records* in one or more *tables*.

Validation rule

A rule that sets limits or conditions on the values that you can enter in a *field* or *record*.

Value list

A fixed list of values that a *lookup field* or *combo box* can display for selection.

Wildcard

A special character that represents one or more other characters in a literal value.

Workbook

A Microsoft Excel file that contains one or more *worksheets*.

Worksheet

The primary document you use to store and work with data in Excel. Also referred to as a spreadsheet.

Yes/No data type

Stores Yes/No, True/False or On/Off values.

Index

literal values 117, 274, 275, 284
logical functions 117, 277
logical operators 276
lookup fields 35–46, 284
   basing on queries 39–41
   creating and modifying manually 41–6
   modifying a lookup field that looks up
      values in another table 45–6
Lookup tab 41
Lookup Wizard 36–9, 40, 41
Lotus 1-2-3 244
lowest values 143–4

Macro window 229–33
macros 227–39, 265, 270, 284
   attaching to control events 233–5
   attaching to form and report events 236–7
   creating 229–33
   synchronizing two forms or a form and a
      report 235–6
main form 190, 191, 284
make-table queries 90, 93–5, 284
many-to-many relationships 64–6, 284
Max function 100, 277
Memo data type 21–2, 284
Memo fields 21–2
menus, custom 268
Min function 100, 277
modification anomalies 6–7
multipart fields 7, 13, 284
multiple criteria 105–6
multi-record calculated controls 181
   creating 184–6
multivalue fields 7, 13–14, 284

name
   control 159, 280
   field 103–4, 253
named range 244
naming conventions 271–3
navigation buttons 197
New Record button 191
normalization 8
Not operator 142, 276

Now() function 277
Null values 129–32, 284
Number data type 22–5, 285
Number fields 22–5
numbering report items 221–2
Nz() function (Null to Zero function) 132, 277

one field, one value principle 13–14
one-to-many relationships 63–4, 285
one-to-one relationships 63, 285
one table, one primary key principle 14–15
one table, one subject principle 12–13
operators 274, 275–6, 285
option button controls 154, 167, 285
option group controls 153, 154, 285
   bound 165–7
Option Group Wizard 165–6
Or operator 276

page breaks 222–3
page footers 207
   creating calculated controls in 216–17
   omitting 223–4
page headers 207
   creating calculated controls in 215–16
   omitting 223–4
Page Numbers dialog box 216
page width warning 209
Paradox tables 242–4, 257
parameter queries 145–9, 285
   creating 146–7
   prompting for a date range 147–8
   returning all records 148–9
   using wildcards 148
Percent format 123
percentages, calculating 217–18
prefixes 272
primary key 14–15, 285
primary tables 66, 285
Print Preview button 211
Print Preview View 285
properties, field *see* field properties
Properties button 122–3, 158
property sheets 156, 158–60
purpose, database 3, 8

queries 4, 285
  basing a lookup field on a query 39–41
  defining relationships in a query 86
  design *see* query design
  refining 128–51
  setting a join type in a query 82–3
Query Builder 42, 45–6, 200
query criteria *see* criteria
query design 89–151, 263–4
  action queries 89–98
  custom calculations 116–27
  refining queries 128–51
  total queries 99–115
Query Properties dialog box 86
Query Type button 92

record selector combo box 170–1
record source 154, 155, 159, 179, 286
  modifying for a subform 199–200
Record Source property 159, 199–200,
    207–8
records 286
  creating a macro that opens blank records
    232–3
  limiting records displayed 105, 107–8
  limiting in total calculations 105, 106
  returning all records with a parameter
    query 148–9
  totalling all records 102–3
  totalling groups of 104–5
redundancy 6, 286
referential integrity 71–4, 96, 286
Regional Settings xx–xxi, 19
relational databases 1–2, 286
relationships 1–2, 4, 61–76, 286
  creating and editing 69–71
  defining in a query 86
  many-to-many 64–6, 284
  one-to-many 63–4, 285
  one-to-one 63, 285
  referential integrity 71–4, 96, 286
  types 63–6
  valid 62

Relationships window 66–8
  creating and editing relationships 69–71
renaming fields 103–4
report design 203–26, 264–5
  Books By Category report 205–8
  calculated controls 204, 209–17
  calculating percentages 217–18
  creating running sums 218–20
  numbering report items 221–2
  omitting page headers and footers 223–4
  report controls 204
  working with page breaks 222–3
report events 228–9, 281
  attaching macros to 236–7
report footer 206–7
  creating calculated controls in 213–14
  omitting page headers/footers 223, 224
  repeating the grand total in 220
  running sums 219–20
report header 205
  creating calculated controls in 215
  omitting page headers/footers 223, 224
report width wider than page width warning
    209
reports 4, 286
  creating a macro that runs a report 231–2
  design *see* report design
  grouped 283
  synchronizing a form and a report 235–6
required fields 57, 286
required values 57–8, 129
results displayed, limiting 105, 107–8
returning all records with a parameter query
    148–9
right outer joins 79–80, 286
Row Source 37, 42, 44, 45, 165
Row Source Type 42, 44, 45
running sums 206, 218-20, 221, 286

select queries 89, 90, 263, 287
self joins 80, 287
  creating 83–6
Show All button 68